THE
STYLISH
LIFE

COWBOYS

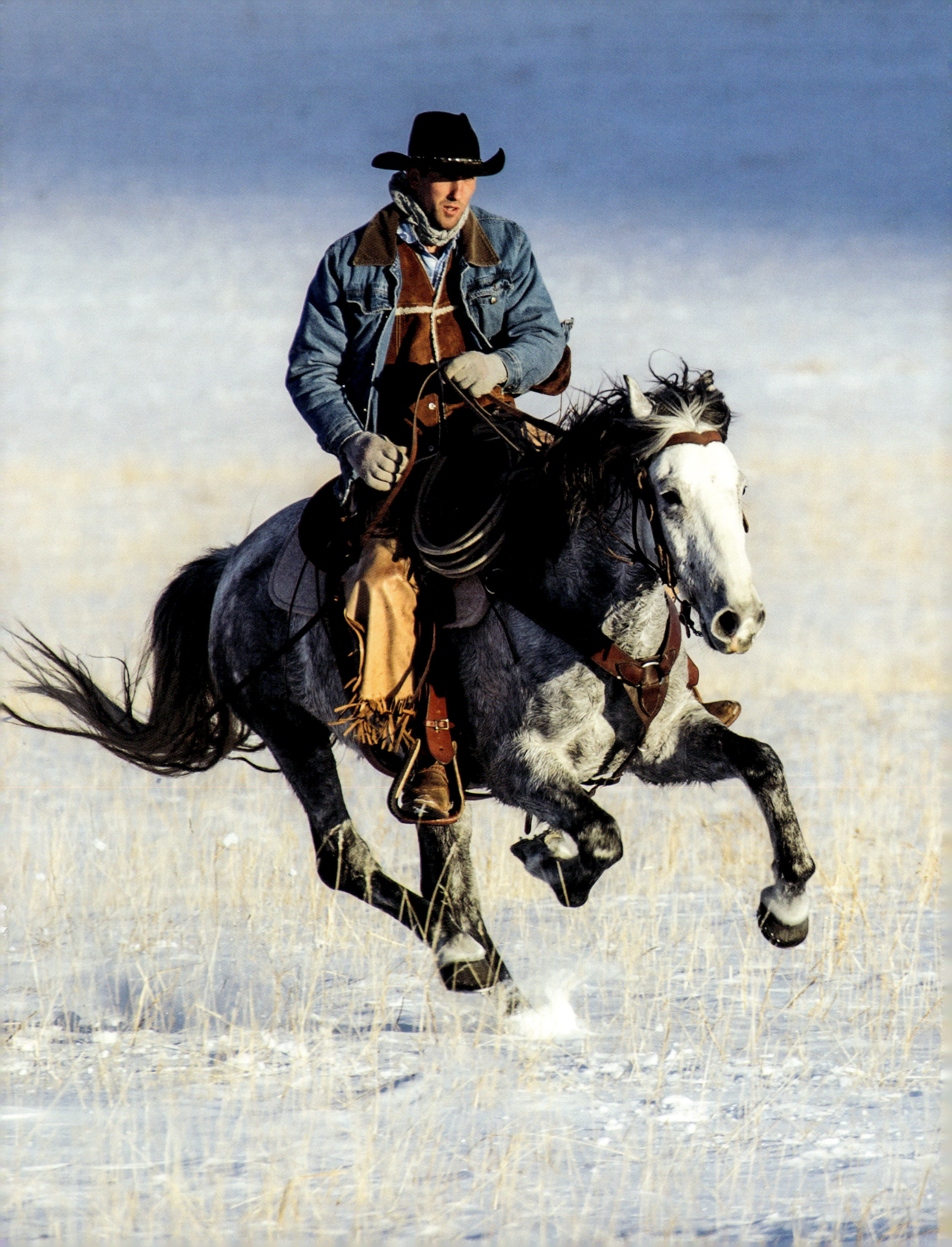

TEXTS BY ABE DAVIES

THE STYLISH LIFE

COWBOYS

teNeues

CONTENTS

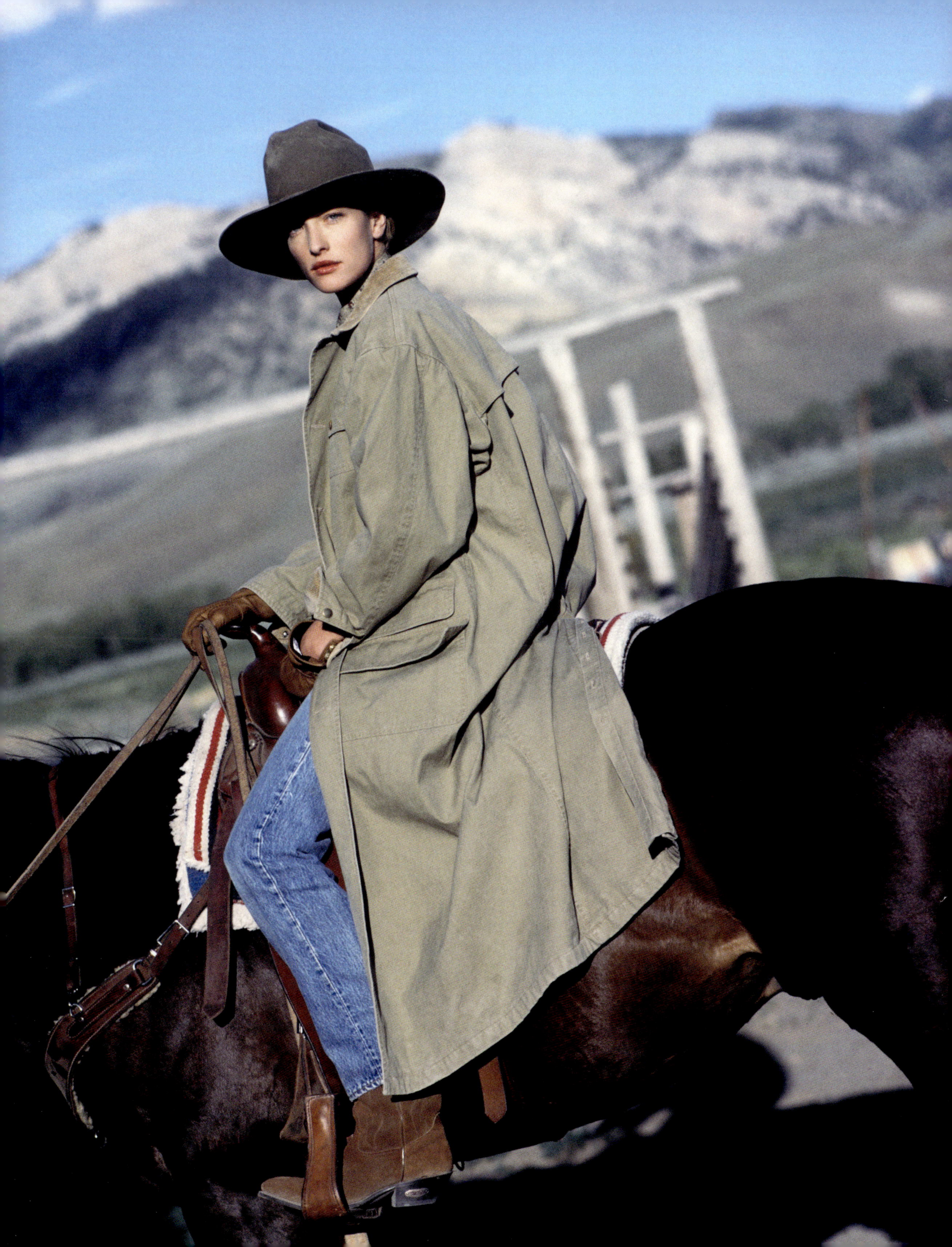

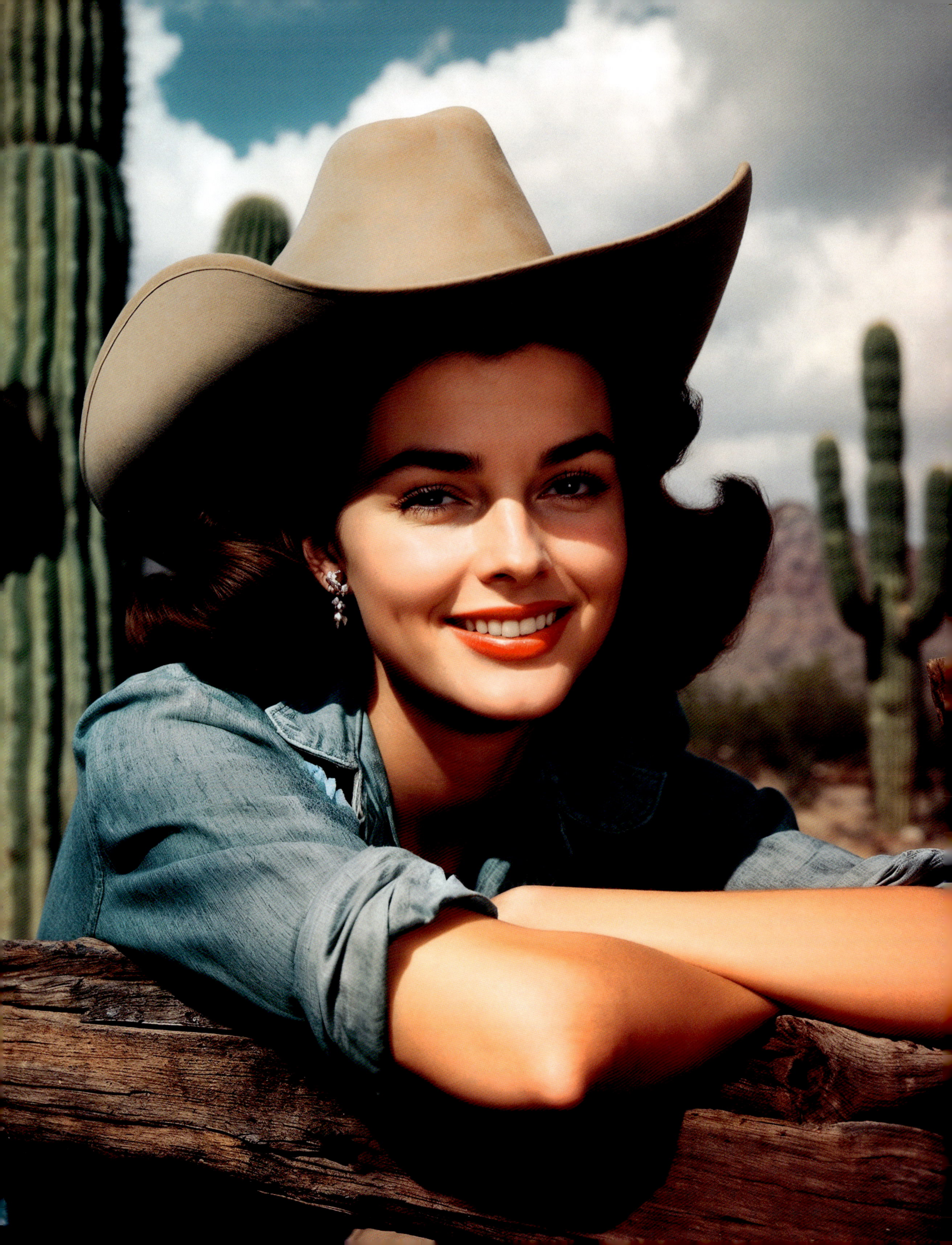

INTRODUCTION

ABE DAVIES

In the 2020s Western wear has burst back onto the global pop culture scene like an unruly outlaw gang descending on a Wild West saloon. From Pharrell Williams' 2024 Louis Vuitton collection to multiple ratings-dominating *Yellowstone* series to thousands of Instagram influencers flaunting rhinestone, tassels and Stetsons, the cowboy—and cowgirl—is everywhere. There's even an Internet-age fashion term for the phenomenon: we're living in the age of what fashion and culture social media have dubbed "cowboy core."

Yet on the other hand cowboy style never went away. Especially visible though it might be today, and in some unexpected places and forms, the Western aesthetic has also permeated global culture at a deep level for more than a century: music, film, fashion and everyday life are all marked in indelible ways by the history, mythology and style of the American West. So, while the recent resurgence in interest in all things cowboy can be striking, it's also just the latest chapter in a very long style story—and one that's got some possible surprises in store for the uninitiated. Let's go back to the start.

No image more immediately evokes the idea of America than the Wild West cowboy. Alone with his quarter horse on the plain, behind him a mountain range stretched across the distant horizon, he's kitted-out with a Stetson, boots, lasso, chaps, revolver, holster, buckskin coat, perhaps a poncho.

Page 2: *A cowboy on a wintry Hideout Ranch in Shell, Wyoming.*

Page 5: *VOGUE, 1989. With the mountains of Wyoming in the background, Tatjana Patitz sits on a bay horse wearing a long riding coat by Ralph Lauren Roughwear, jeans by Guess?, brown suede boots, and a brown cowboy hat.*

Opposite: *A young woman in a cowboy hat leans on a fence.*

There's a faraway look in his eyes that evokes the national values of steadfast self-reliance, stoic calm and a deep kinship with the land: instinctively, from a thousand movies and tall tales, we know this is a simple man with an unerring sense of justice, a man of fortitude in the face of life's challenges and setbacks. He's slow to anger, yet willing and able to fight for any cause in which he believes, whether a damsel in distress or a peaceful community threatened by forces it cannot resist alone.

This figure—alongside the cowgirl, of course, his female counterpart—is the original and avatar of Western style, the subject to which this entire book is devoted. But there's a possible irony here, which is that to such a person the idea of a book such as this one might seem rather alien. What we call cowboy "style" was to its original wearers simply the clothing and equipment they needed to survive, and the same could be said of their modern-day descendants. In fact, to the archetypal figure we're imagining on the plains, the very idea of "style" might seem antithetical, the kind of thing mollycoddled big-city folks care about because their lives are excessive, luxurious, trivial. To "style" oneself as something is to adopt a pretense, and pretense is alien to the world of cowboys and cowgirls. Function—and the survival it enables—is all.

Or is that really the case? All style evolves out of function, after all: even the most elaborate *haute couture* creation is the gaudy descendant of an animal skin or simple woven item donned to keep the prehistoric wearer warm and protected. And even the most ascetic historical cultures—even those whose governing virtues are the ability to live off the land, to survive the elements, to eschew the comfortable trappings of modern life—have developed a sense of the aesthetic value and appeal of their (ostensibly) purely functional equipment and clothing. Which is to say they have developed a sense of *style*.

For all their ruggedness and self-reliance, wouldn't a cowboy or girl take pride in the brushed coat of their horse, the gleam of a well-maintained revolver, the fabric of a Sunday-best dress, the high-quality leather of hat, chaps and boots? It's not hard to imagine even the most hard-bitten man or woman of the plains casting an approving glance at their reflection as they passed a mirror or window on a trip into town for supplies. A sense of style is everywhere, even in the places we might least expect to find it.

This is still a long way from fashion Instagram or the catwalk. But in fact it's hardly surprising that Western style has the influence and profile that it does. For one thing, what could be more glamorous—and thus more irresistible to the world of fashion—than the style of a charismatic figure with no apparent regard for glamor?

What could be more rich with style possibilities than an aesthetic that's rugged, down-to-earth and practical, infused with exciting history a million miles away from the sophistication and self-consciousness of the fashion world?

For another thing: like many great cultural symbols, the cowboy and their Wild West home can be many things to many people, and are capable of being constantly adapted, adopted, employed and subverted in different and unexpected ways. From the heteronormative, overwhelmingly white world of John Wayne and *Yellowstone* to the playful Queer provocations of Lil Nas X or Beyoncé's recent take on Country & Western; from the gentle optimism of *Little House on the Prairie* to the jaundiced despair of *Midnight Cowboy*; from traditional depictions of the Wild West that tell reassuring stories about America to more recent visions of it as a place of violence, sin and corruption: the image of the cowboy can be interpreted in a great many sometimes contradictory ways, which means that its capacity to be remade and reconfigured is never exhausted.

That capacity is amply in evidence throughout *The Stylish Life: Cowboys*. The fascinating photographs collected here trace the story of cowboy style from the beginning: from a time when you could hardly call it "fashion" at all right through to a present day in which ideas and imagery of the Wild West have been processed through a century-and-a-half of mythmaking in the form of books, movies, TV, music, advertising, and fashion trends. Full of jeans and leathers, bolo ties and western-style belts, checked shirts and rhinestone, rodeos and ranches, everyday people and global stars, this is a tour through cowboy style that will captivate anyone who's ever imagined themselves out on the open range—or even just yearned to indulge their inner cowpoke with a tasselled jacket or pair of snakeskin boots.

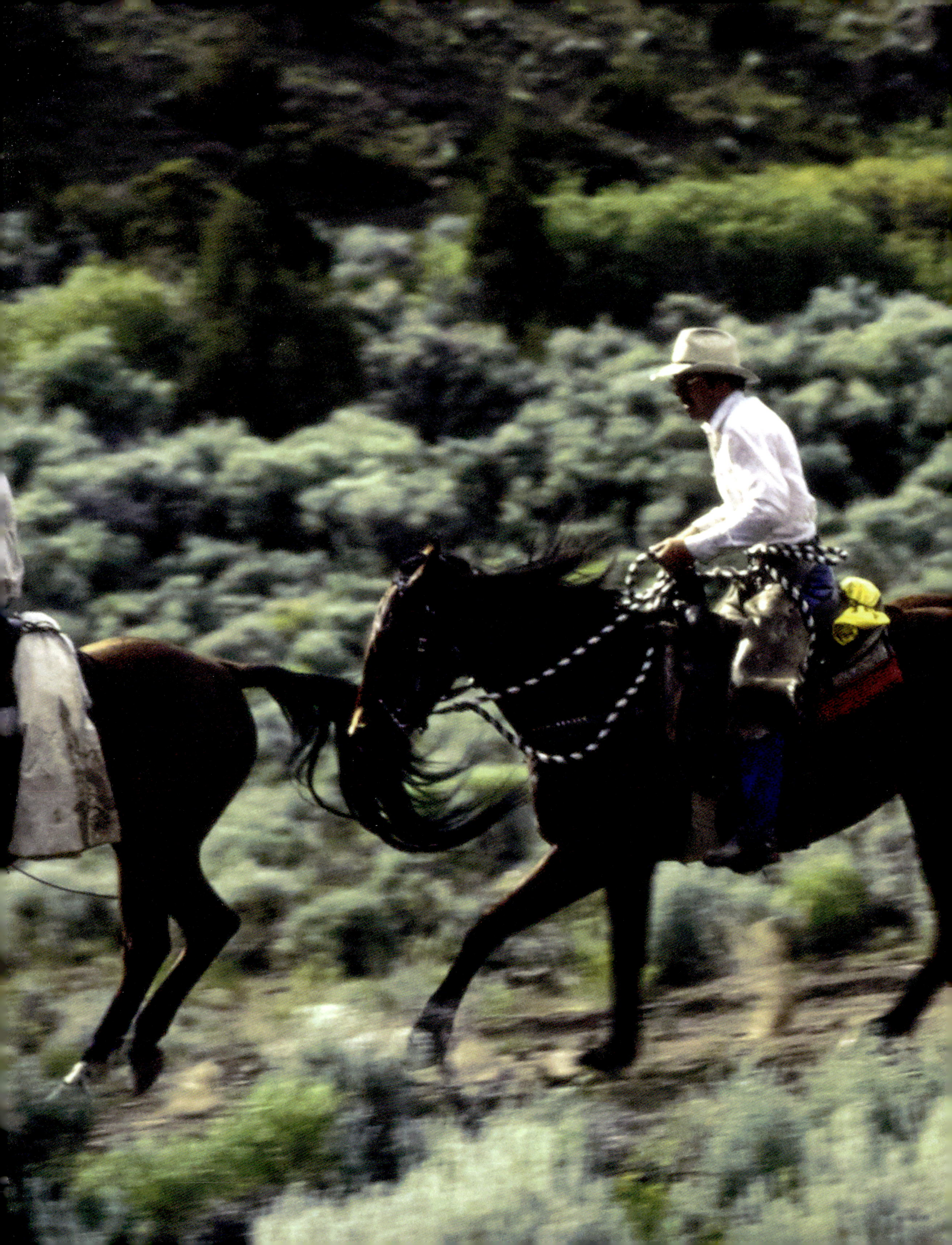

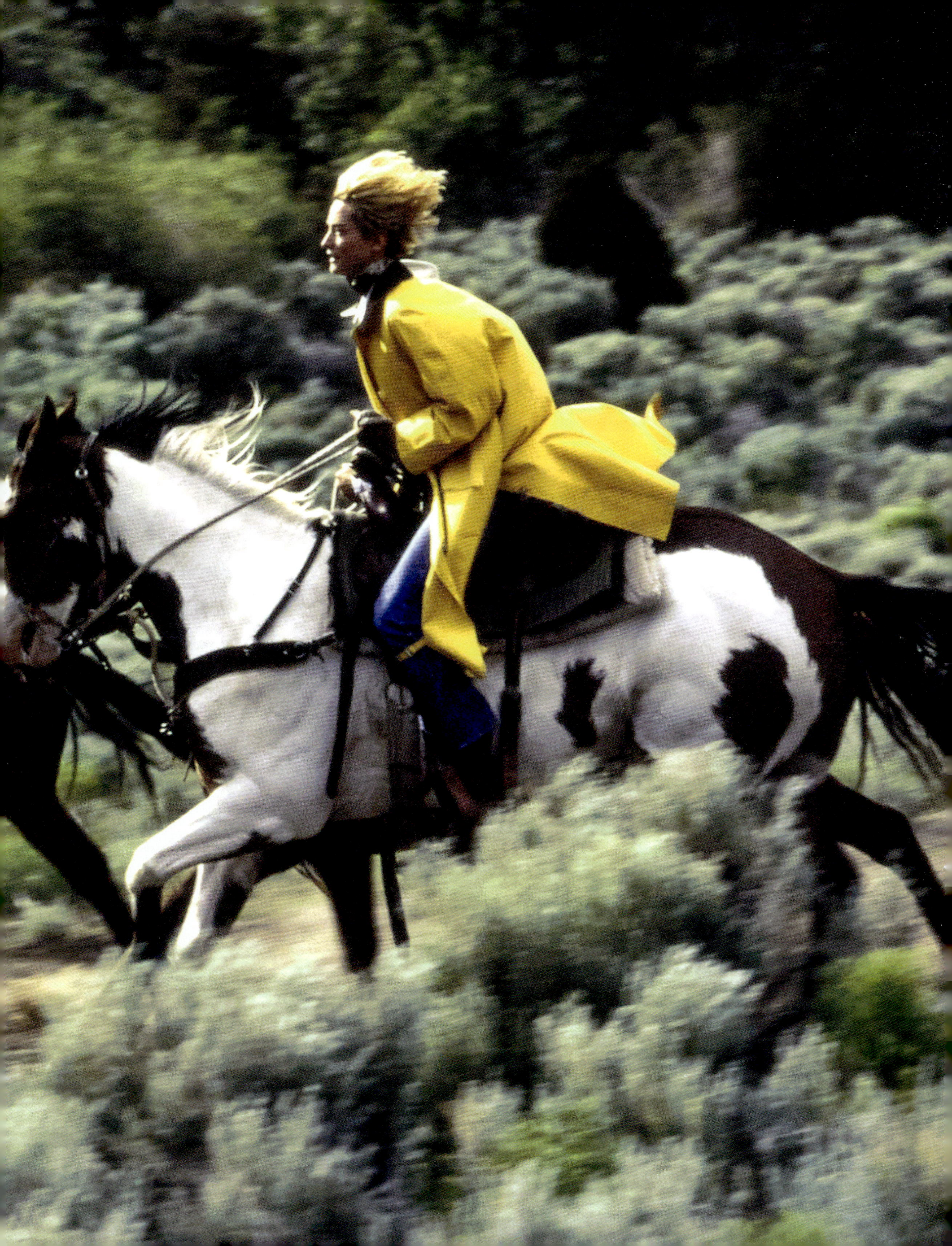

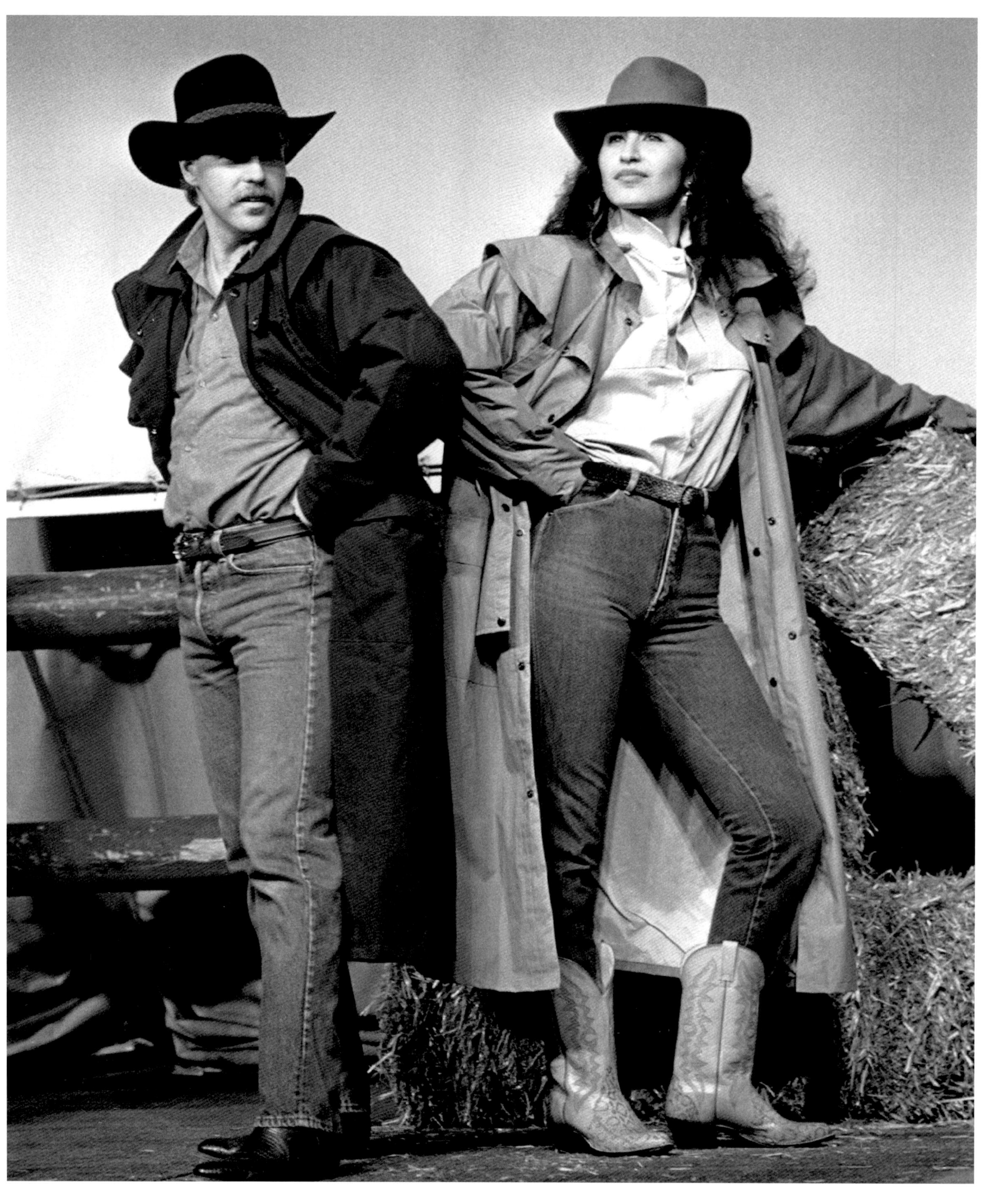

Opposite: *Florida cowgirl, c. 1945: full-length portrait of a young woman wearing a fringed crop top with matching fringed shorts and white boots, holding her cowboy hat aloft.*

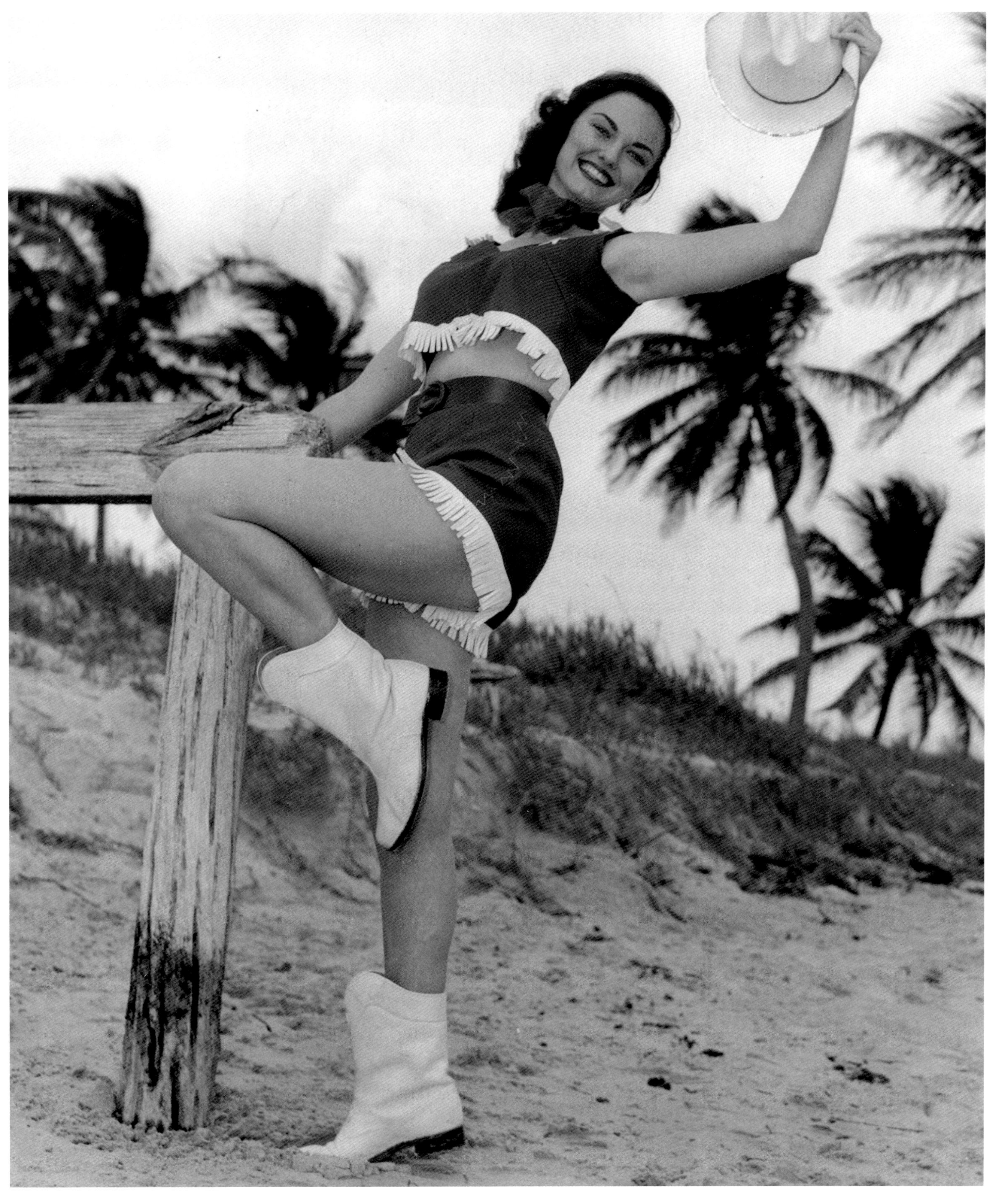

Following pages: *The Beatles pose for a portrait on the set of their movie HELP!, released on August 25, 1965. From left to right: John Lennon, Paul McCartney, Ringo Starr, George Harrison.*

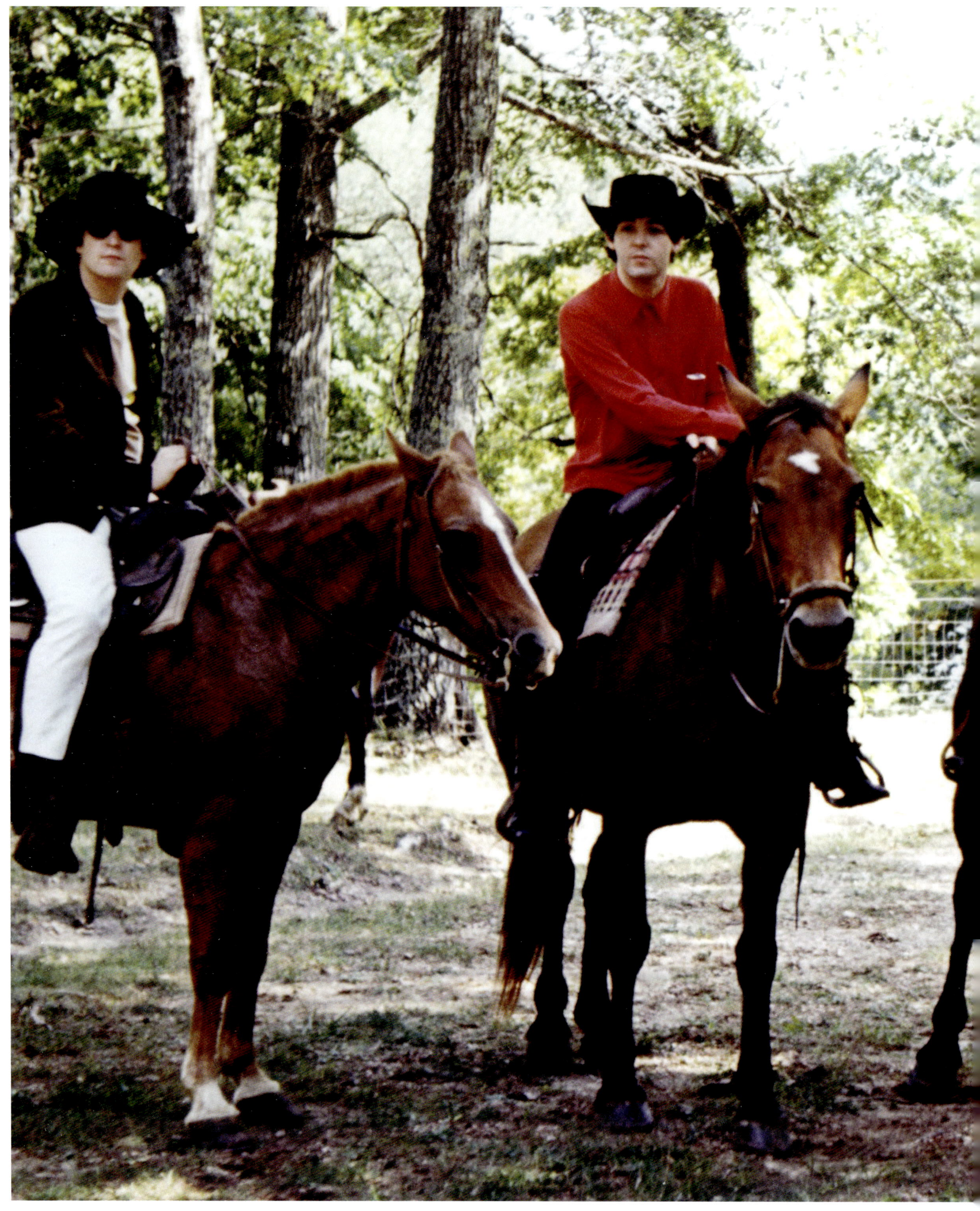

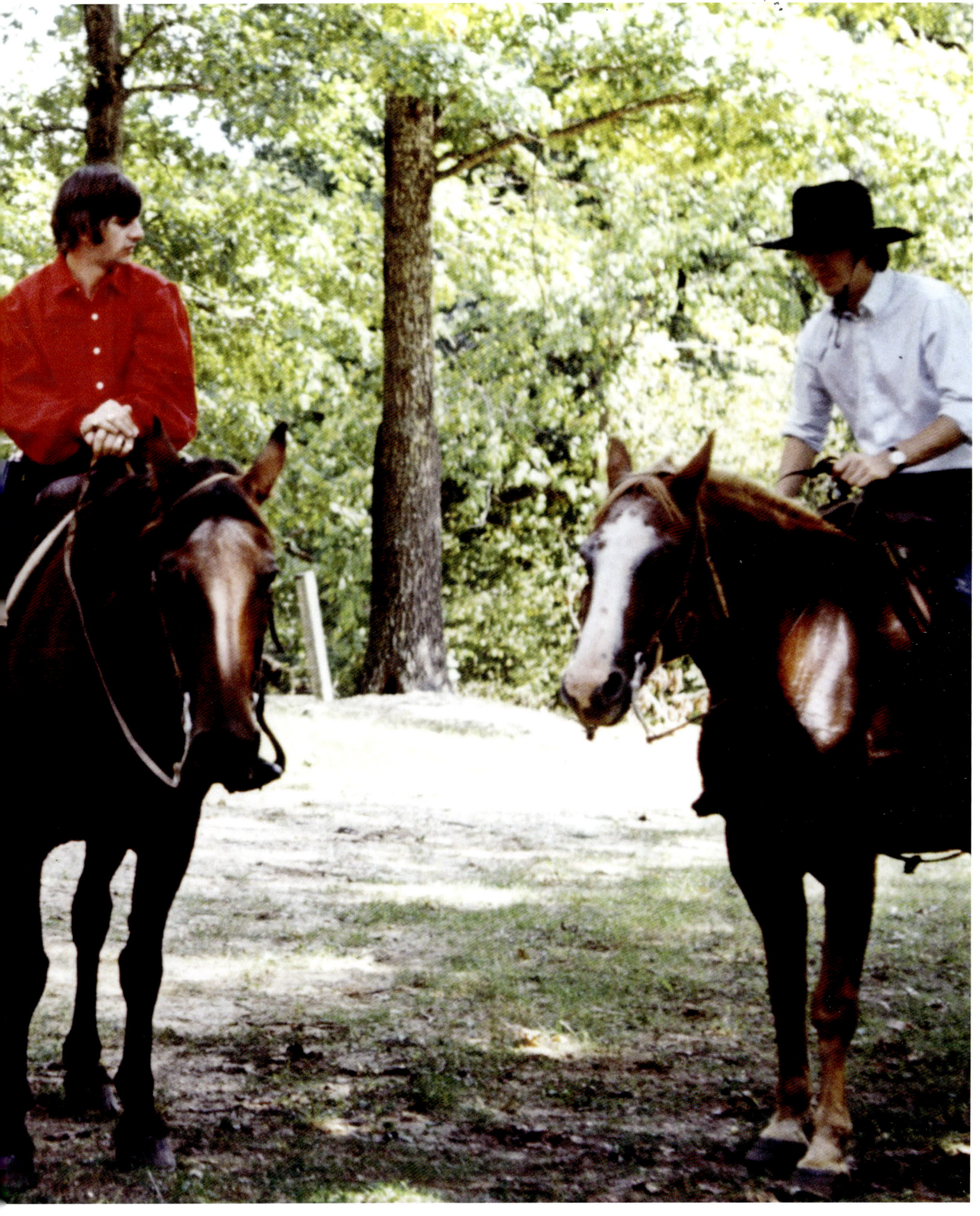

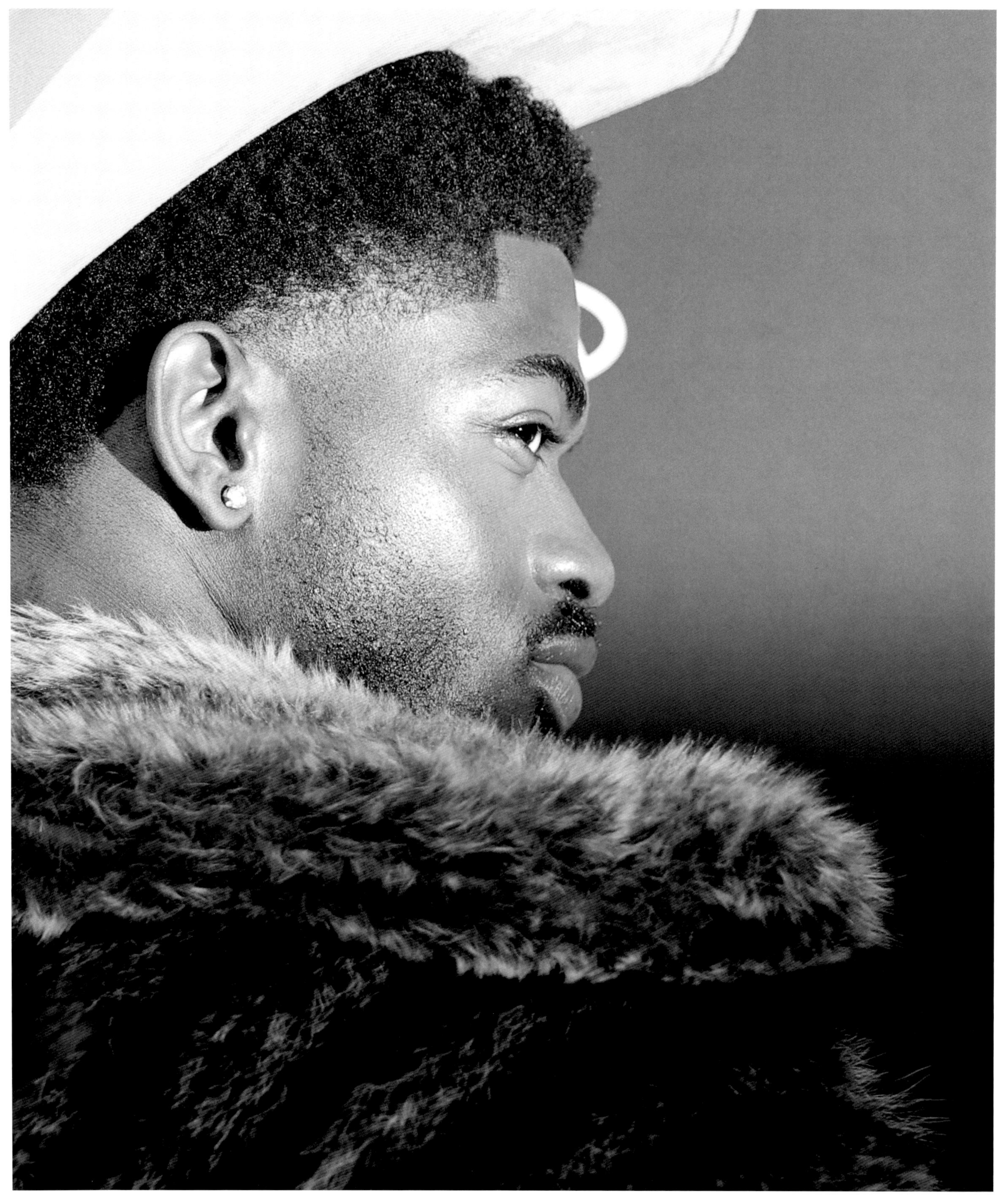

This page: *Lil Nas X attends the 36th Annual GLAAD Media Awards at the Beverly Hilton on March 27, 2025.*

Opposite: *Journalist Sheinelle Jones in her Beyoncé costume at NBC's "Today" Halloween celebration at Rockefeller Plaza in New York City on October 31, 2025.*

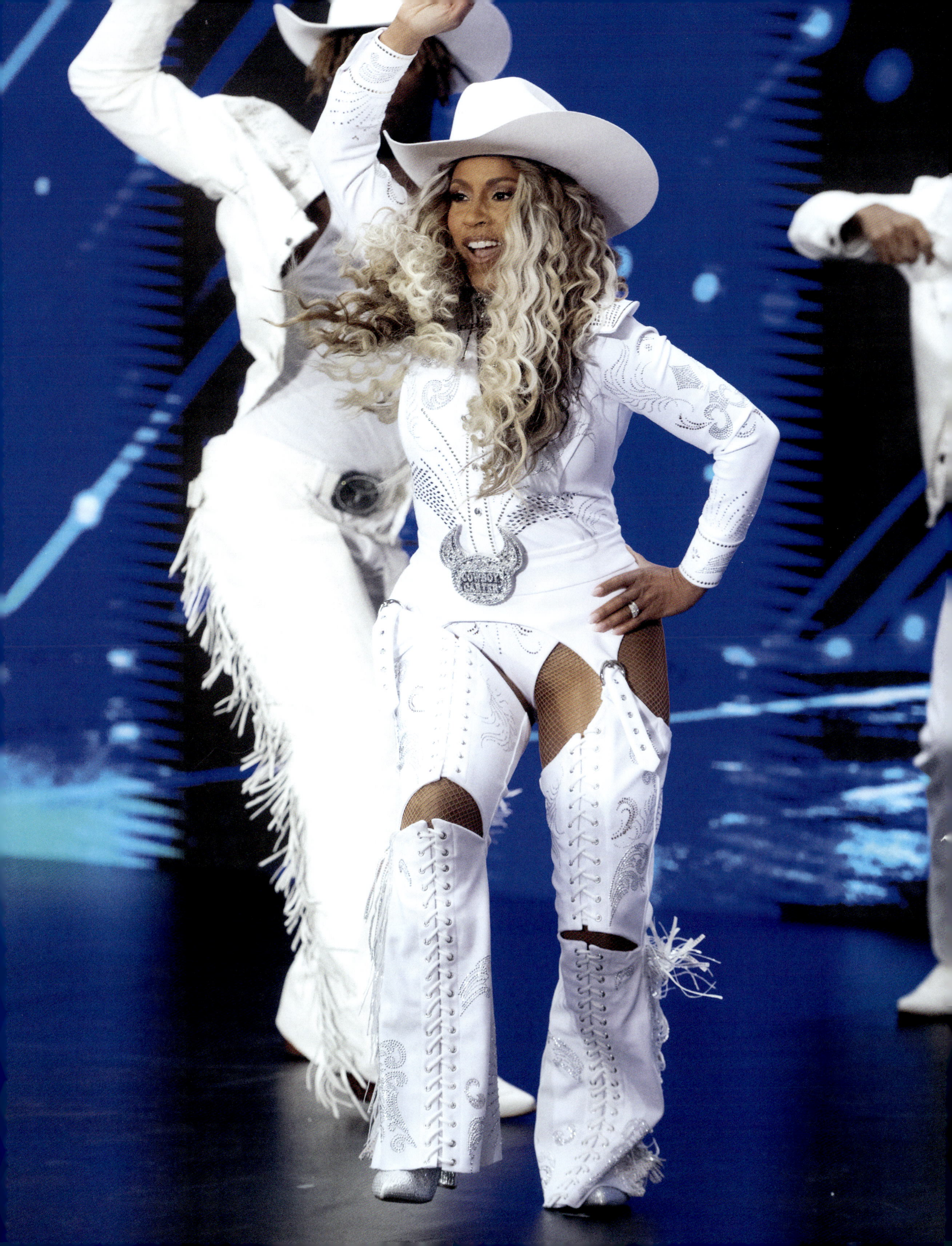

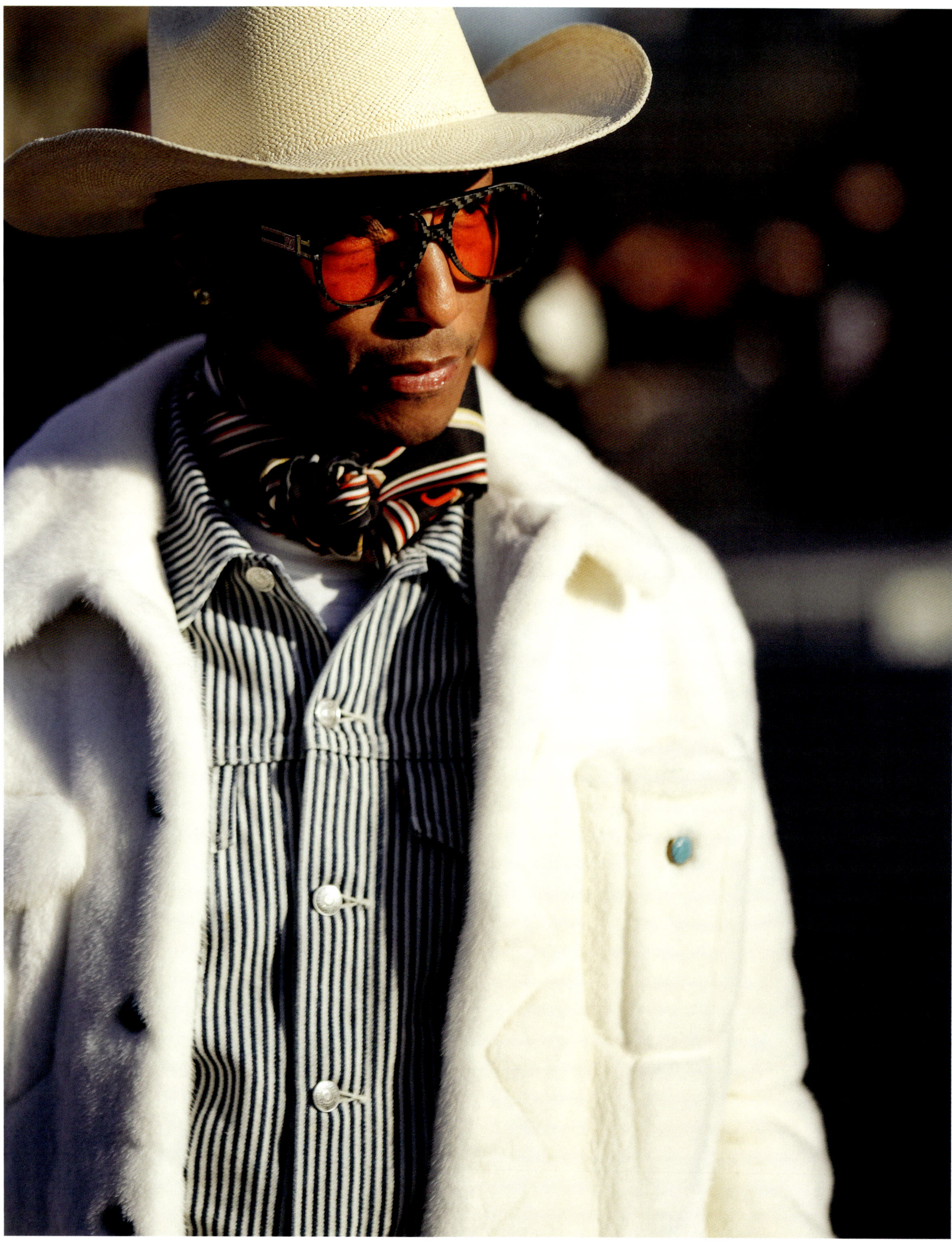

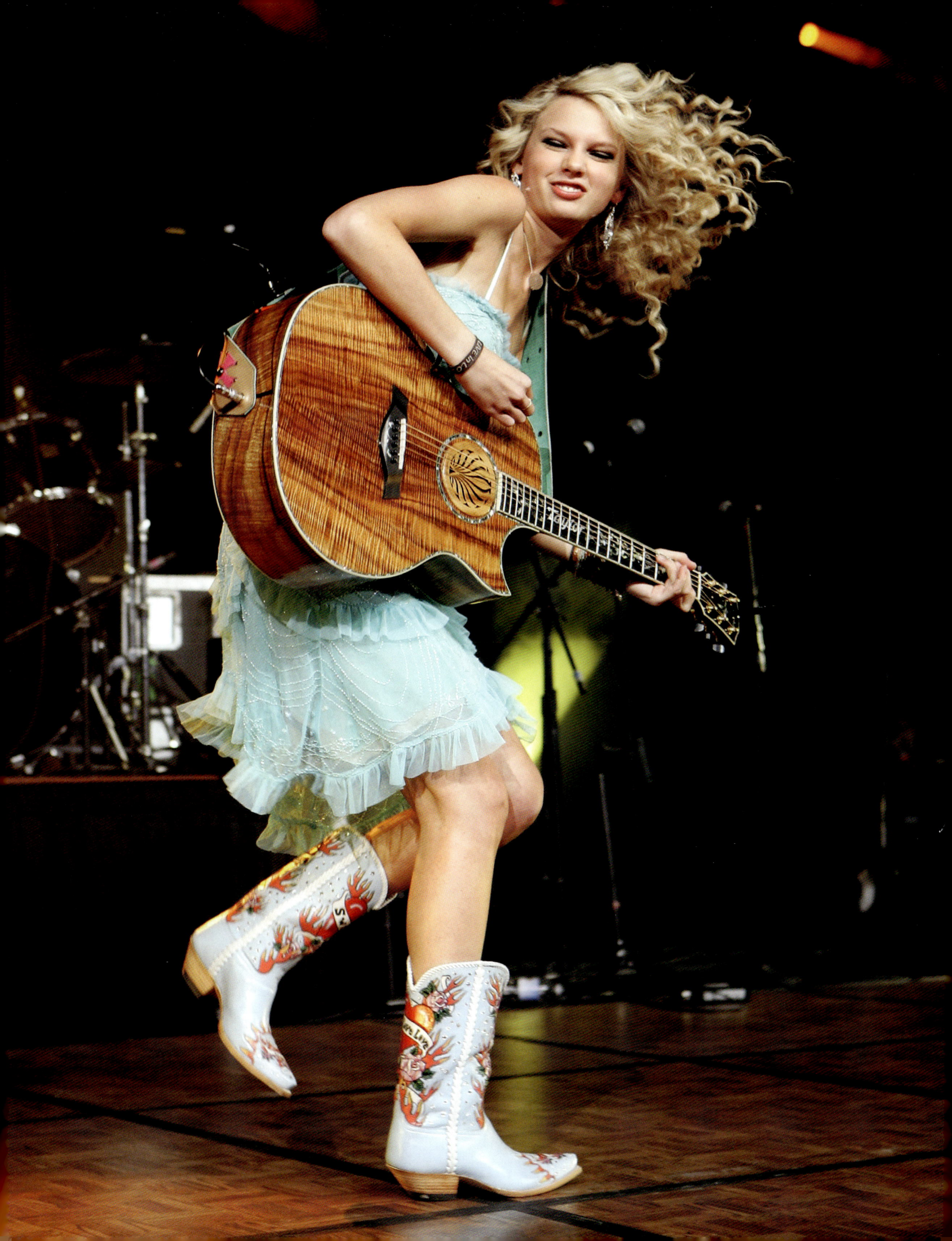

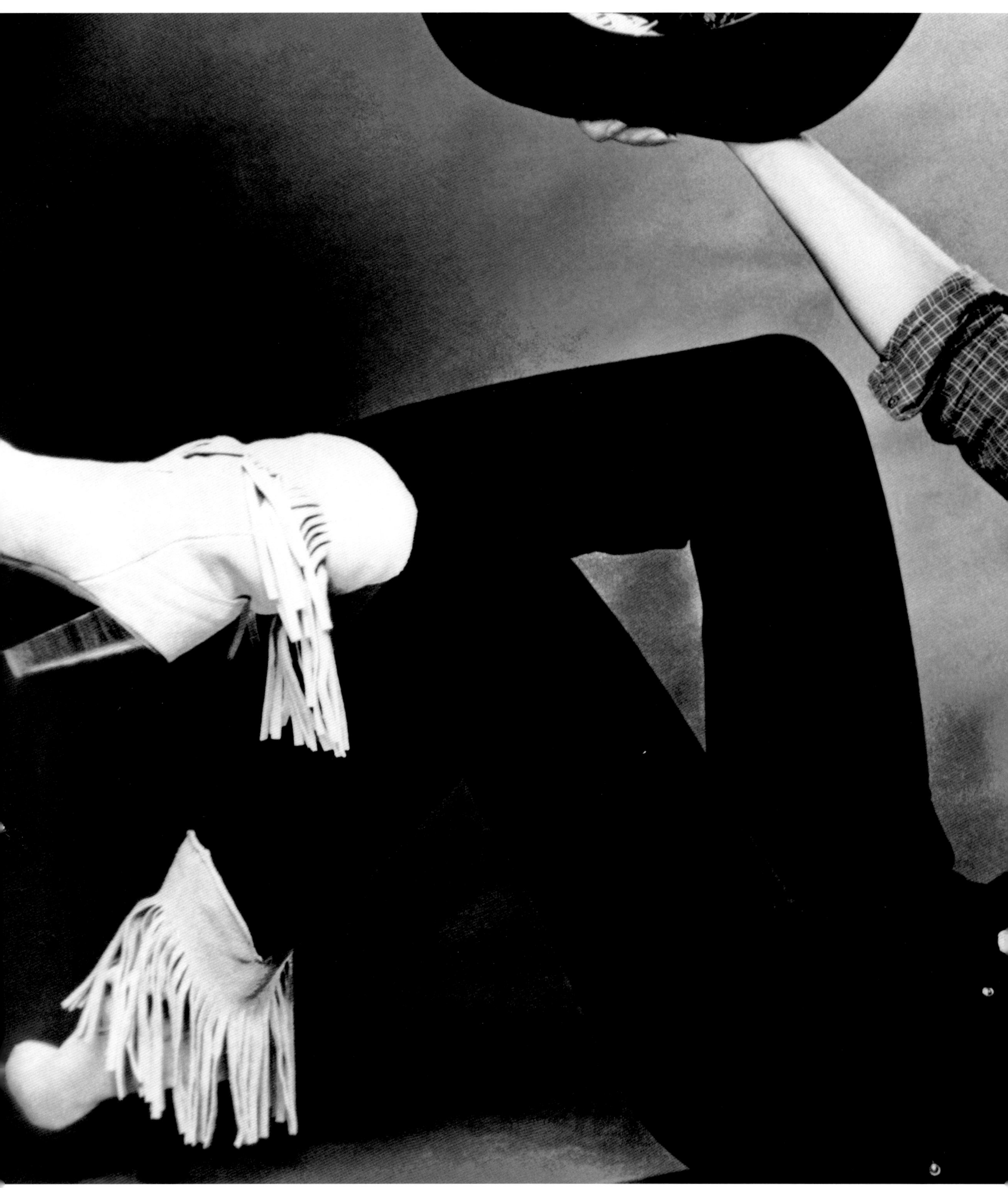

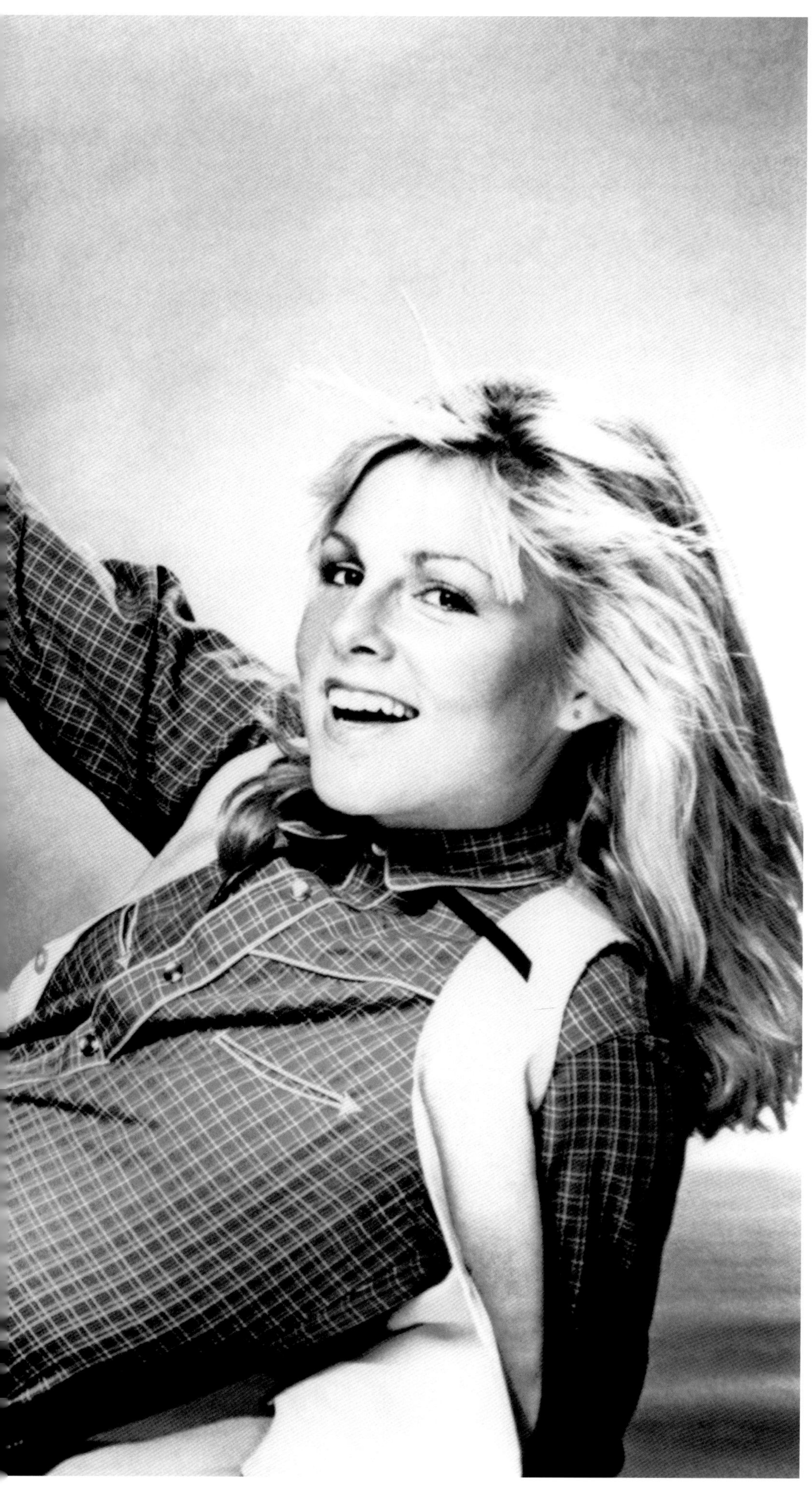

Page 18: *Pharrell Williams wears a white cowboy hat, scarf, black and white striped shirt, white fluffy coat and sunglasses at Paris Fashion Week on January 19, 2024.*

Page 19: *Taylor Swift performs during the first ever Academy of Country Music New Artists' Show Party for a Cause, held at the MGM Grand Conference Center in Las Vegas on May 14, 2007.*

These pages: *Mia Kovacs, daughter of Ernie Kovacs and Edie Adams, poses for a studio portrait in cowboy attire c. 1980 in Los Angeles.*

Following pages: *East Hampton, New York, November 1977. Ralph Lauren with his wife Ricky as he puts on a pair of cowboy boots in the bedroom of their home.*

Pages 24/25: *Angela Lindvall sits on the back of a horse behind a cowboy dressed in denim and leather chaps; she wears a strapless floral print ball gown by Escada with a black cowboy hat and boots.*

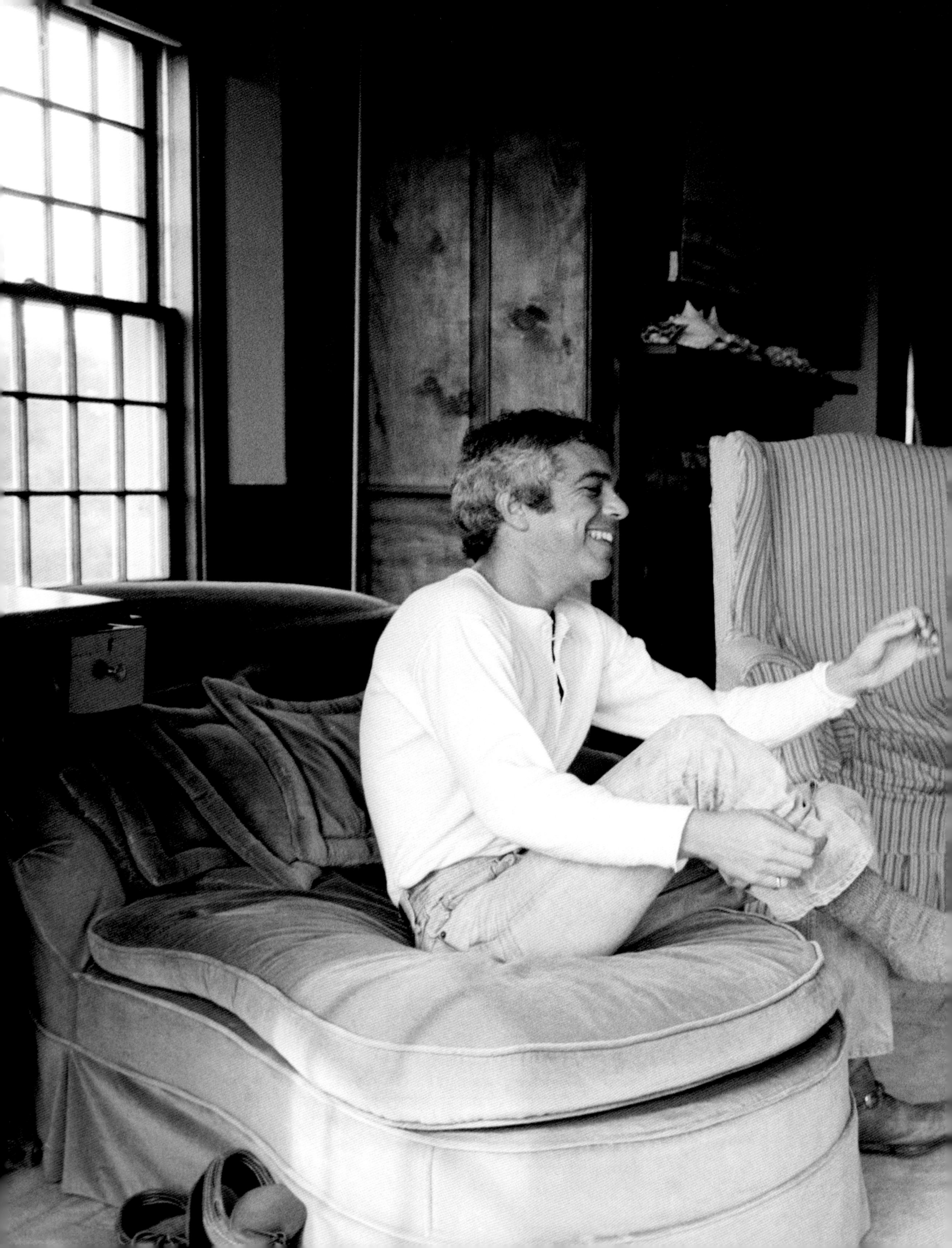

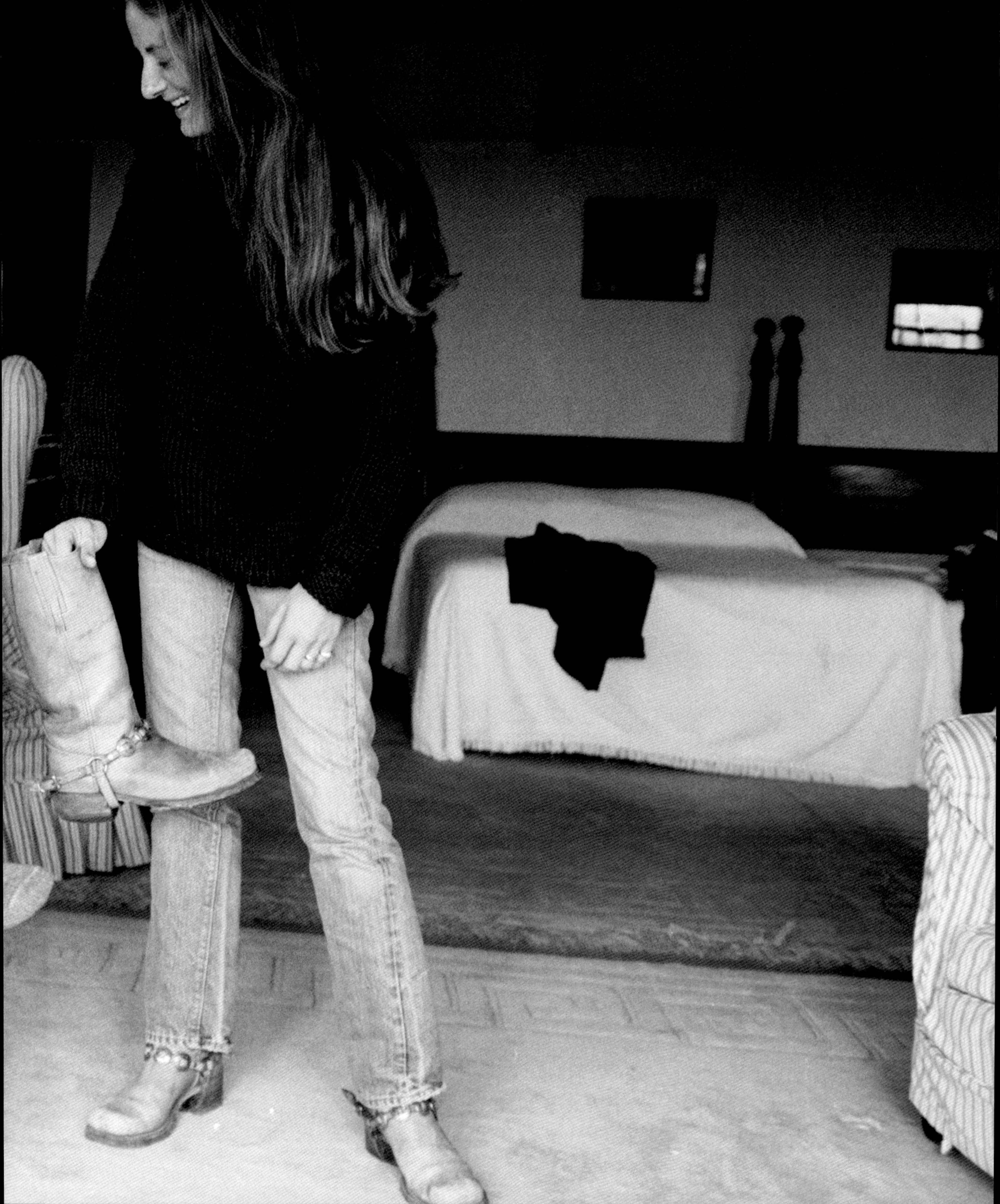

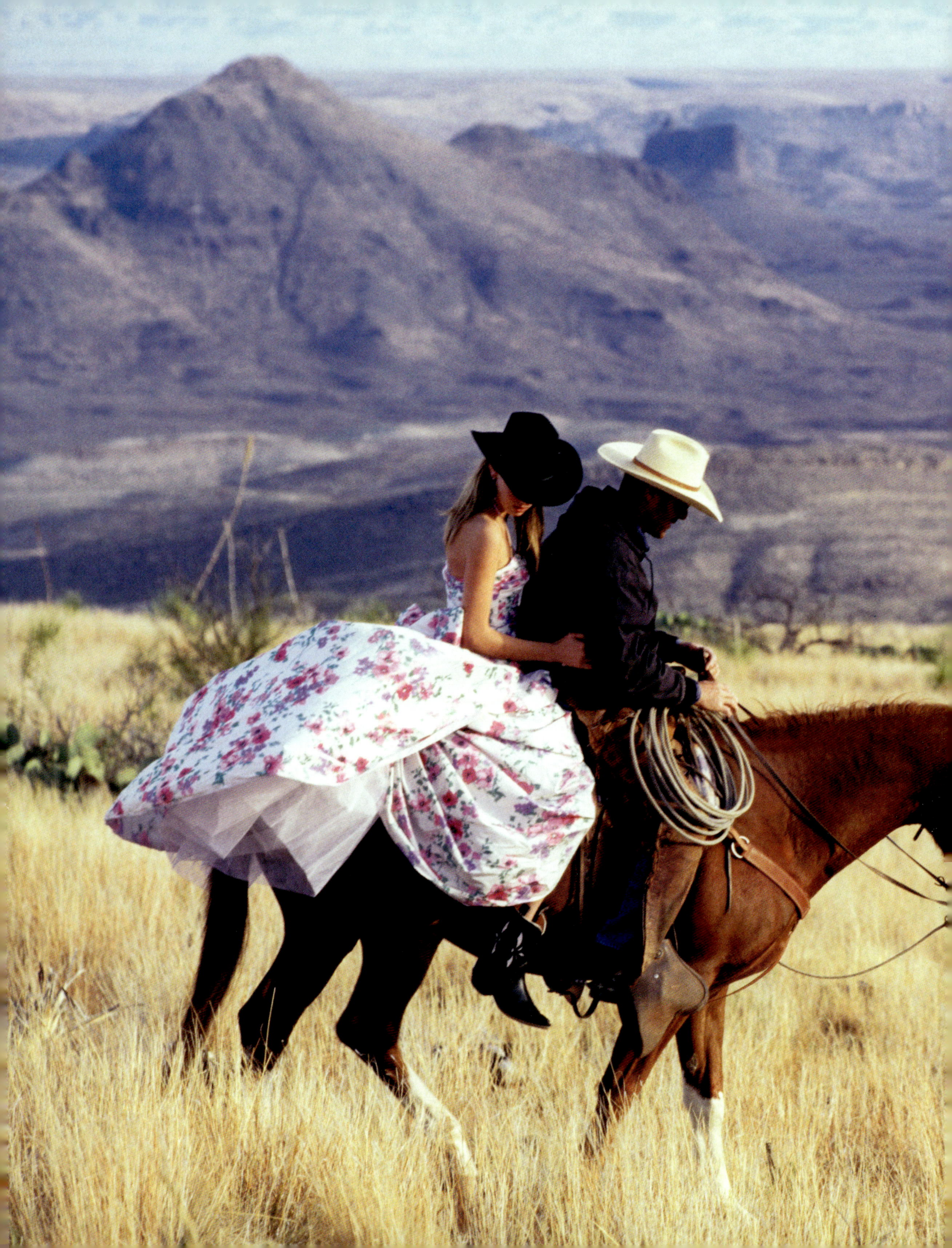

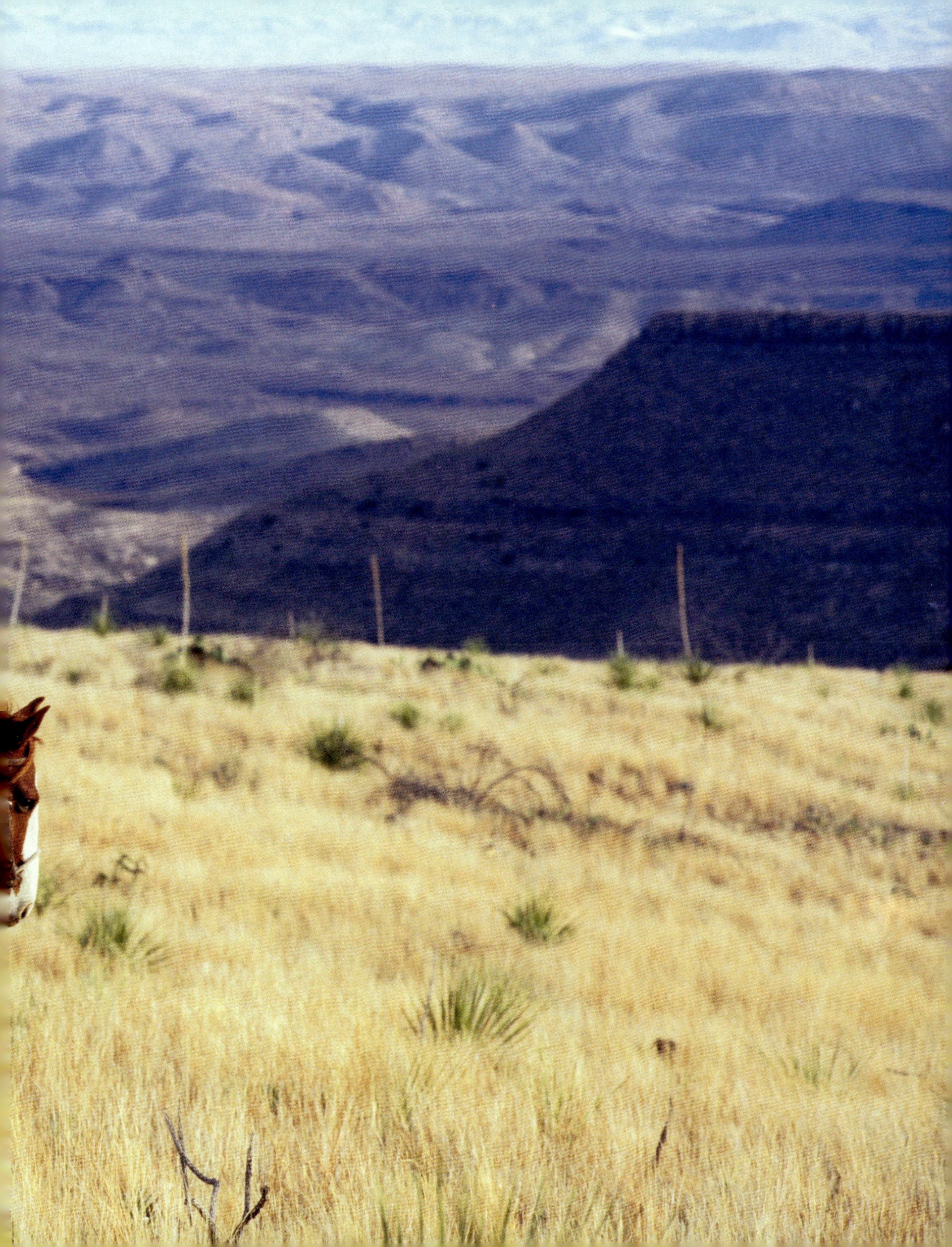

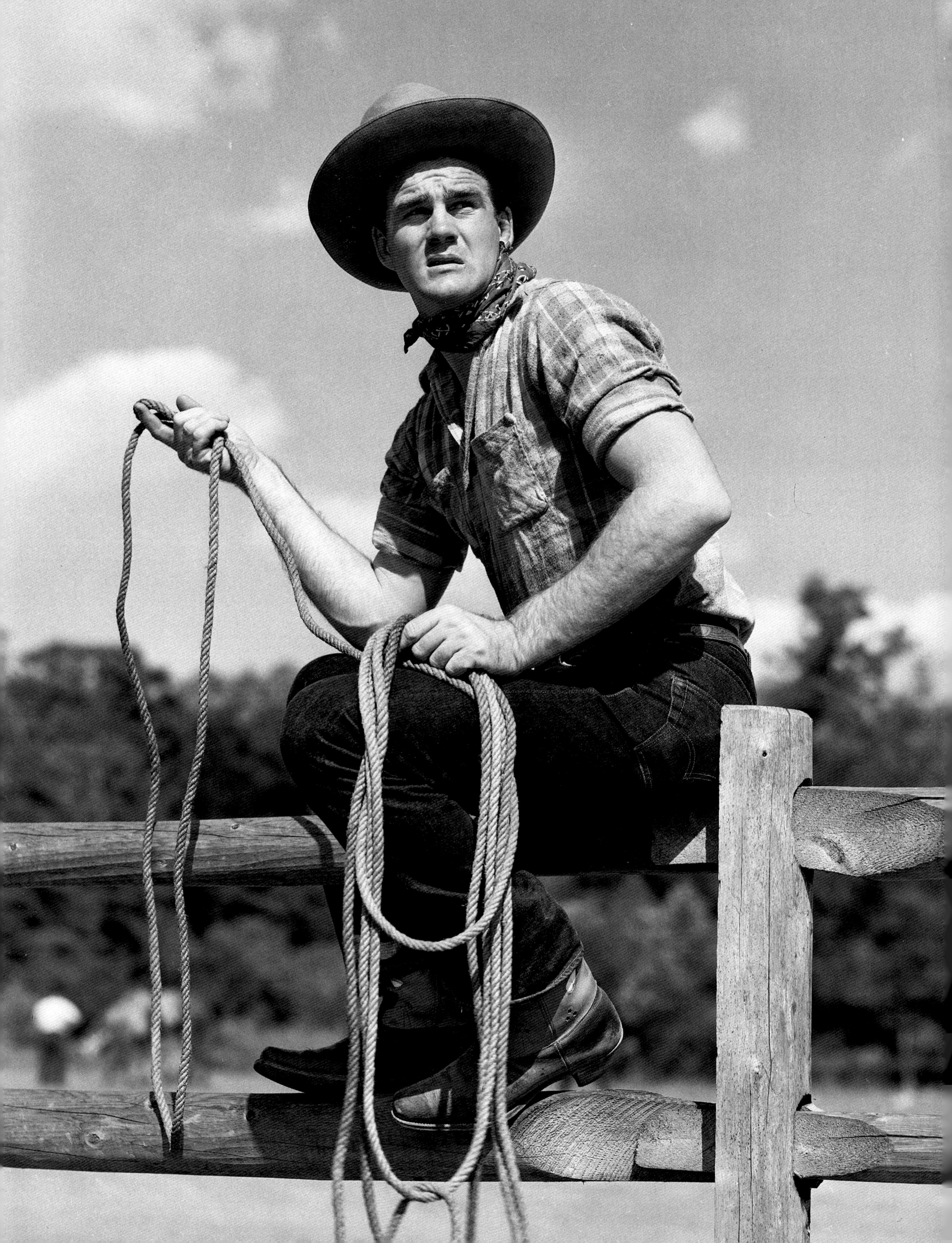

REAL
COWBOYS

ORIGINS, CULTURE, STYLE

Who were the real people whose lives and culture lie behind modern-day Western style? What was life like for the real cowboys and girls of the Wild West? When was their heyday, do they still exist in the modern world—and if so, what do they look like now?

In the contemporary imagination, it's worth noting, the figure of the cowboy is a bit of an amalgam: a combination of "cowboys" as such and other defining figures of the Old West such as gunslingers, sheriffs, outlaws and bounty hunters. But for the purposes of this book, there's no need to be too fussy over historical semantics. When we talk about Western wear or cowboy core we really just mean the iconic looks that have evolved out of the traditions of life as it was lived in the Old West.

So when did "cowboys" appear? In fact, there's no straightforward answer to that question. The cowboy as we think of him—the wearer of Stetson and chaps, the wielder of a six-shooter—was a figure of the mid- to late-nineteenth-century American West, but the term "cowboys" as it was first used in America referred to a group of fighters loyal to the British during the War of Independence—so originally this quintessentially All-American figure was something quite different! Even earlier, in seventeenth-century England "cowboy" seems to have meant a young child employed to herd cattle, as it would later do when the English settled Australia and New Zealand.

None of those early versions of the cowboy, however, have left much of an impression on modern-day culture. Instead, it was as the United States spread west and north in the mid-1800s, settling the remaining unclaimed territories between Mexico and what would later become Canada, that the cowboy as we think of him today appeared on the scene. A skilled cattleman and equestrian, his main function was to look after herds—up to 20,000 strong, first on the open range and later on large ranches—and to lead them on long "drives" to fresh pastures or to railway hubs for transportation east, where their meat would feed large urban centers such as New York, Philadelphia or Cleveland. At the same time, the figures with which cowboys would later become muddled also began to proliferate (lawmen, sharpshooters, outlaws and the rest), policing, profiting from or terrorizing the emerging territories.

This was the cultural context from which the iconic styles of the West emerged. Whether in the wilderness or the small "cattletowns" that sprang up along established drive routes such as the Chisholm Trail, this was a rough-hewn and perilous place to live—one that required not only extraordinary survival skills, grit and endurance but also a very specific set of practical, durable garments and accessories. Broad-brimmed hats and bandanas for the sun; jeans, boots, ponchos, leather jackets and thick cotton or wool shirts for the cold; spurs, chaps and lariats for riding; gun-belts, holsters and revolvers for fighting: all the familiar elements of 2020s cowboy core were present and correct.

But if there's a lot that's familiar here, there are also some more unexpected aspects of the story of Western life and style. It's true that cow*boy* is overwhelmingly the correct term: while women did participate in the cowboy life, and could become renowned for doing so, this was a heavily male-dominated world. False, though, is the popular image of the cowboy as nearly exclusively white: in fact, historians think that as much as a quarter of the cowboy population was Black, and despite the conventional notion of cowboys and "Indians" as enemies, a huge number of cowboys had Indigenous backgrounds. Along similar lines, it was from the Mexican *vaquero* tradition that many Northern American cowboy methods and style traditions grew, which itself had roots—via Moorish Spain— in North African culture. Again, there is more to the "All American" cowboy and their look than meets the eye.

Why did the original era of cowboy style come to an end? Well, in fact it didn't. True, the age of cattle drives had largely passed by the later nineteenth century, with processing facilities now operating closer to the grazing lands and the invention of barbed wire and the expansion of the railways having rendered many of the traditional functions of the cowboy obsolete. Similarly, figures such as the outlaw and bounty hunter faded from the scene as populations grew and state authorities became established. But "cowboy" life and style continued on ranches and in Western towns and cities, where they can still be observed today. A lot has changed with the advent of cell phones, pick-up trucks, university agricultural programs and modern veterinary science. But equally many features of cowboy life have been transmitted mostly unchanged down the generations, from seasonal events such as branding or spring calving to the distinctive and much-mimicked sartorial styles that go along with them.

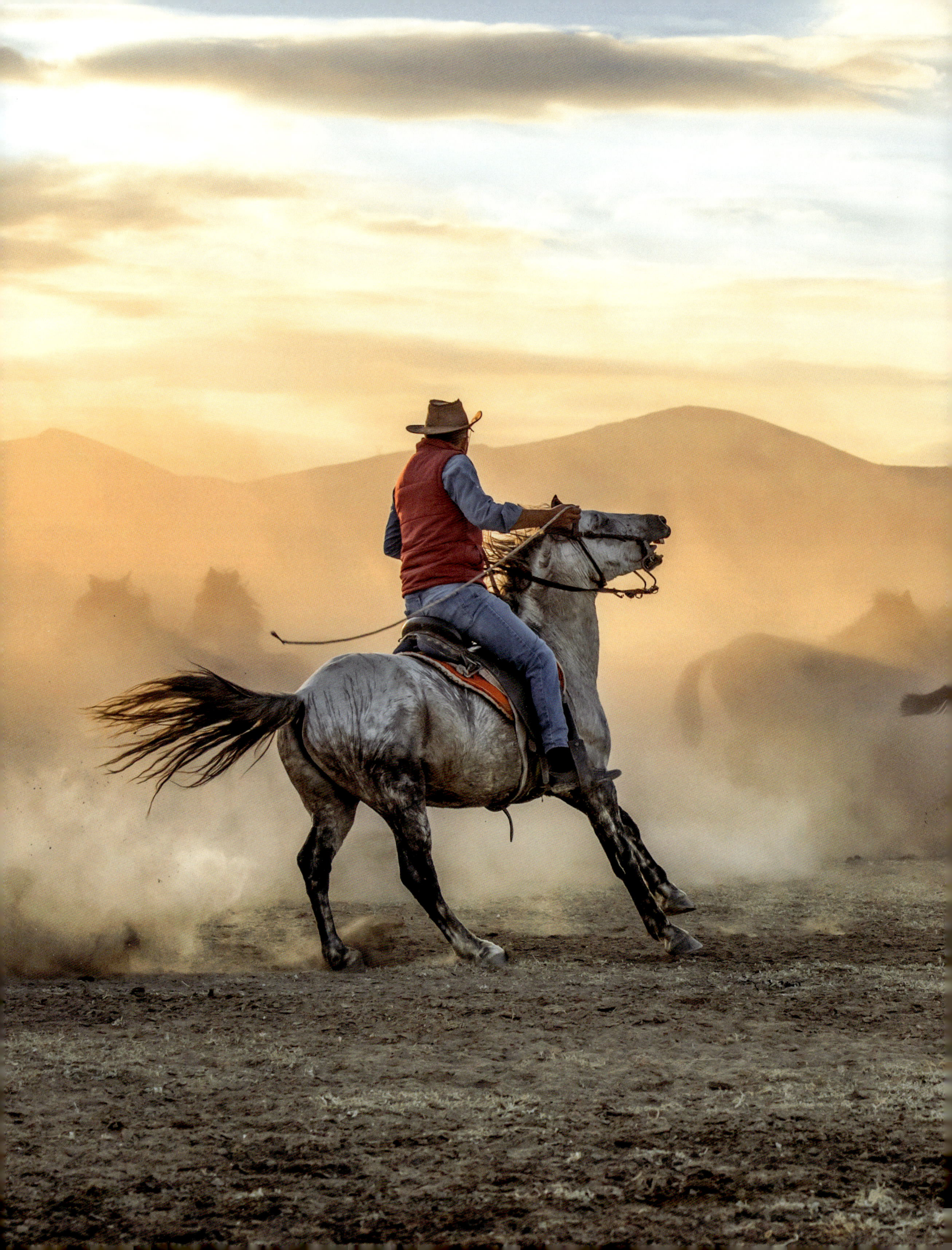

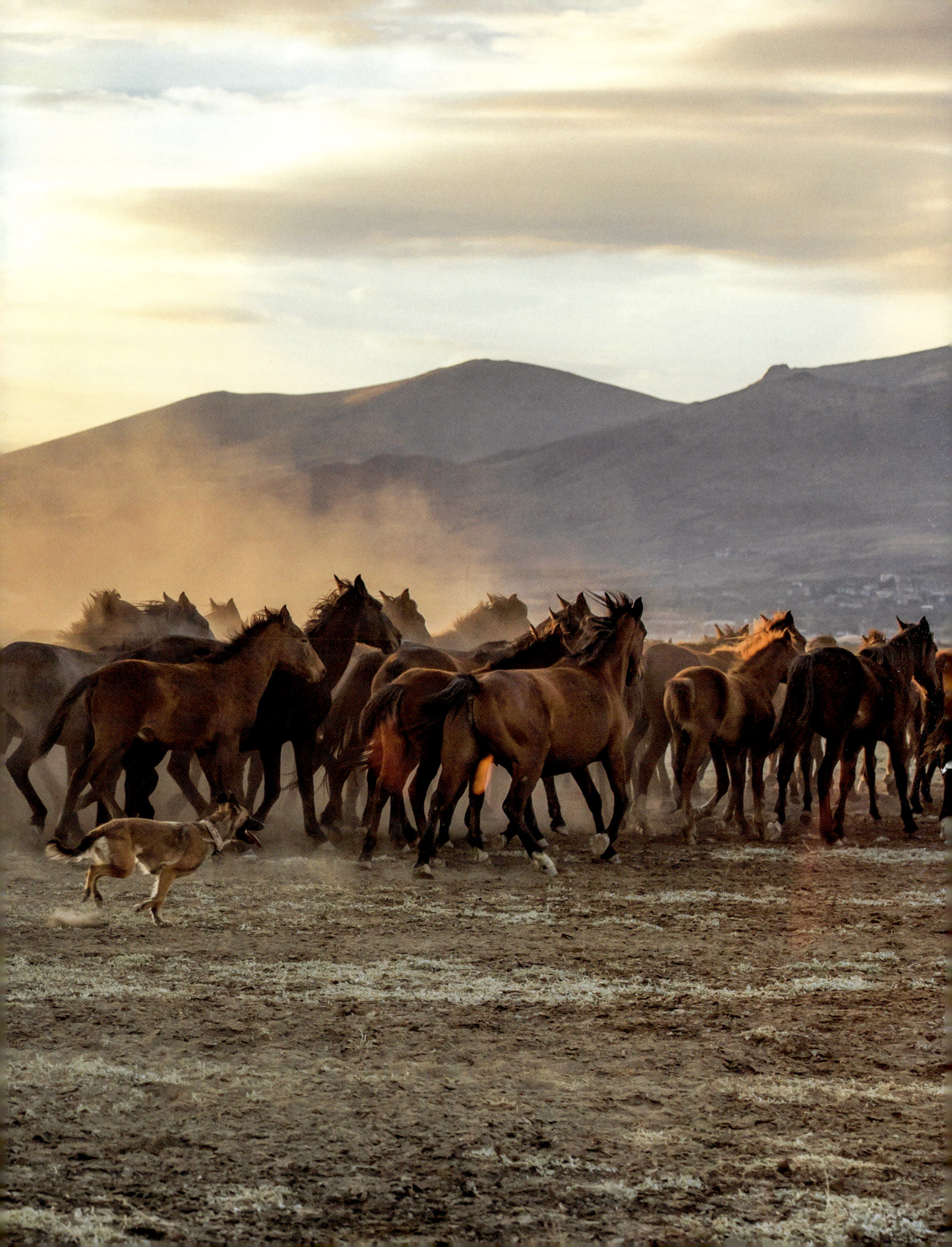

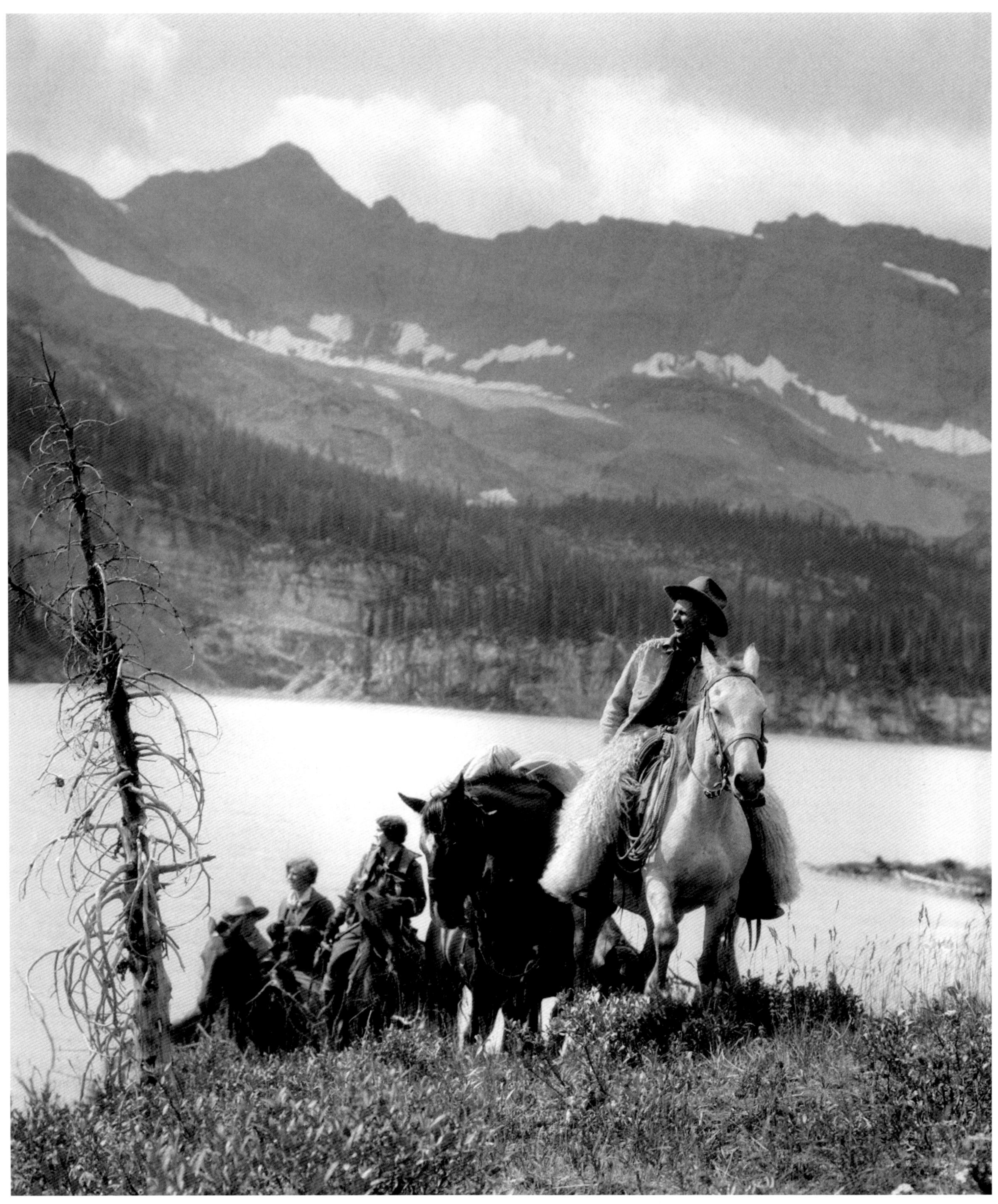

This page: *Two cowgirls and a cowboy in woolen chaps in the 1920s or 1930s in Canada.*

Opposite: *A group in cowboy dress makes camp for the night near two very large cacti, cooking sausages over an open fire (c. 1955).*

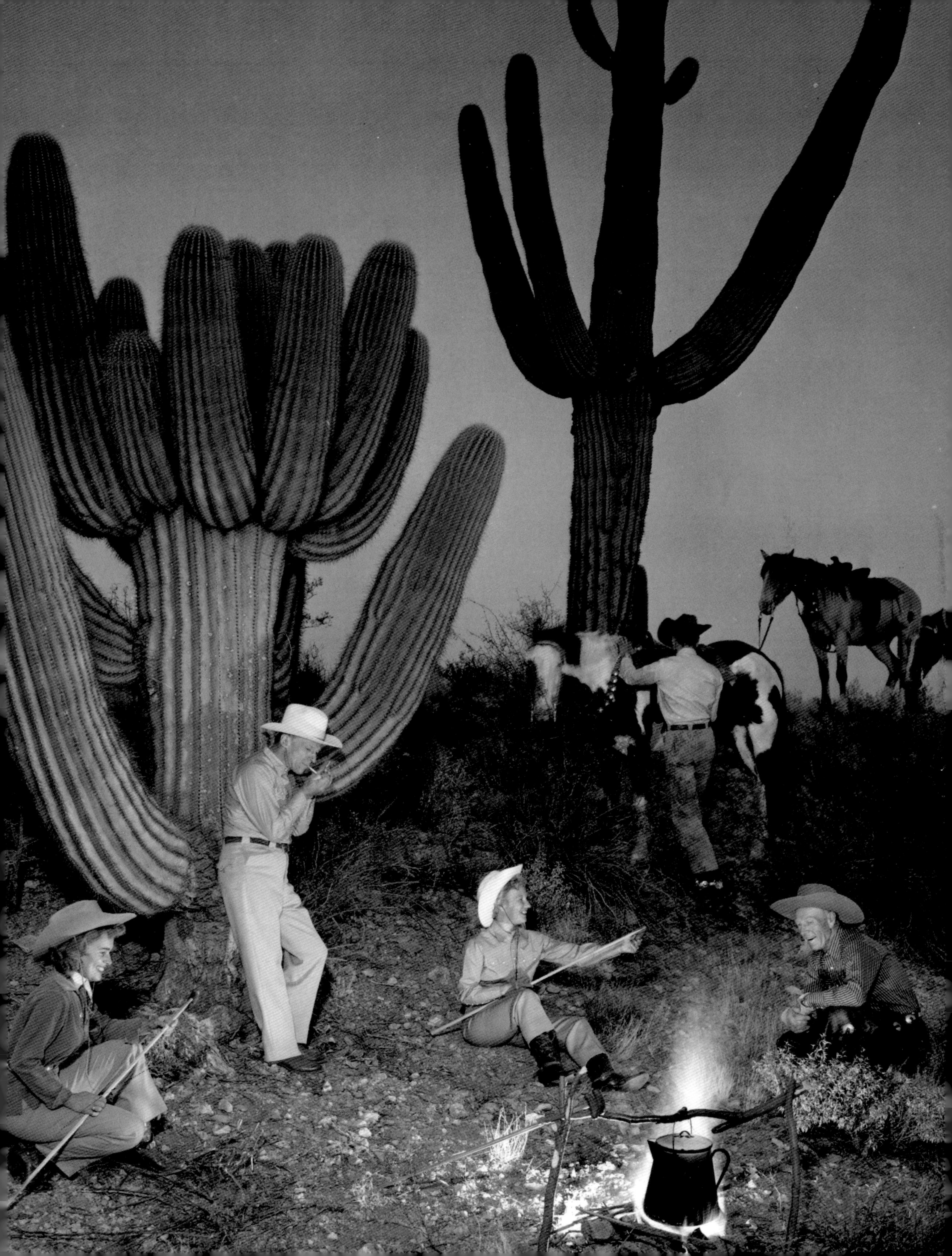

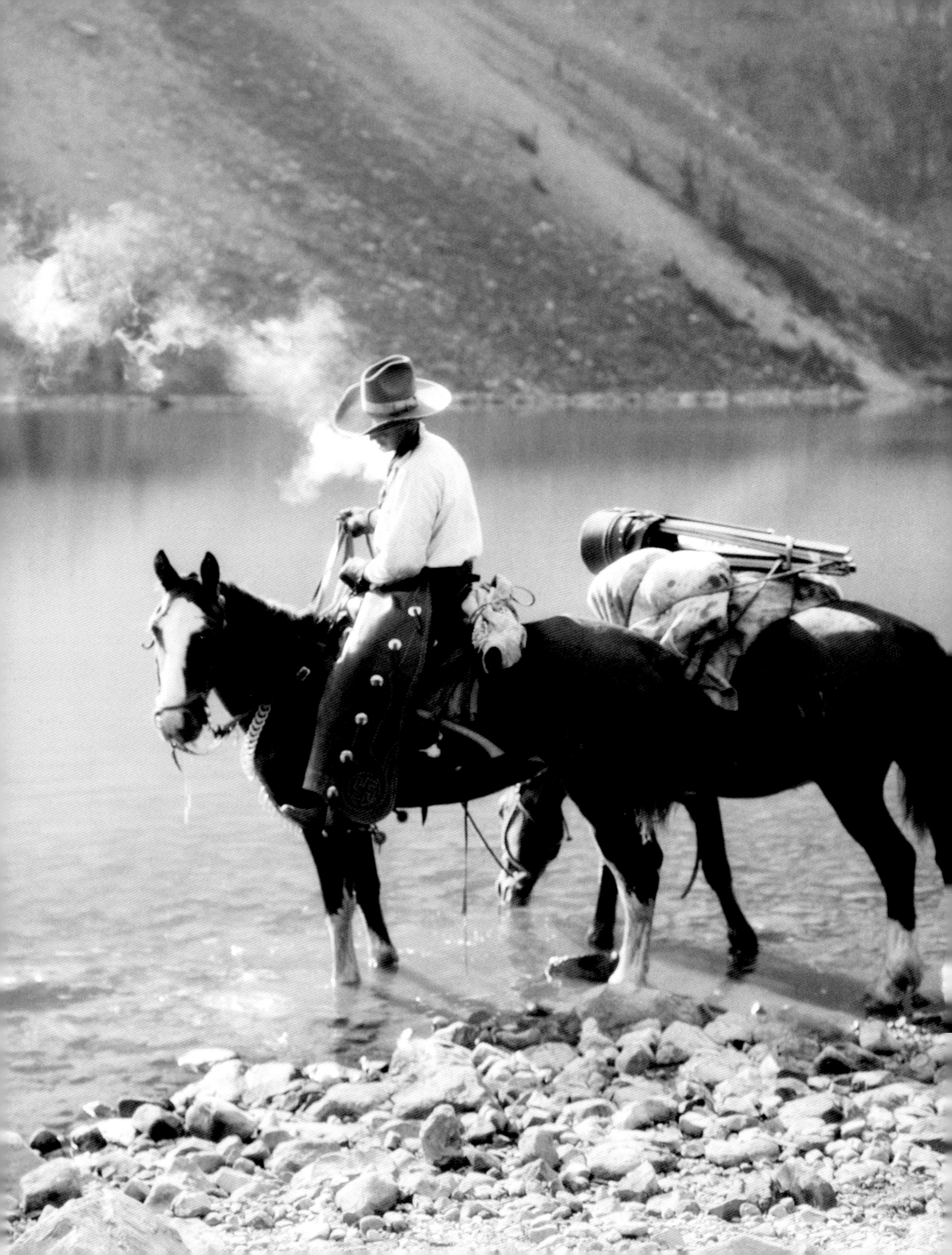

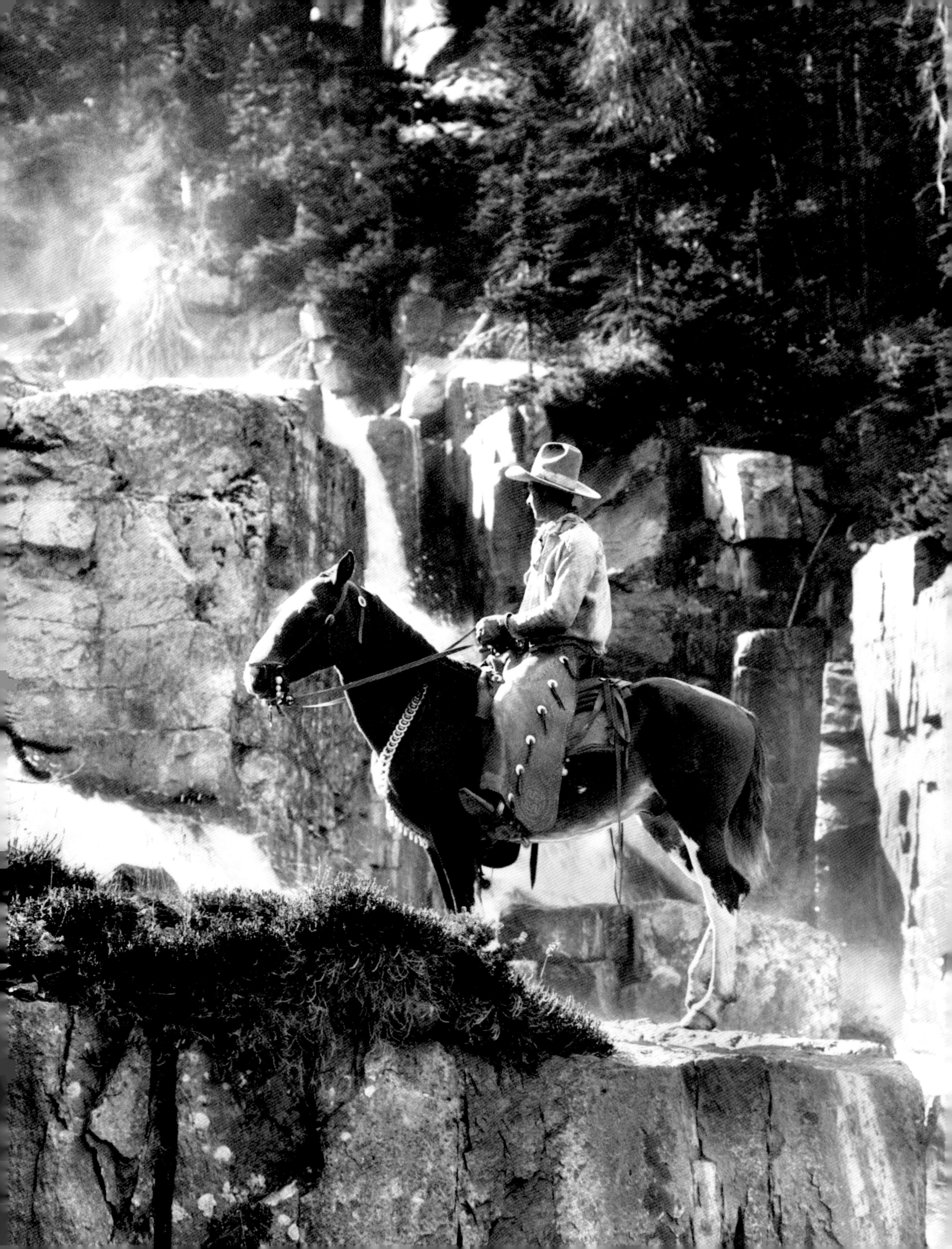

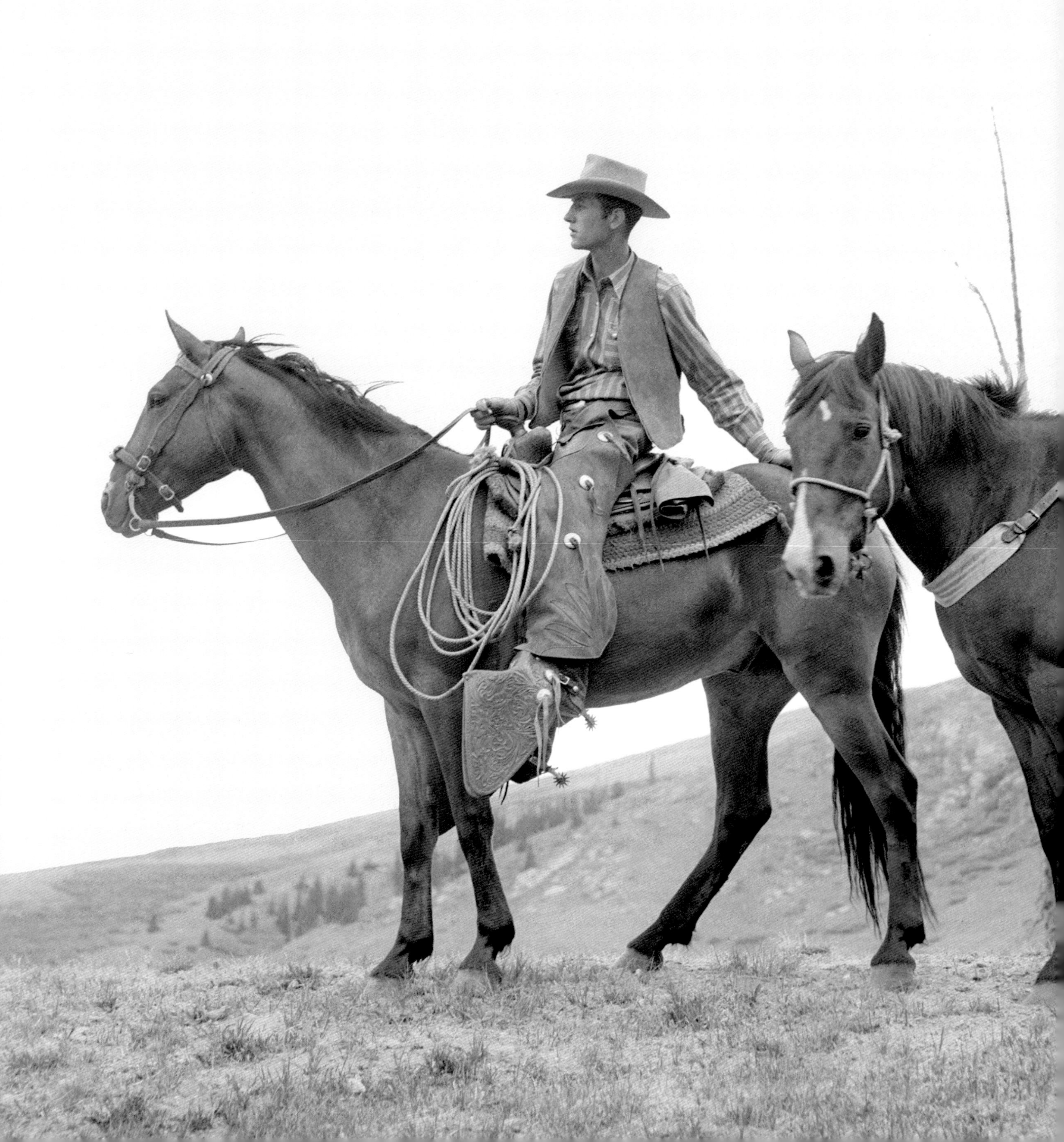

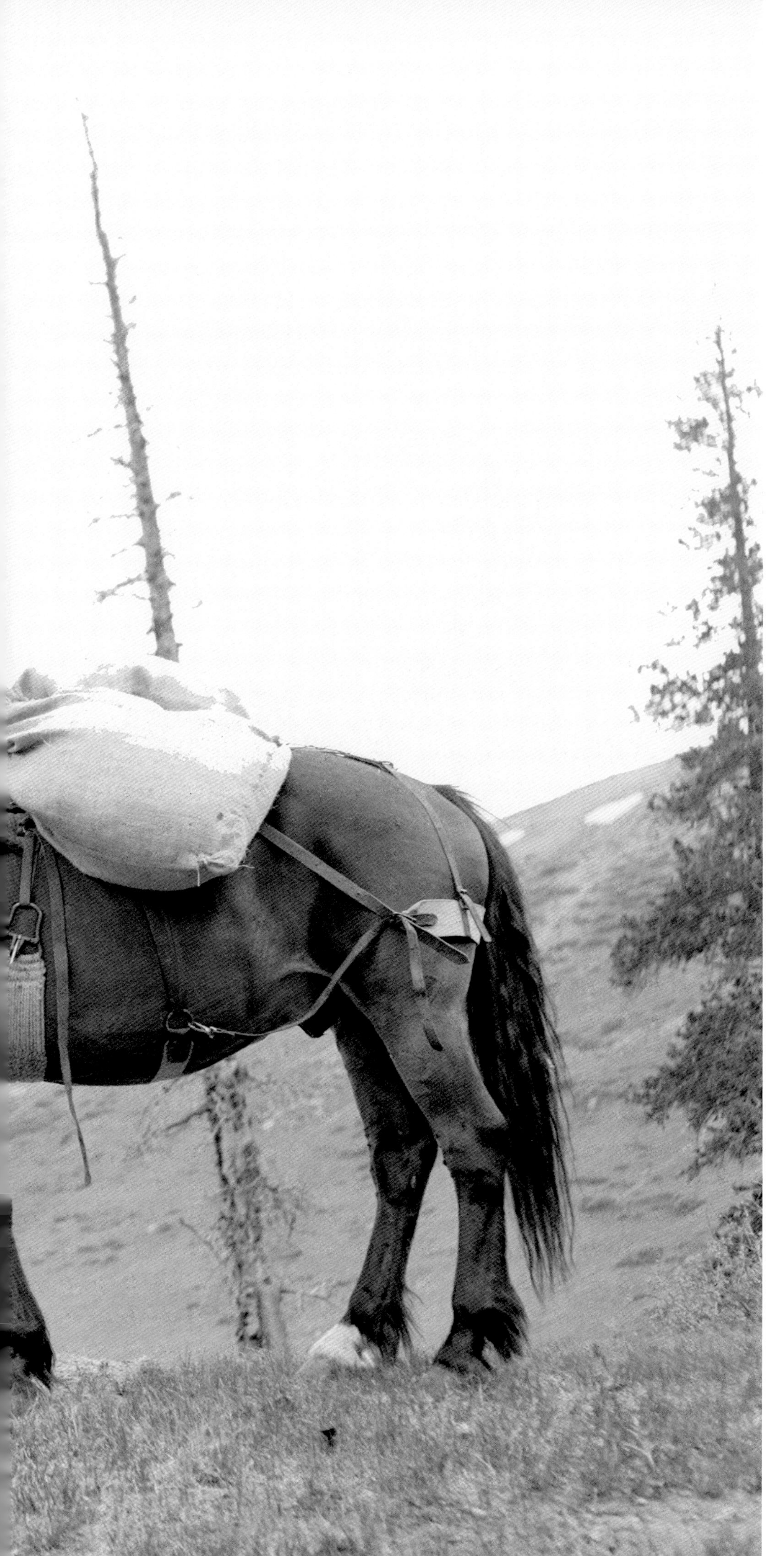

Page 34: *A cowboy on the shores of Moraine Lake, Alberta, Canada, 1920s or 1930s.*

Page 35: *A cowboy in front of a waterfall in Paradise Valley, Alberta, Canada.*

These pages: *A cowboy and pack horse in the 1920s or 1930s.*

Page 38, top: *Two cowboys drinking coffee by campfire in Bow Summit, Alberta, Canada.*

Page 38, bottom: *Two trail hands and two female guests eating lunch in Alberta, Canada.*

Page 39: *Cowboys preparing their meal over a campfire in Brazeau River, Alberta, Canada.*

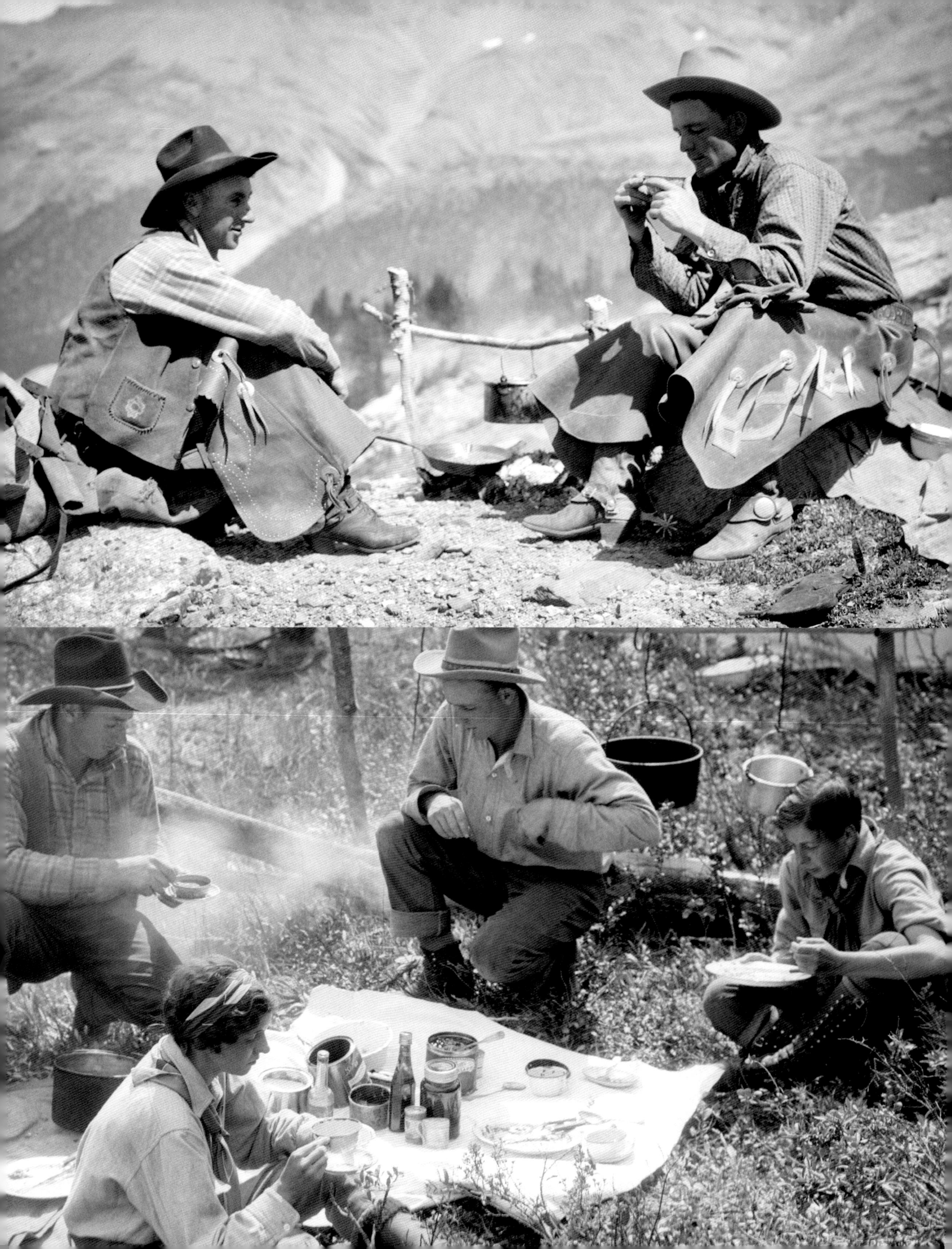

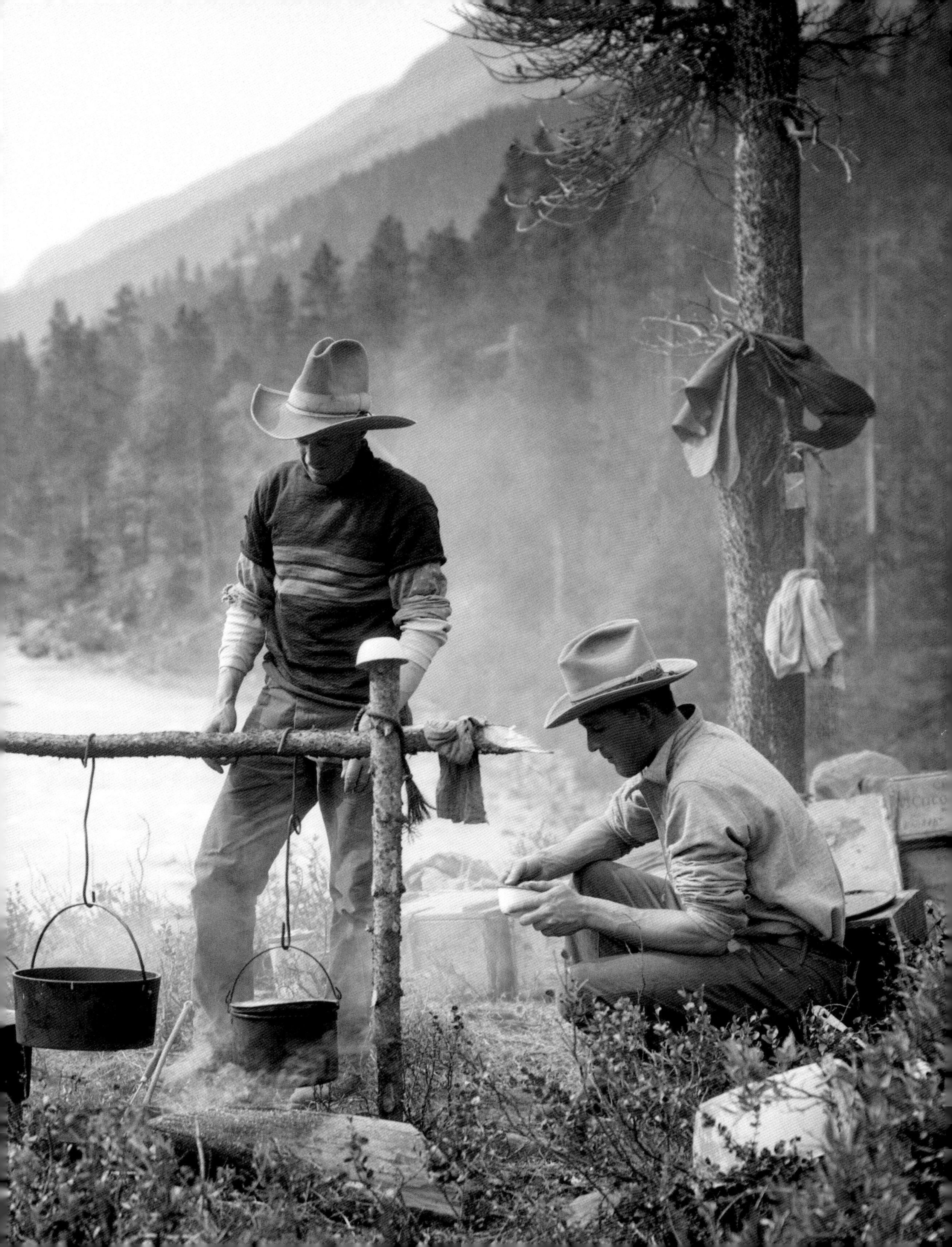

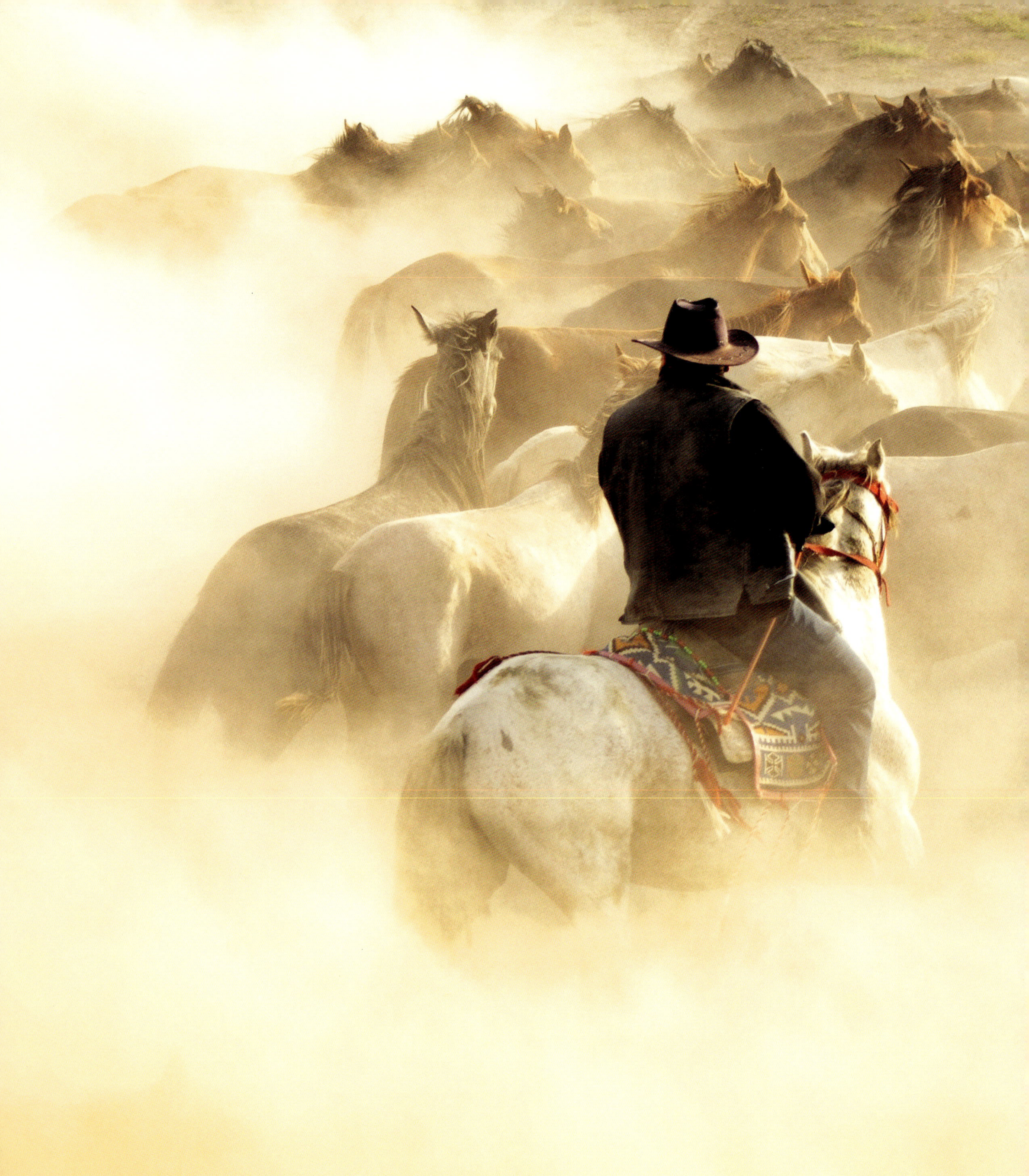

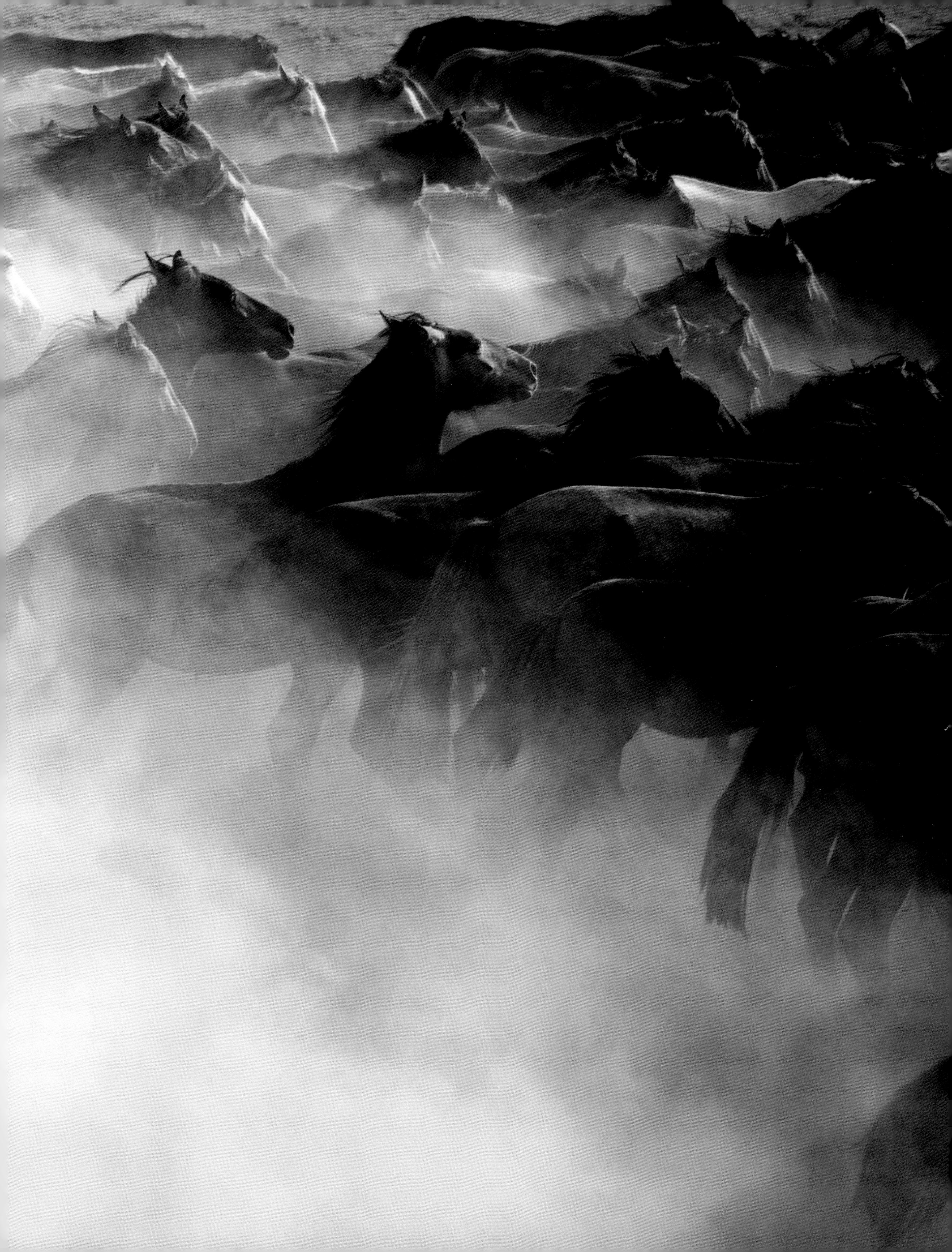

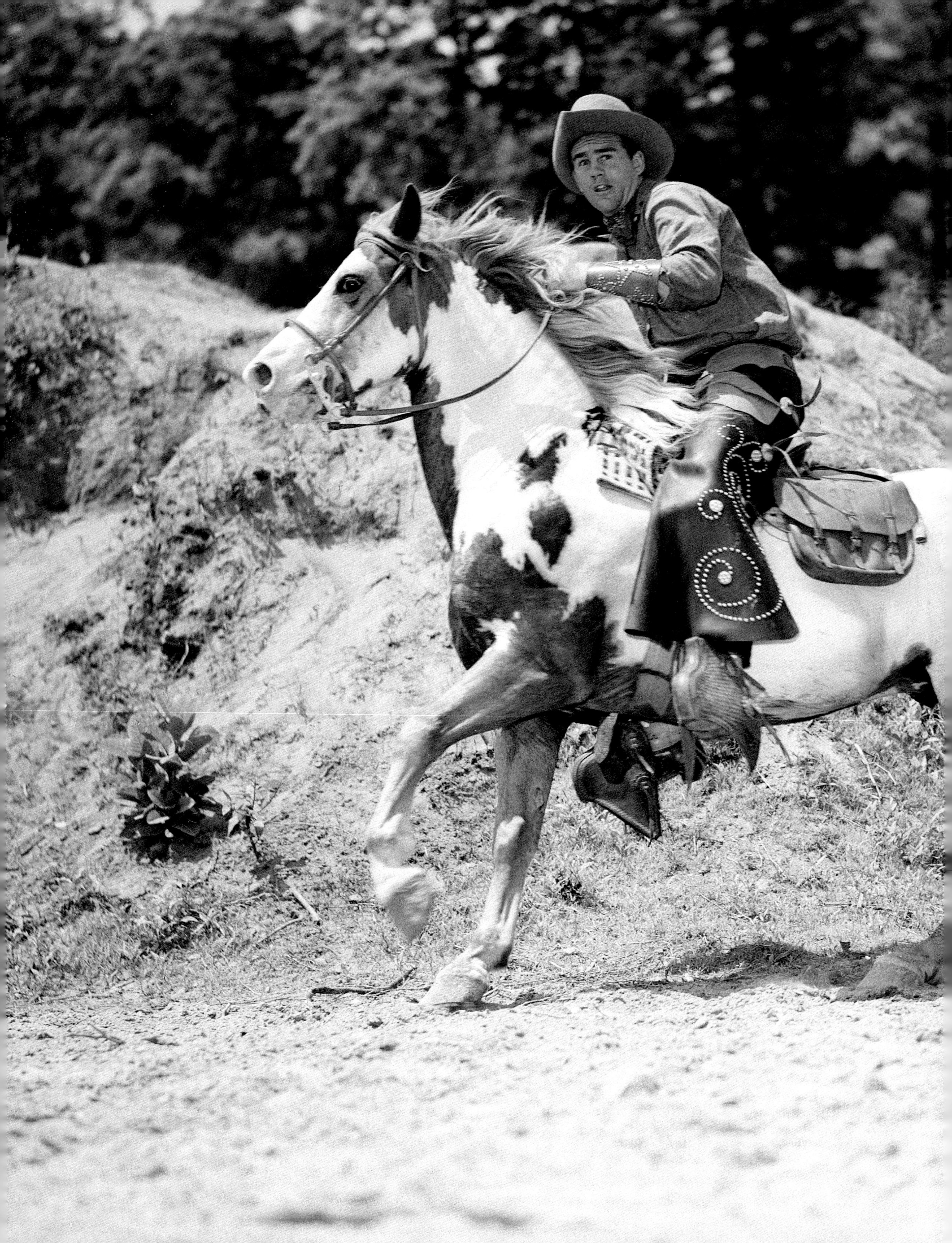

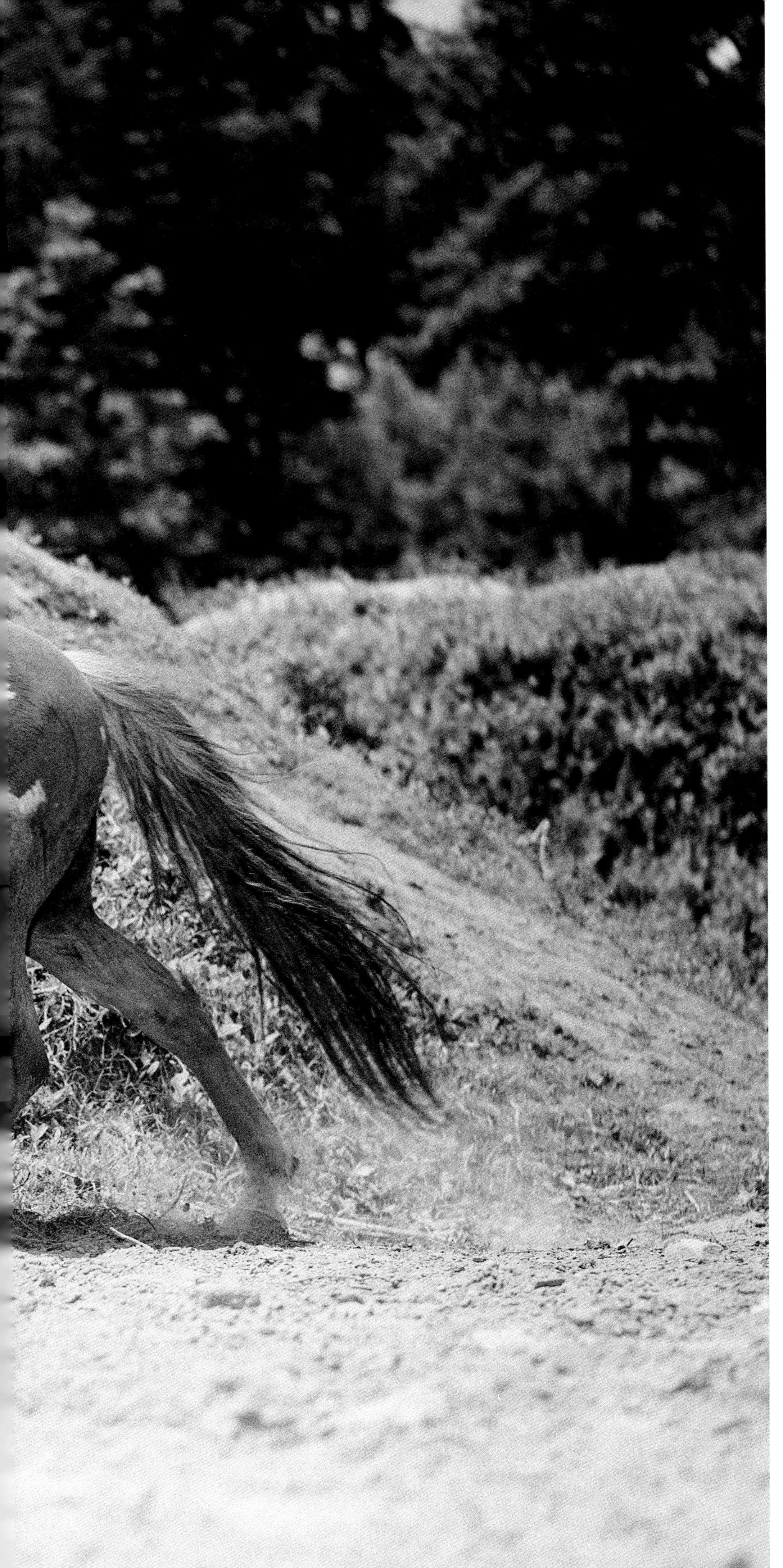

Pages 40/41: *A cowboy leading horses.*

These pages: *A cowboy on horseback.*

Page 44, top: *Two teenage boys prepare a meal at a campfire as two older men look on from beside a chuck wagon, c. 1945.*

Page 44, bottom: *Group of cowboys standing and kneeling around a campfire, 1950s.*

Page 45: *Cowboys (one standing in batwing chaps) and a woman groom a horse, 1930s.*

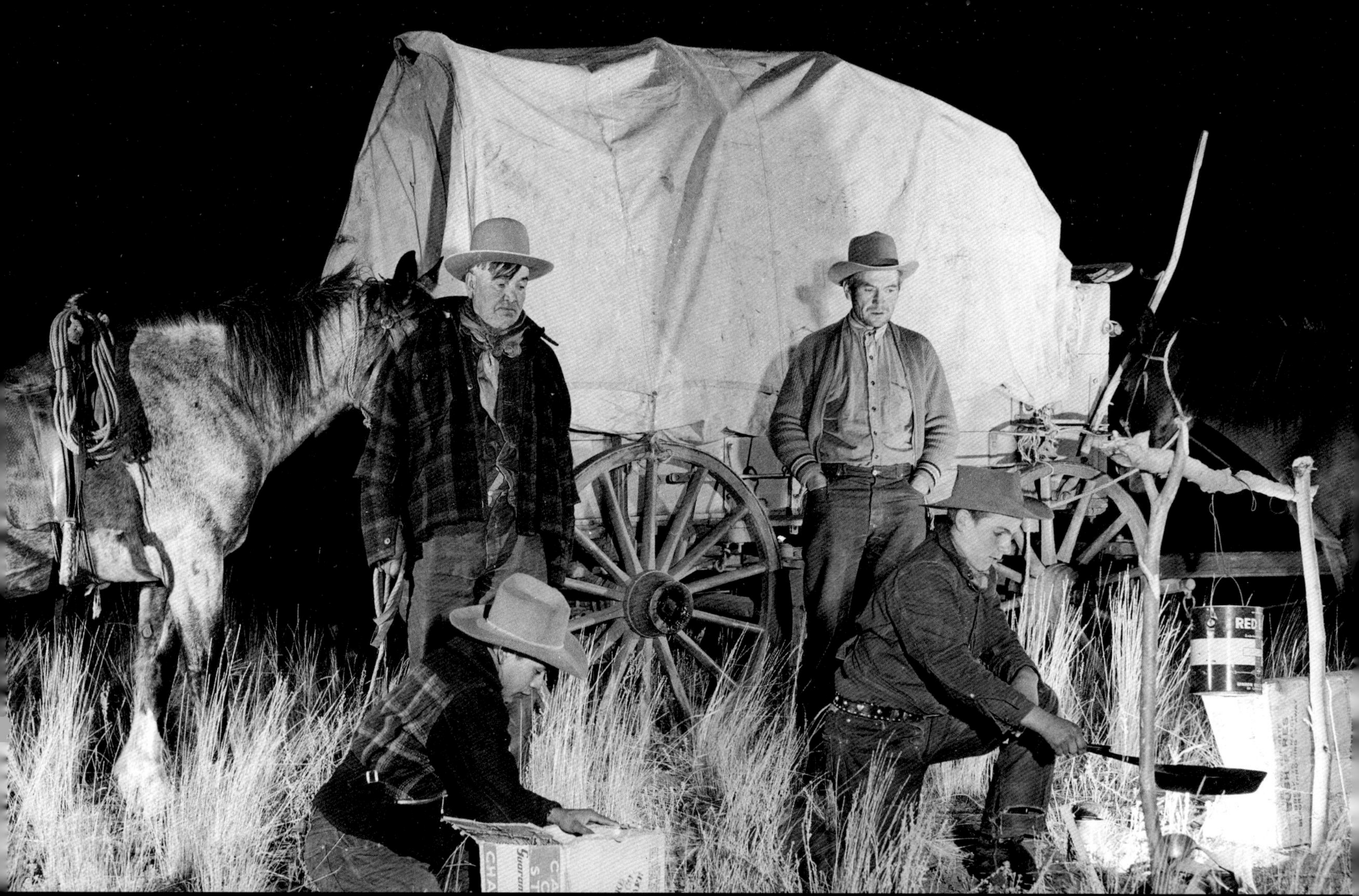

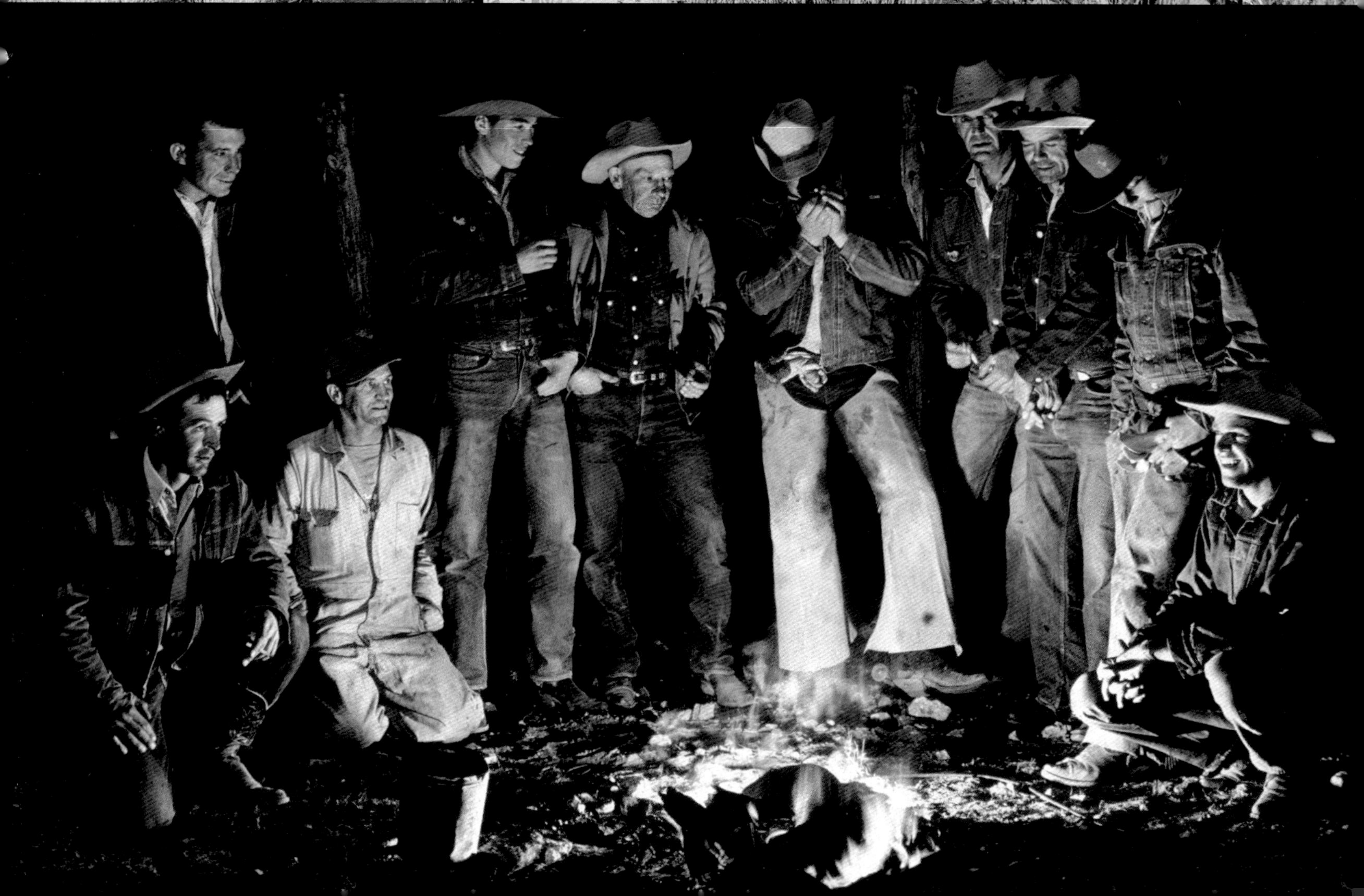

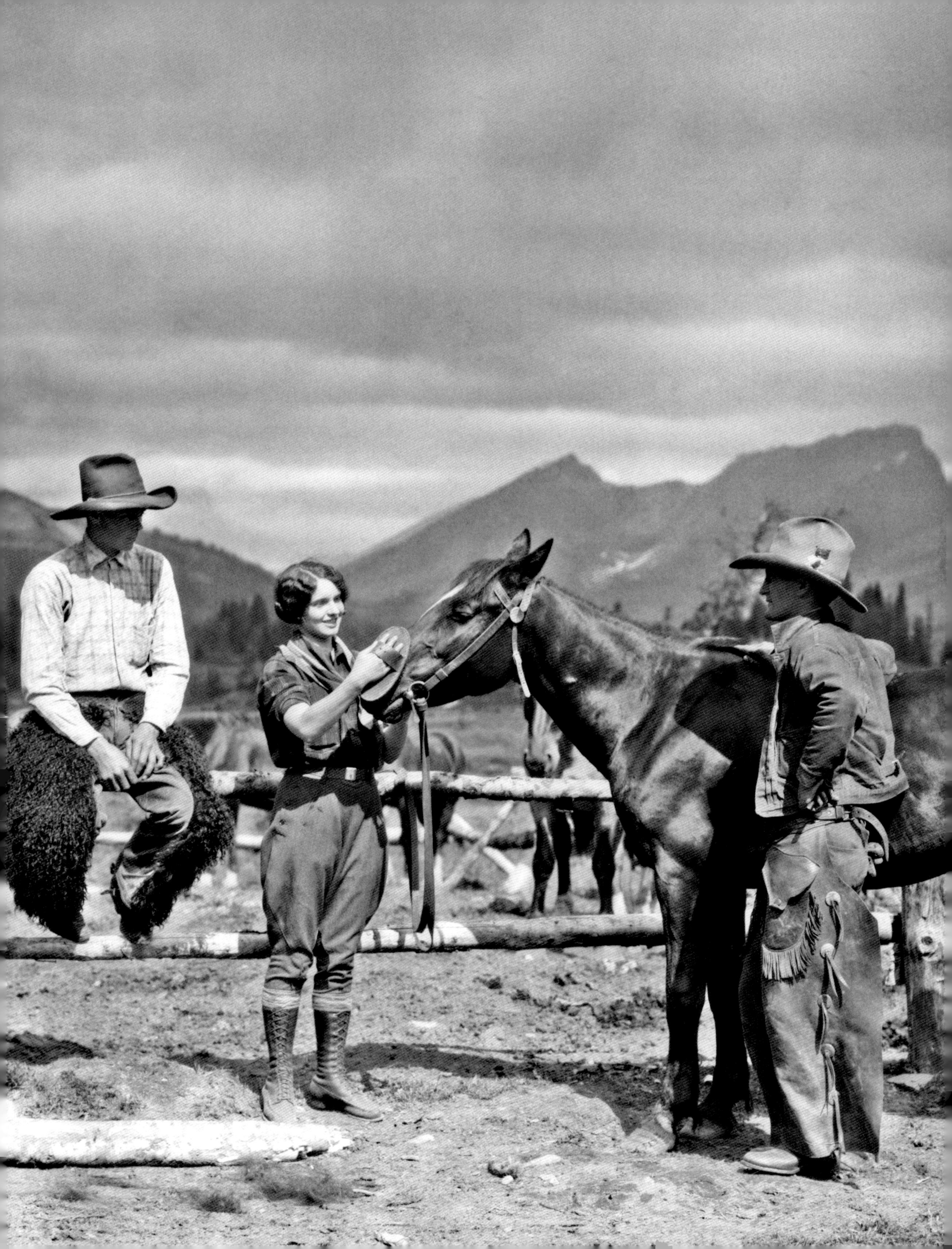

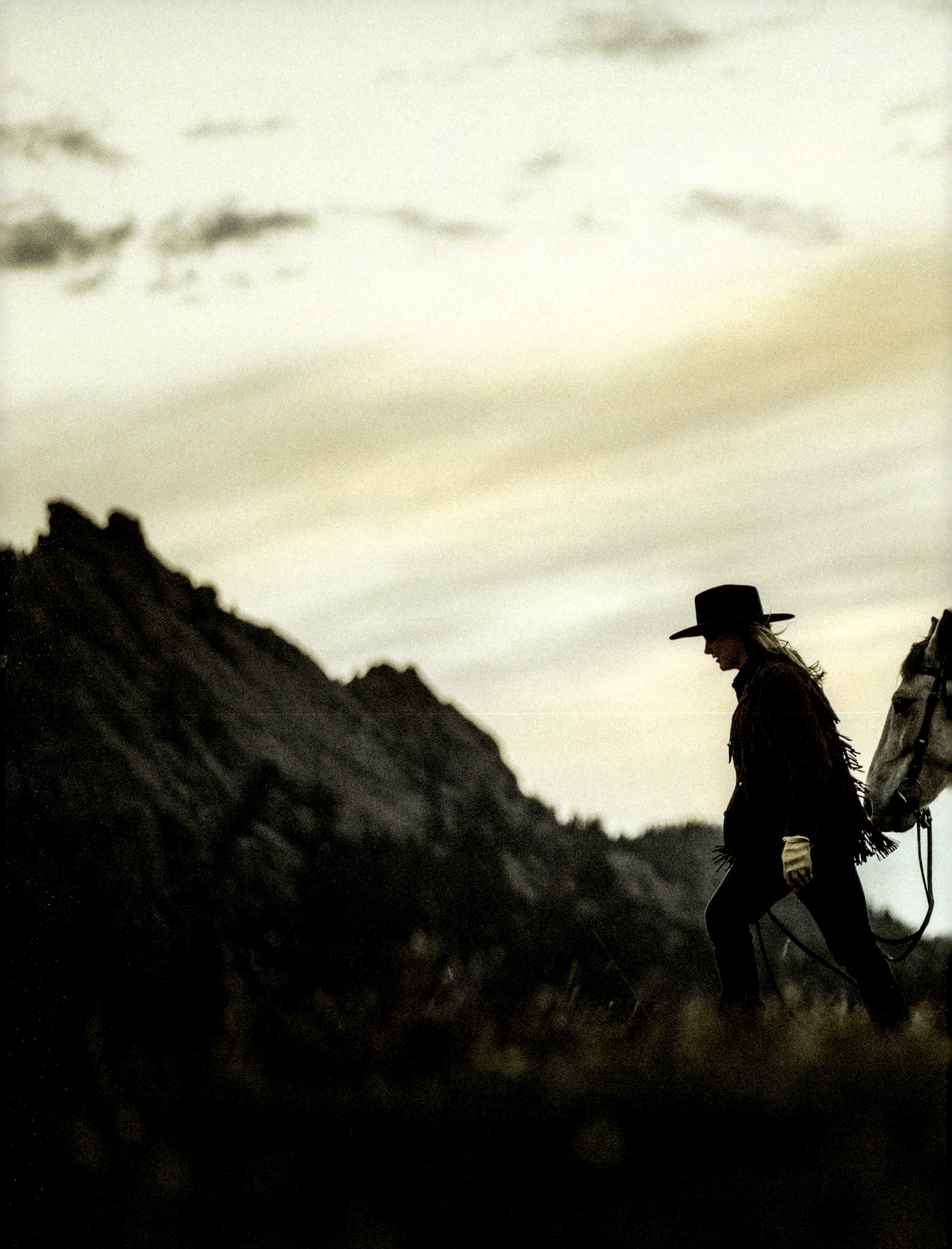

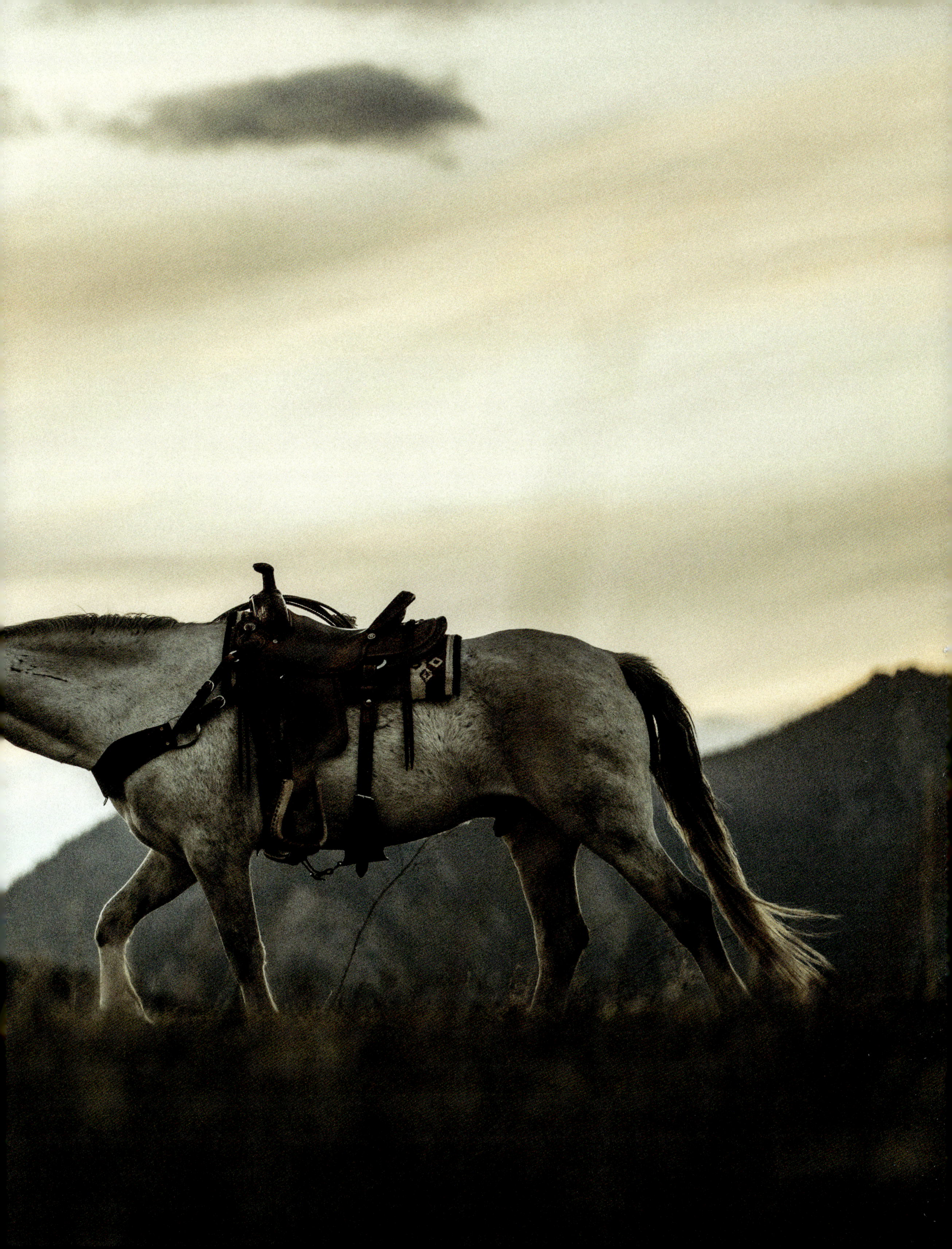

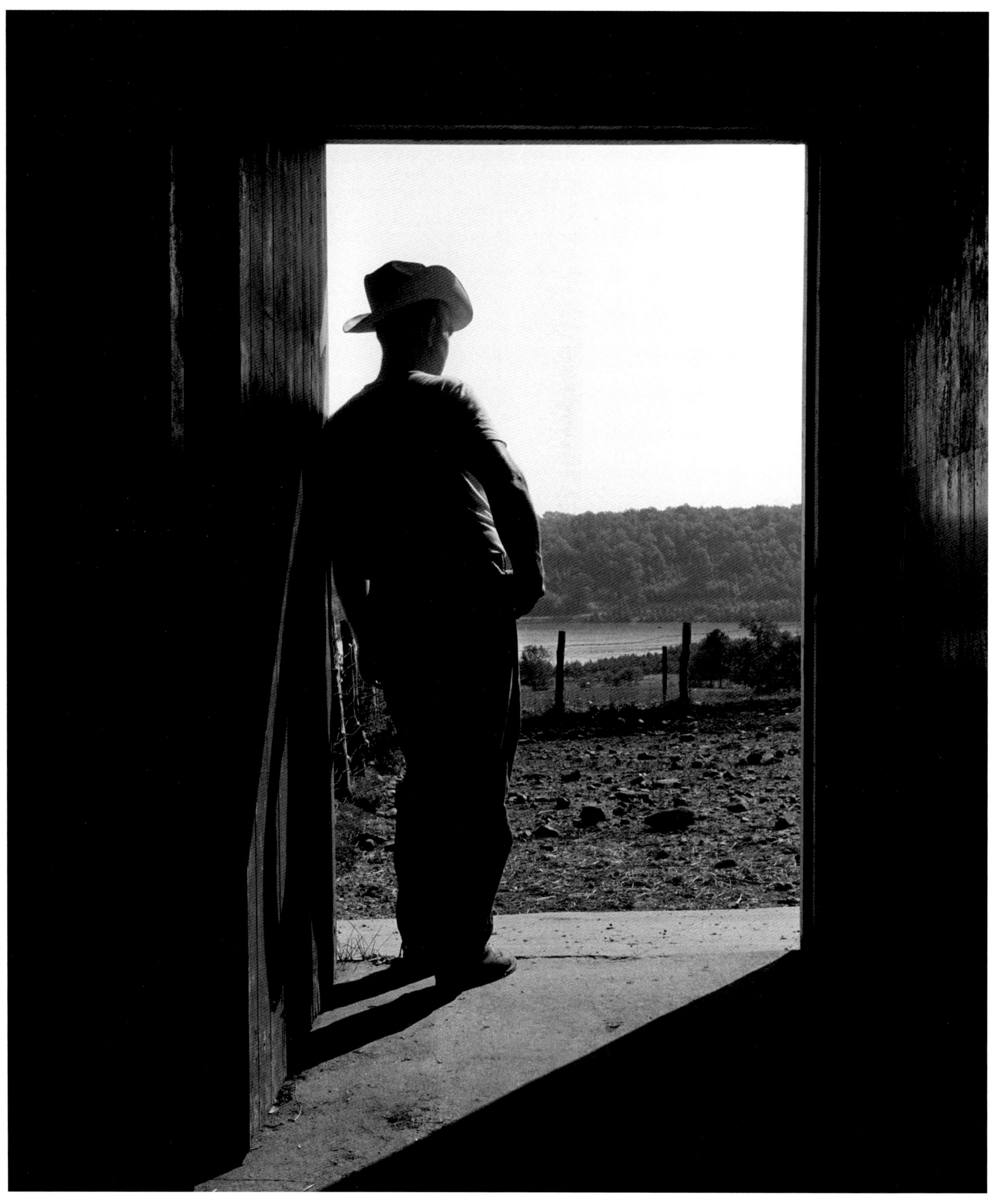

This page, opposite: *Vintage photographs of classic cowboys.*

Page 50, top: *The "ghost town" of Galilee, Saskatchewan, Canada.* Page 50, bottom: *Mounted cowboys roping wild horses.* Page 50, bottom: *Valley of Fire State Park, Nevada's oldest and largest state park, located 50 miles northeast of Las Vegas.*

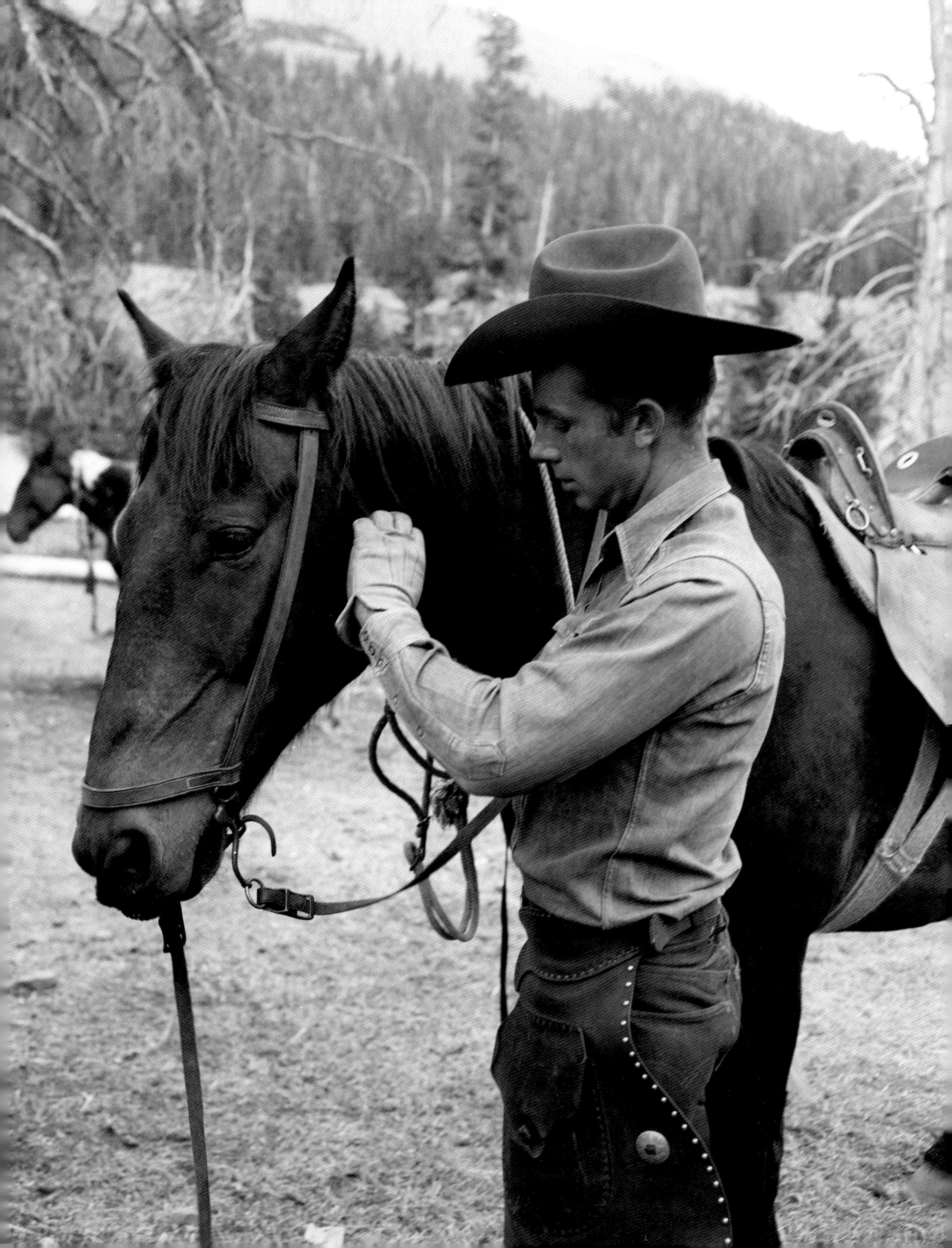

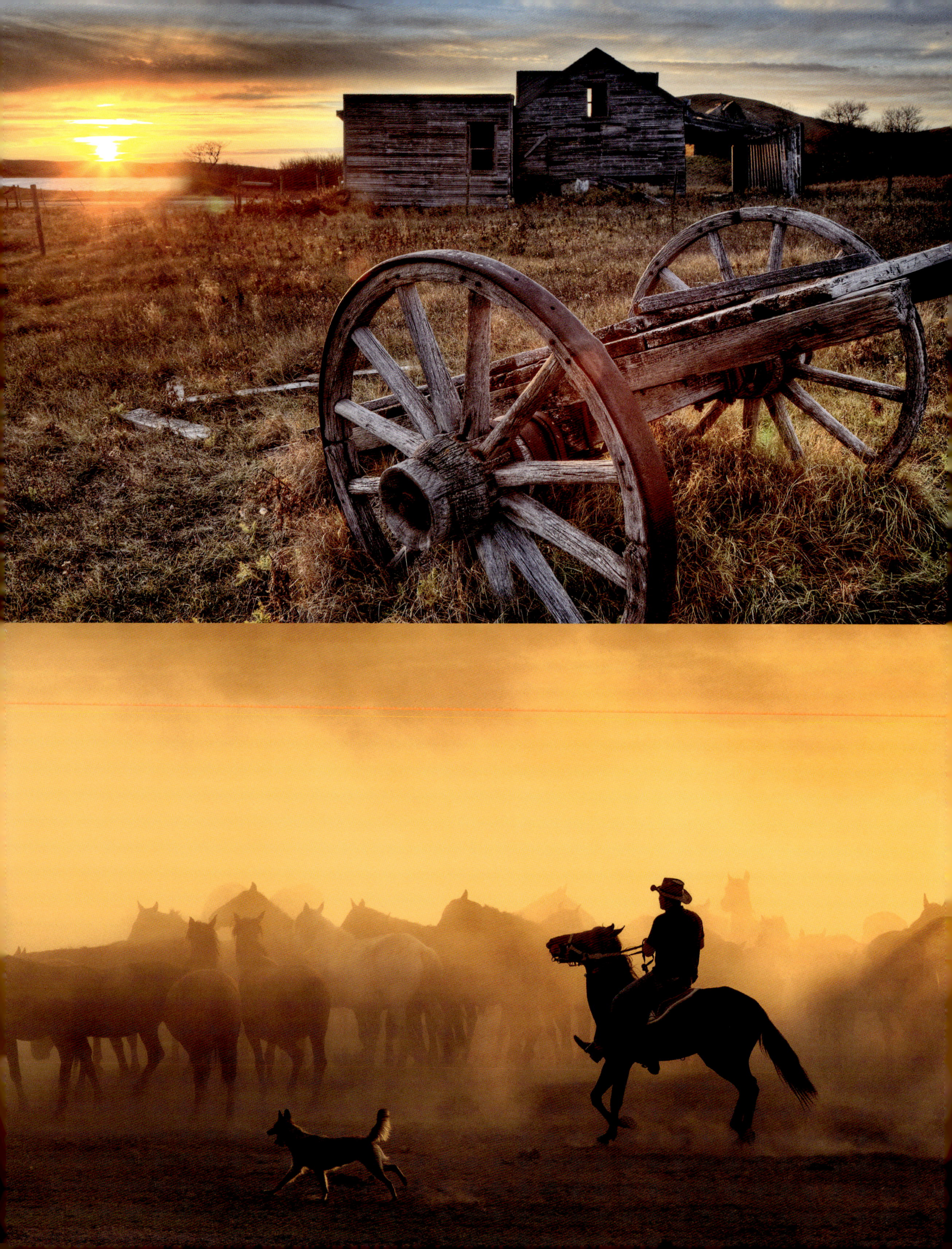

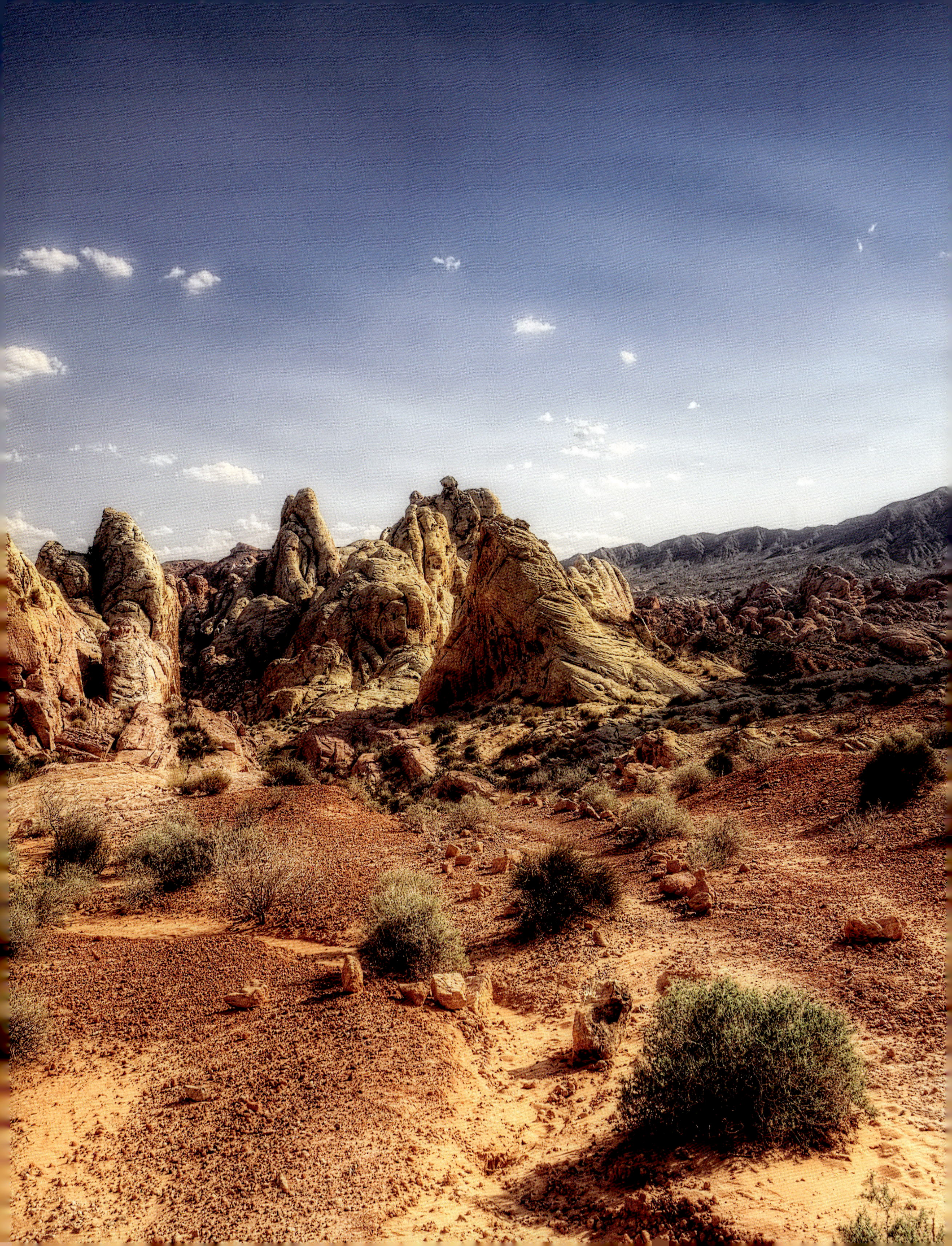

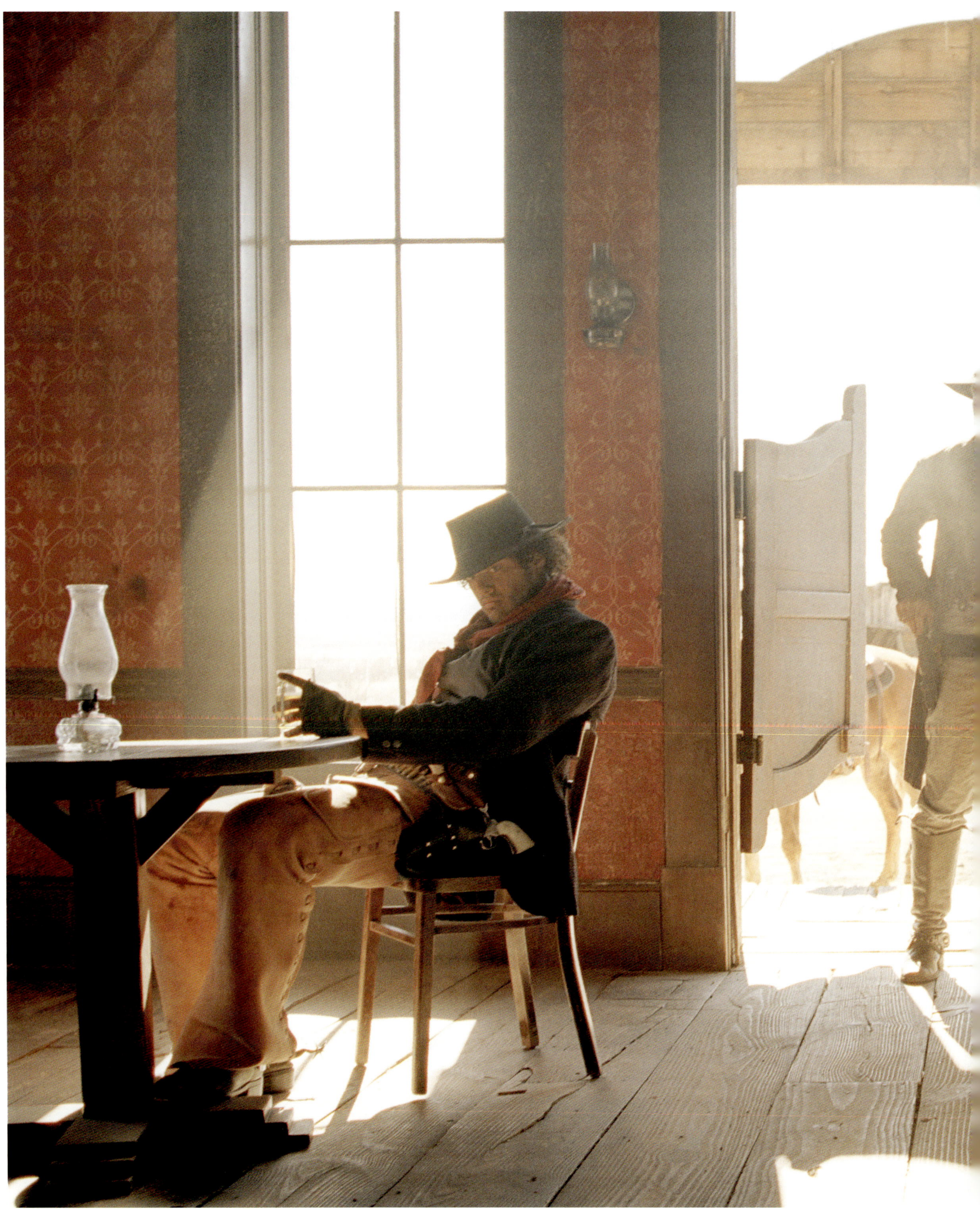

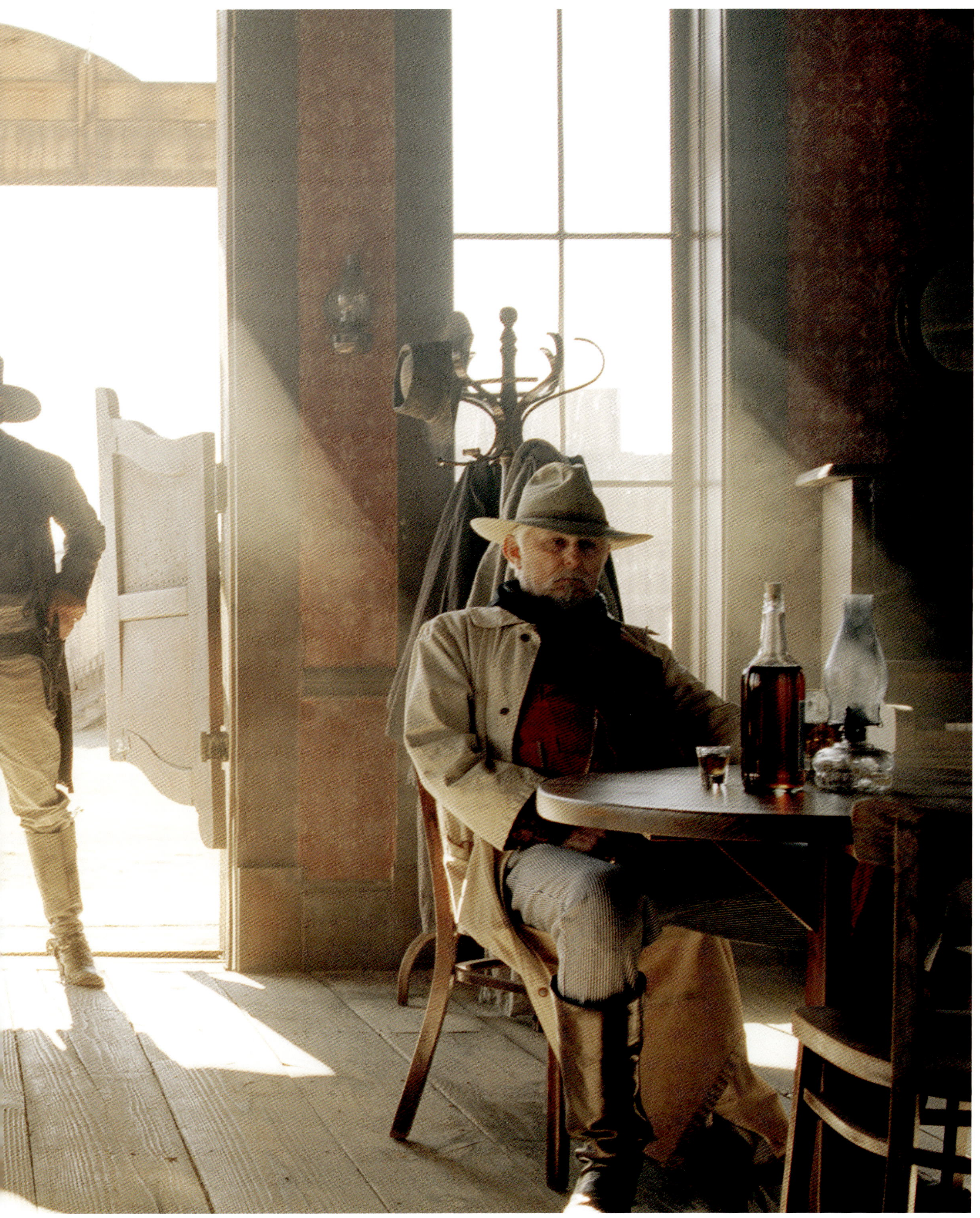

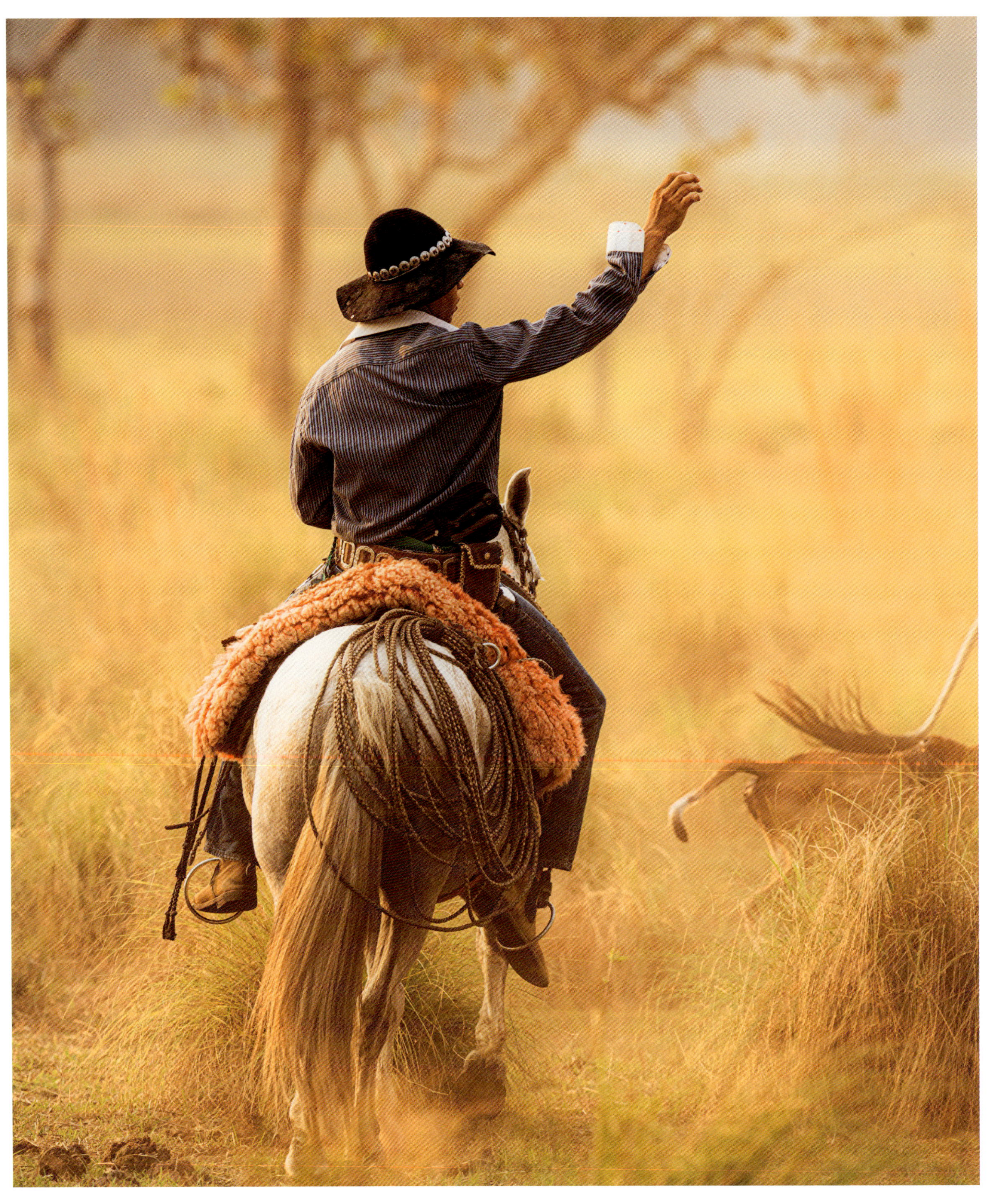

This page: *A PANTANEIRO (a cowboy from Brazil's Pantanal wetlands) on horseback. Though the term primarily refers to a Brazilian cattle breed, it can also mean the horse of the same name or the traditional cowboys of the region.*

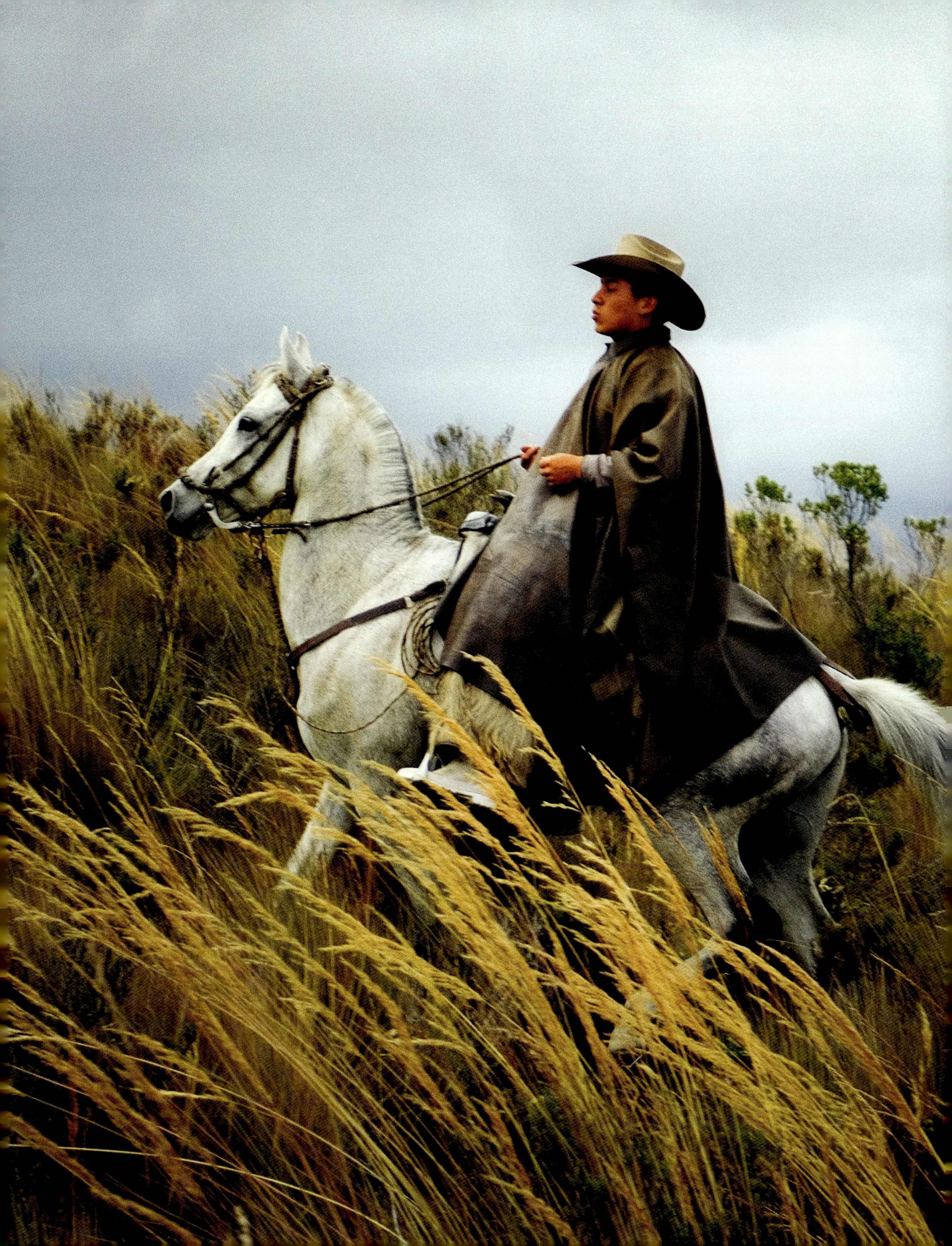

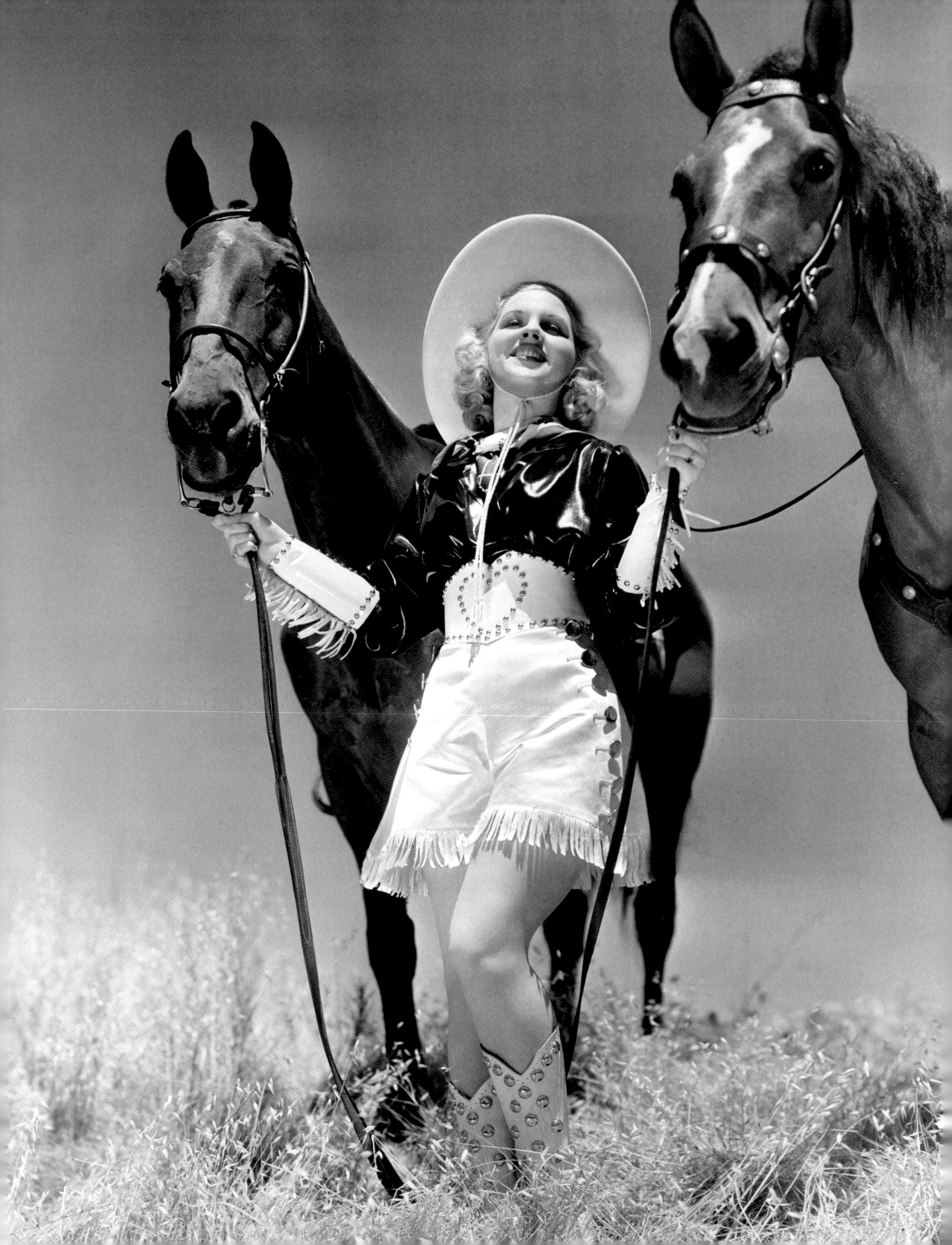

LEGENDARY FIGURES OF THE WILD WEST

No single figure or group "invented" cowboy culture: instead, it emerged piecemeal over a long period of time and hundreds of thousands of square miles of territory. Yet with that said, the history of the Wild West is a firmament in which some stars burned brighter than others. These were looming figures who became legends in their own time and helped to establish the basics of cowboy style for posterity—though, of course, most didn't make a living out of working with cattle, and some weren't "boys" at all.

Few names are more synonymous with the Wild West than Wild Bill Hickok. The fame of his protégé and namesake Buffalo Bill Cody eventually came to exceed his own, certainly. But Hickok paved the way with a life that included stints as a soldier, gunslinger, lawman, outlaw, cattle rustler, gambler and performer: nearly every pursuit we've come to associate with the Old West. Wild Bill's example also suggests how complicit the great figures of the period often were in the development of their own legends, with the "Wild" of his nickname apparently his own invention and many of the exploits he recounted apparently fabricated. Yet even with that said, there's no doubt that Wild Bill had a life— and a style—that matched the outsized persona he created for himself.

To imagine the Wild West is to picture expansive and sparsely-populated landscapes: empty prairie, arid desert, forbidding mountains. At the same time, however, it was also a surprisingly small world in which the best-known figures often crossed paths. Buffalo Bill Cody seems to have met his early mentor Wild Bill Hickok when they worked together on wagon trains in Kansas, and there's a legend that their lifelong friendship began when the latter defended his younger colleague from an attack. But if Hickok was initially the senior figure in the friendship, Buffalo Bill would go on to achieve greater prominence, first as a legendary hunter of buffalo and then with his global theatrical sensation *Buffalo Bill's Wild West Show*—doing more than perhaps any other individual to brand the American West on the popular imagination.

But the Wild West wasn't only about men named Bill. Phoebe Ann Mosey, who would rise to enormous fame as Annie Oakley, lived a life seemingly destined for the movies. Rented out as a young child to a family so cruel she afterwards referred to them only as "the wolves," Annie was an accomplished trapper and woodswoman by the age of seven, and as a sharpshooter would later become one of the top celebrities of the day. A key moment in her rise to fame was victory in a shooting match—at the age of 15—against the renowned marksman Frank E. Butler. Yet this episode further underscores the legend-building that was part of the Wild West from the start, since it's speculated that Oakley's youth was in fact exaggerated by five years to make her more marketable. Entirely authentic or not, however, marketable she certainly was: by the end of her career she was the second-highest-paid performer in *Wild Bill's Wild West Show*, and became a style icon for her insistence on modest dresses that stood in stark contrast to the burlesque costumes often worn by her contemporaries.

If questions remain about the details of Annie Oakley's life, with Calamity Jane we're certain of even less. Did she, as her highly "creative" autobiography claimed, work as a scout in Wyoming, at one point rescuing her commanding officer after he'd been shot? Historians aren't convinced—and regarding her alleged marriage to Wild Bill Hickok they're even less so. There's general agreement, however, on a few questions. She does seem to have earned her reputation for charity, for instance, caring for the sick of Deadwood during an outbreak of smallpox; while she probably wasn't romantically involved with Wild Bill, she did really know him; and there's no doubt whatsoever that tales of her prodigious drinking were rooted in fact. What's also beyond dispute is the striking style contrast she provides with Annie Oakley, generally preferring a man's buckskin suit and declining to ride sidesaddle as was usually expected of ladies. A very different image of the Wild West cowgirl!

What every character discussed so far has in common is that they appeared at one time or another in a Wild West show. But one figure who became legendary without participating in such myth-building exercises was Billy the Kid. Born Henry McCarty, later changing his name to William H. Bonney, Billy's life perfectly encapsulates the philosopher Thomas Hobbes' characterisation of human existence as "nasty, brutish and short." Orphaned at the age of 15, first arrested a year later and not long afterwards a federal fugitive, by the time of his death at the age of only 21 he was responsible for as many as nine killings. Though Billy the Kid's brutal existence and early death meant that he never took part in a Wild West show, however, that certainly didn't prevent compelling tall tales from gathering around him—perhaps the most memorable recounting that when a judge sentenced him to hang until he was "dead, dead, dead," Billy responded that the judge could go to "hell, hell, hell."

John Wesley Hardin is a similar case—though he lived much longer and had the body-count to match. Hardin took his first life at the age of 15, and more than 20 killings were attributed to him by the time he died at the age of 42. (In fact his murderous career almost began earlier: two years previously Hardin stabbed a fellow student nearly to death in an argument over a girl's honor.) His was a chequered career of gunfighting, brawling and gambling, and the incident that seems to have defined him in the popular imagination emphasized his psychotic heartlessness. Having become enraged one night in a Kansas hotel at a neighboring guest's snoring, so the story goes, Hardin shot several bullets through the adjoining wall and killed him. Interestingly, though, Hardin is also a great illustration of the strange afterlives of Wild West myths. "So mean he once shot a man for snoring" he may have been thought, but nowadays perceptions of Hardin are often colored by the Bob Dylan song in which he's presented as a kind of Wild West Robin Hood, a "friend to the poor" who was "never known to hurt an honest man."

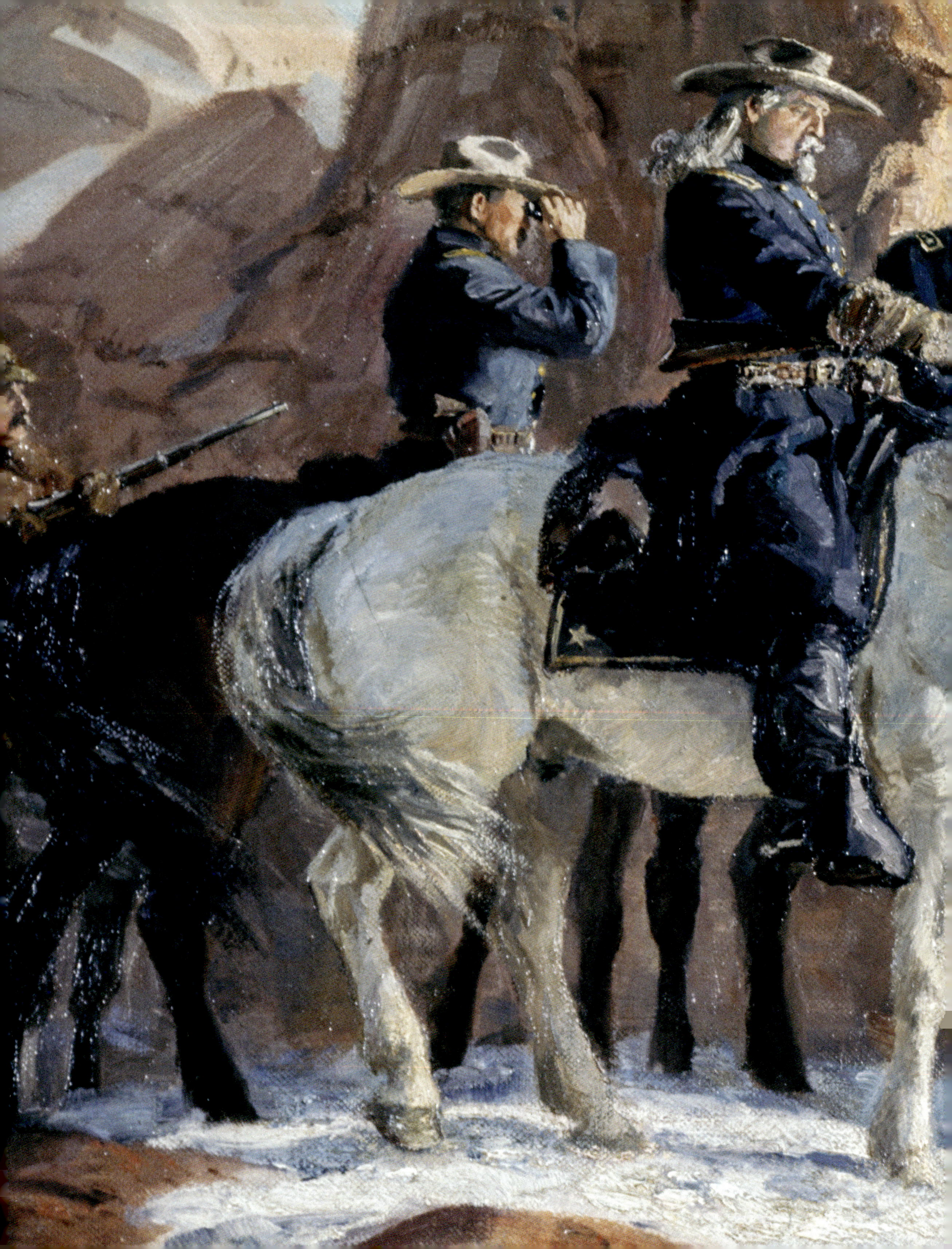

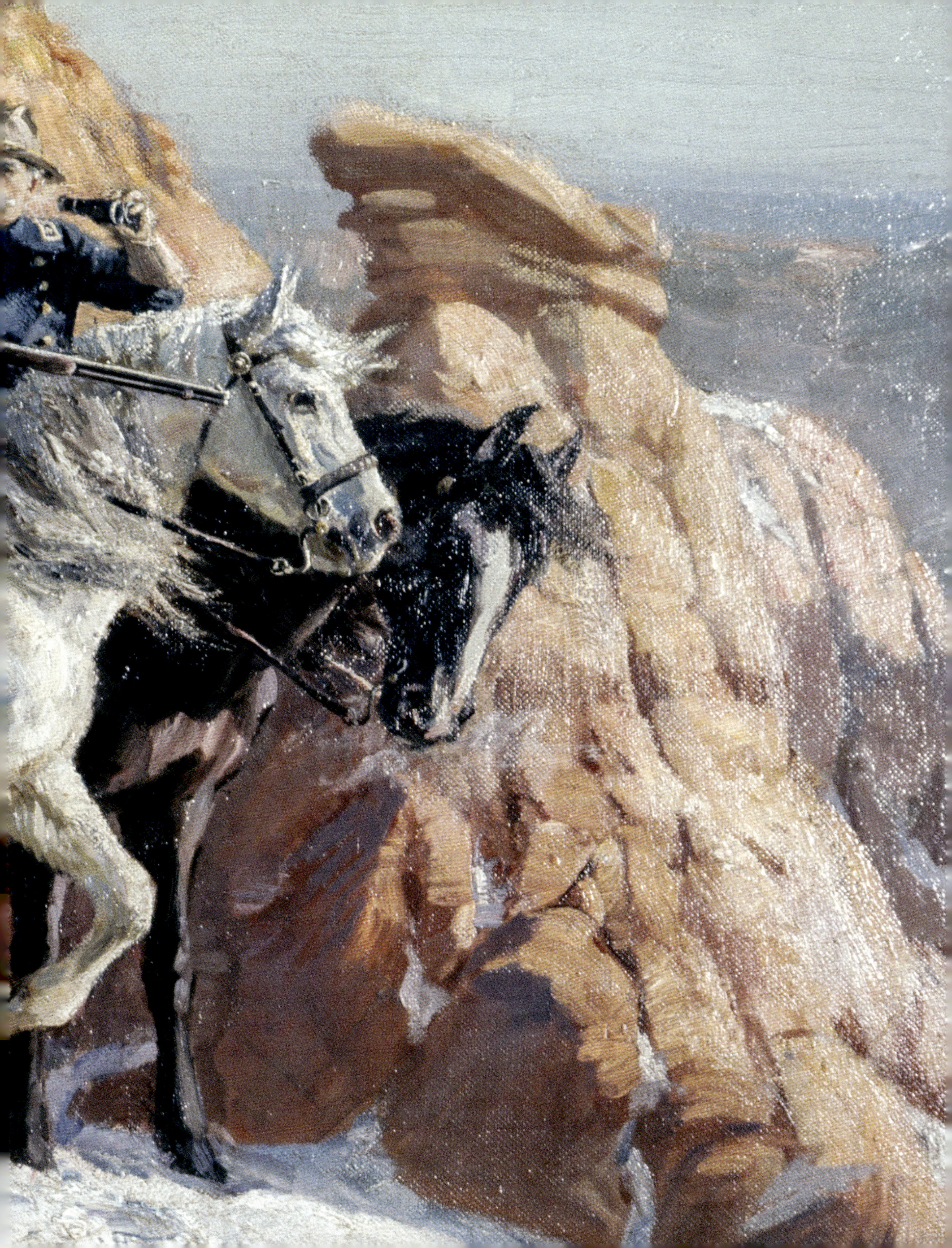

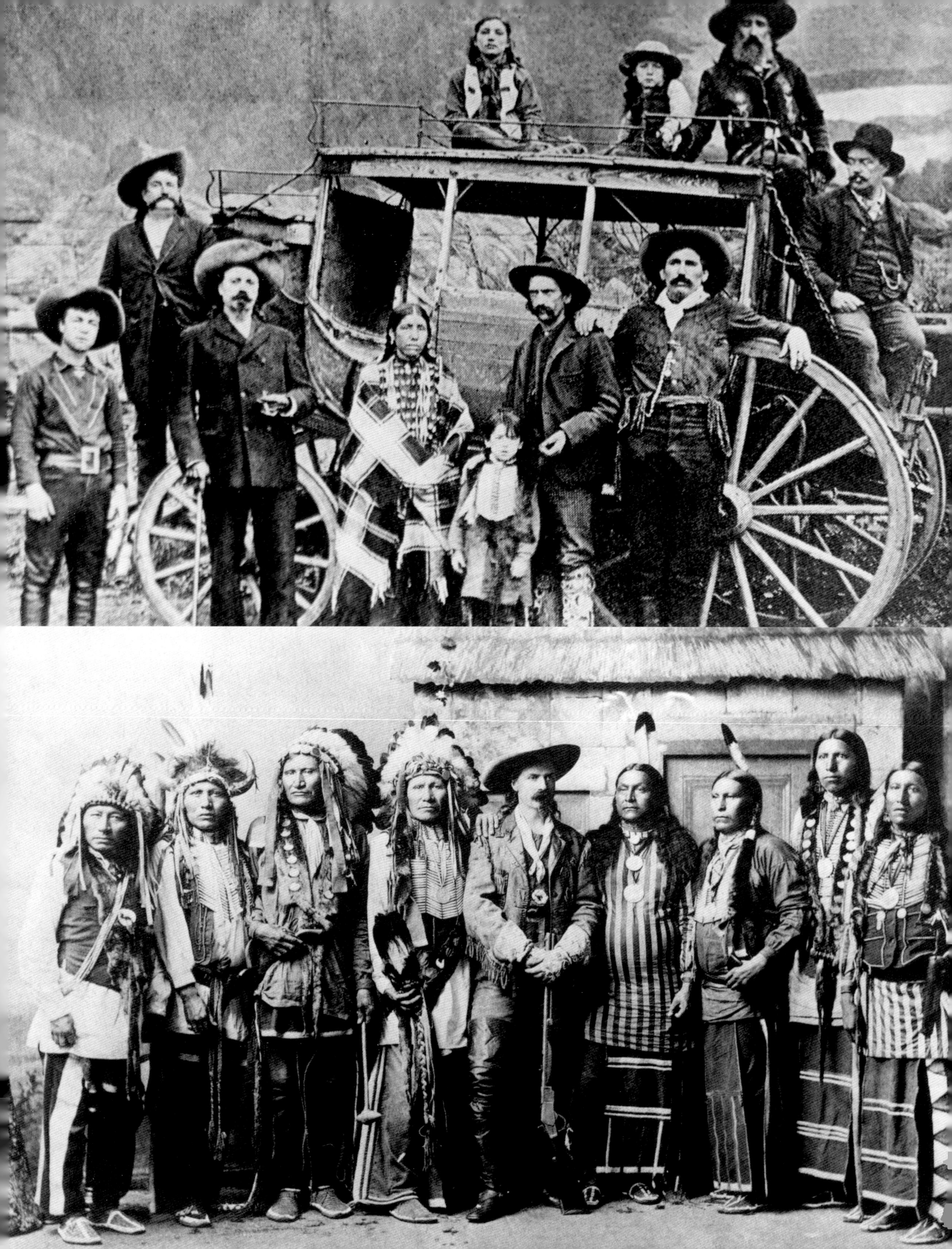

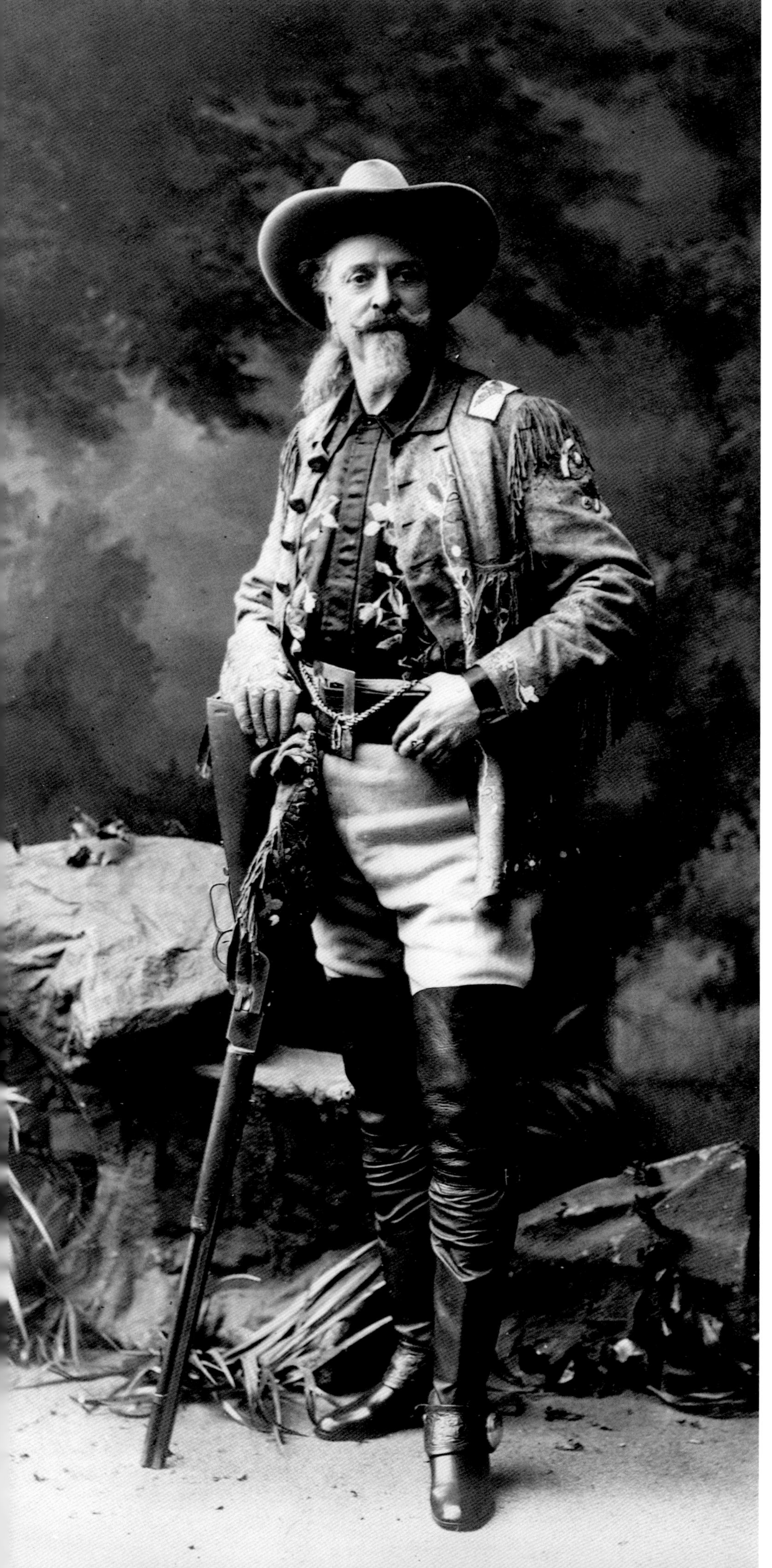

Pages 60/61: *A painting by Irving R. Bacon of Colonel William F. Cody, also known as Buffalo Bill, during a winter military campaign.*

Page 62, top: *Buffalo Bill Cody's Wild West Troupe, 1883.*

Page 62, bottom: *Buffalo Bill Cody with group of Native Americans, 1870.*

Page 63: *A portrait of Buffalo Bill Cody, 1899.*

Following page: *A poster for BUFFALO BILL'S WILD WEST AND CONGRESS OF ROUGH RIDERS OF THE WORLD show.*

Page 66: *An illustration titled "Buffalo Bill" (c. 1952) shows a man in Western attire on a horse with its front legs in the air as if in panic as the man brandishes a gun. In the background we see dead Native Americans lying in the grass and other horses off in the distance.*

Page 67: *Another poster for BUFFALO BILL'S WILD WEST AND CONGRESS OF ROUGH RIDERS OF THE WORLD (c. 1885).*

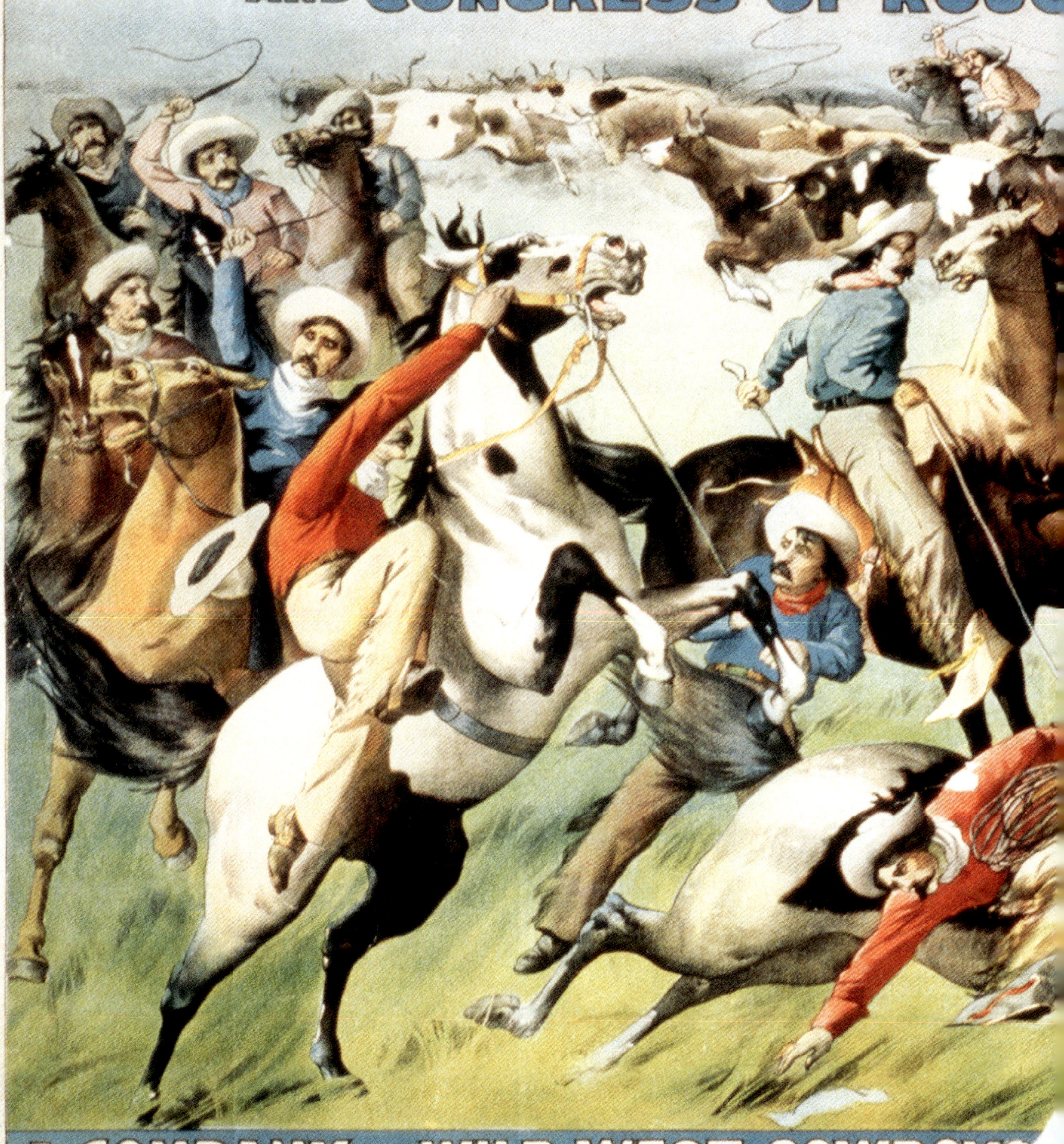

BUFFALO BIL
AND CONGRESS OF ROUG
A COMPANY OF WILD WEST COWBOYS.

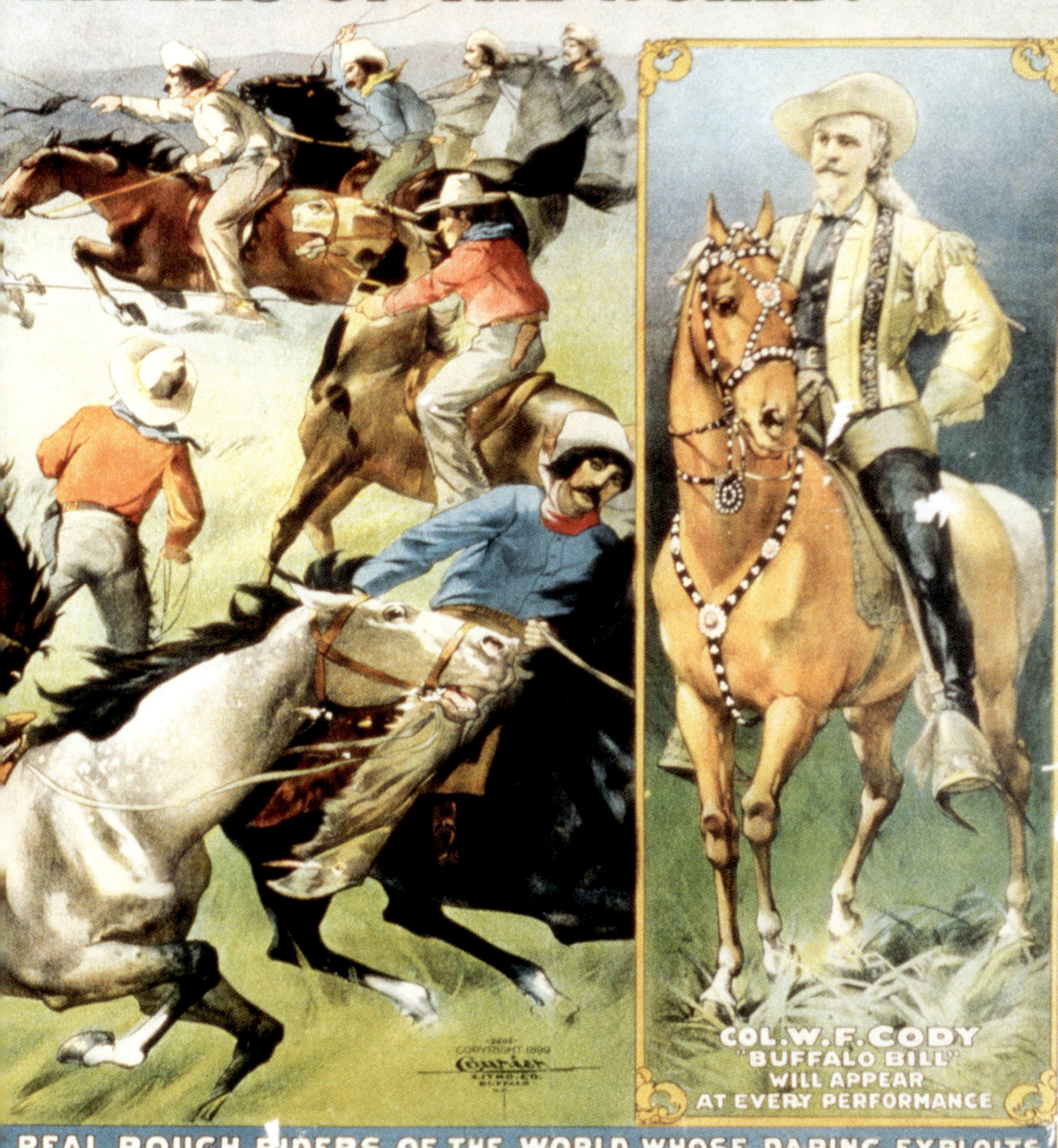

'S WILD WEST
RIDERS OF THE WORLD.
COL. W. F. CODY
"BUFFALO BILL"
WILL APPEAR
AT EVERY PERFORMANCE
REAL ROUGH RIDERS OF THE WORLD WHOSE DARING EXPLOITS
E MADE THEIR VERY NAMES SYNONYMOUS WITH DEEDS OF BRAVERY.
COPYRIGHT 1899
COURIER
LITHO. CO.
BUFFALO

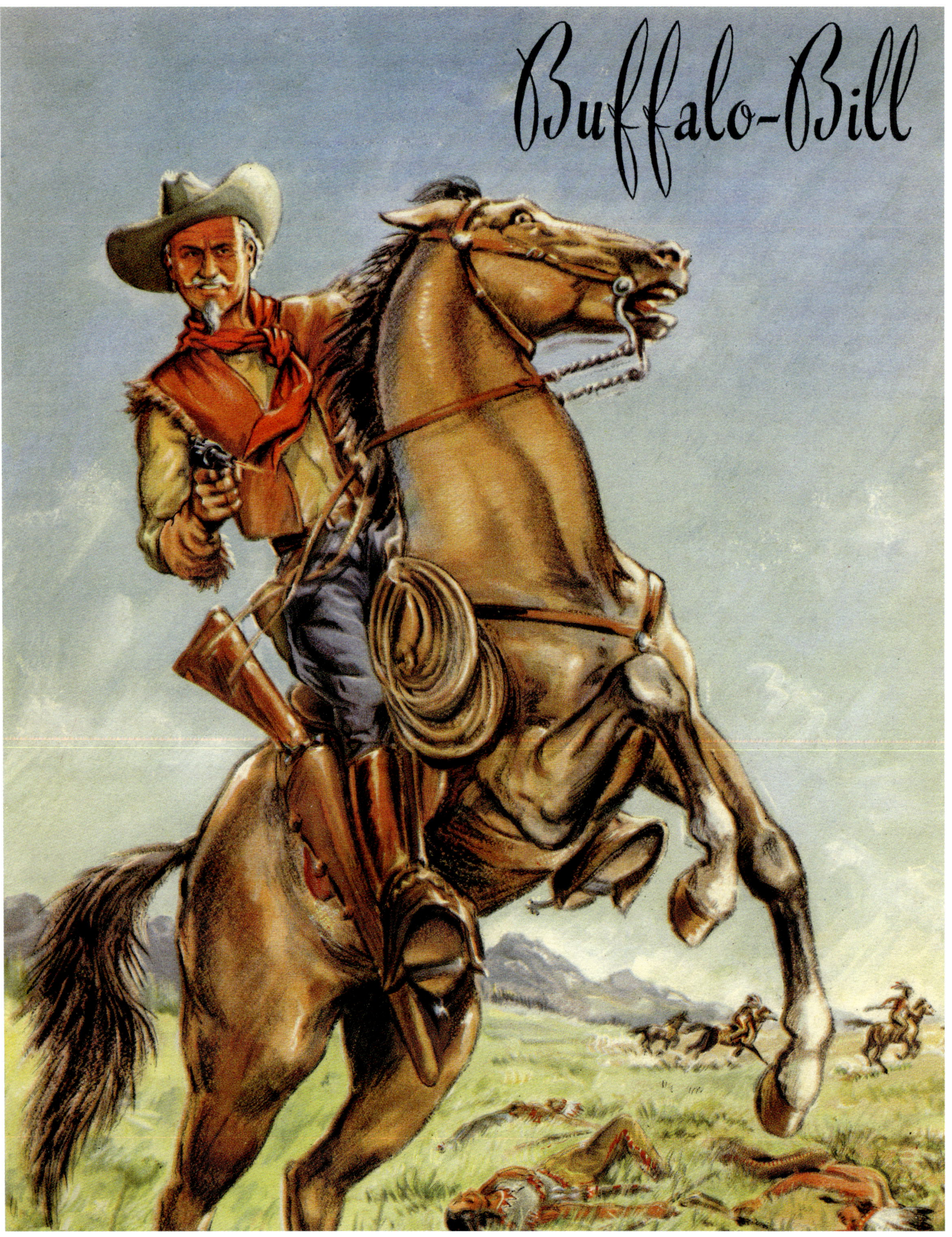
Buffalo-Bill

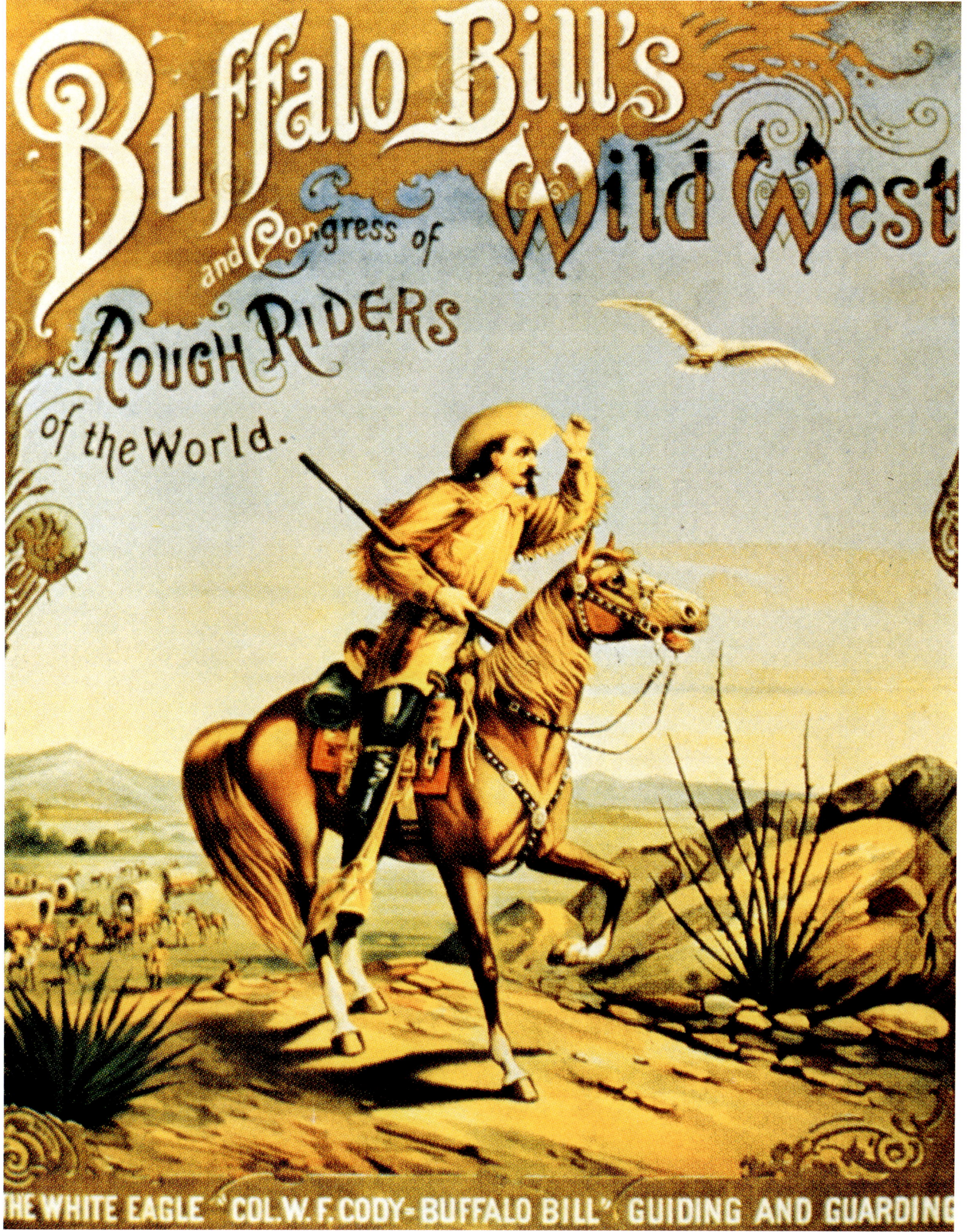

Buffalo Bill's Wild West
and Congress of Rough Riders of the World.
THE WHITE EAGLE "COL. W. F. CODY - BUFFALO BILL" GUIDING AND GUARDING

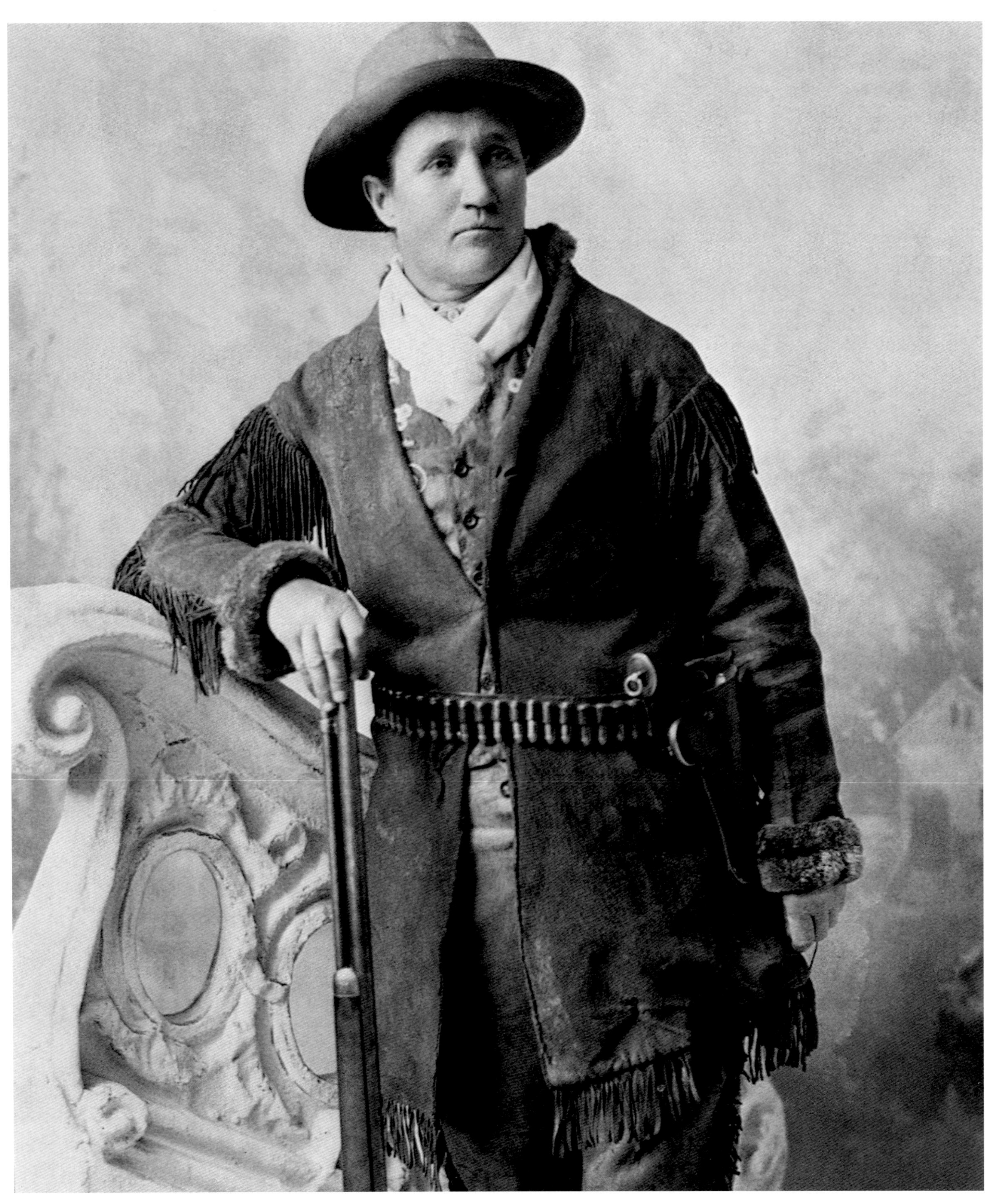

This page: *A portrait of Calamity Jane, a frontierswoman who supposedly scouted for General Custer and later traveled with Wild Bill Hickok, 1895.*

Opposite: *Annie Oakley, star of BUFFALO BILL'S WILD WEST SHOW, shown holding a rifle, 1899.*

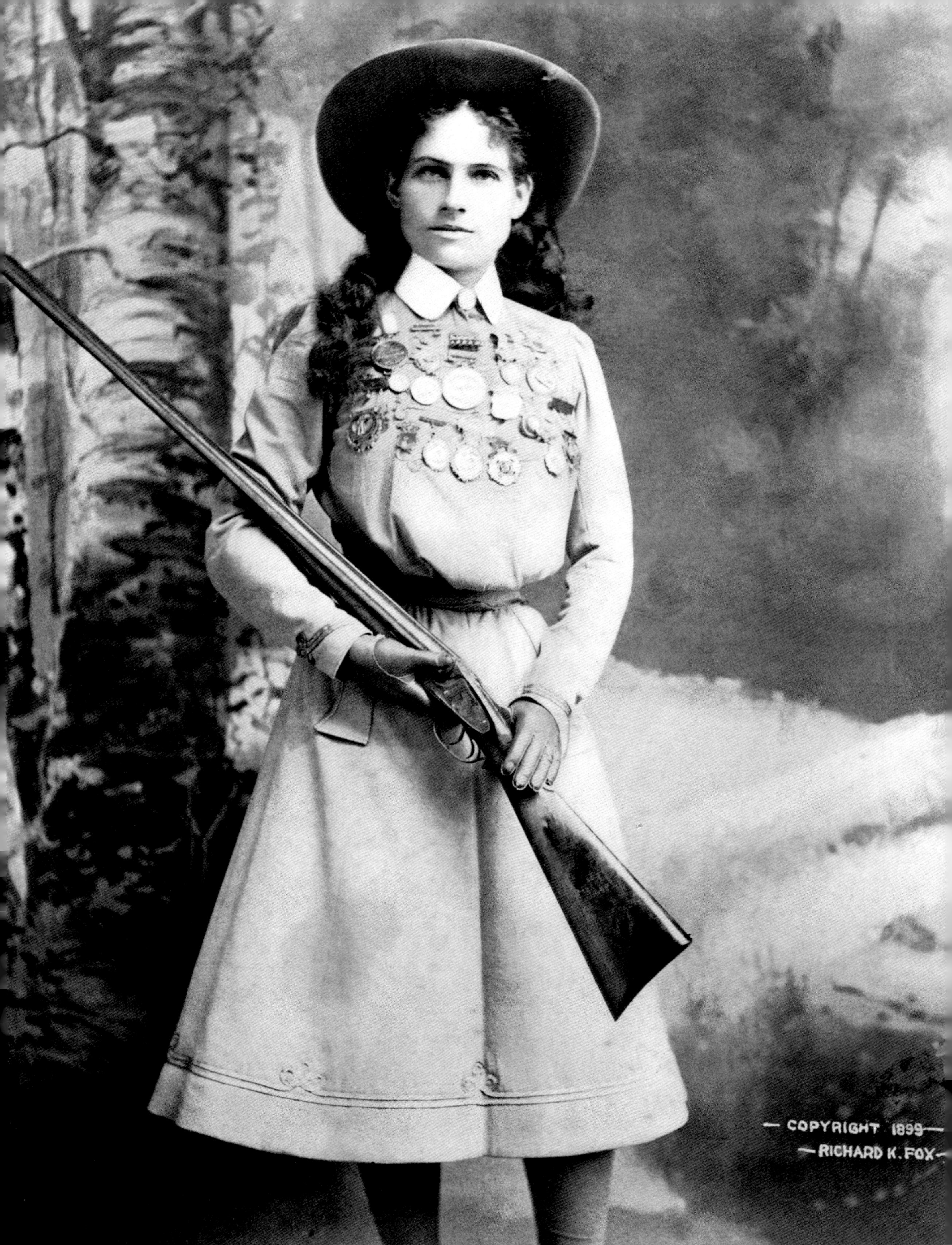

— COPYRIGHT 1899 —
— RICHARD K. FOX —

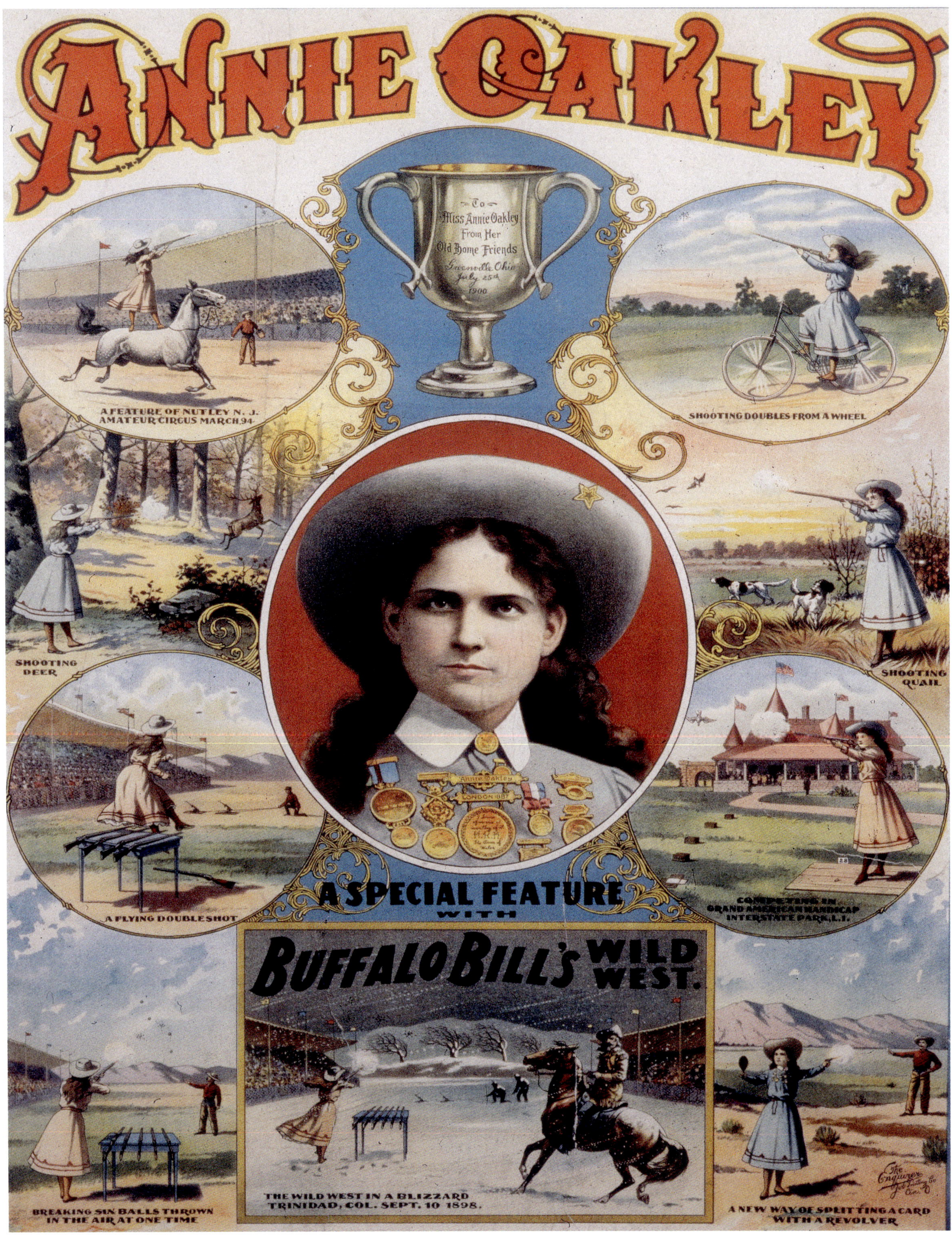

ANNIE OAKLEY
To Miss Annie Oakley From Her Old Home Friends Greenville Ohio July 25th 1900
A FEATURE OF NUTLEY N. J. AMATEUR CIRCUS MARCH 94
SHOOTING DOUBLES FROM A WHEEL
SHOOTING DEER
SHOOTING QUAIL
A FLYING DOUBLE SHOT
COMPETING IN GRAND AMERICAN HANDICAP INTERSTATE PARK, L. I.
A SPECIAL FEATURE
WITH
BUFFALO BILL'S WILD WEST.
THE WILD WEST IN A BLIZZARD TRINIDAD, COL. SEPT. 10 1898.
BREAKING SIX BALLS THROWN IN THE AIR AT ONE TIME
A NEW WAY OF SPLITTING A CARD WITH A REVOLVER

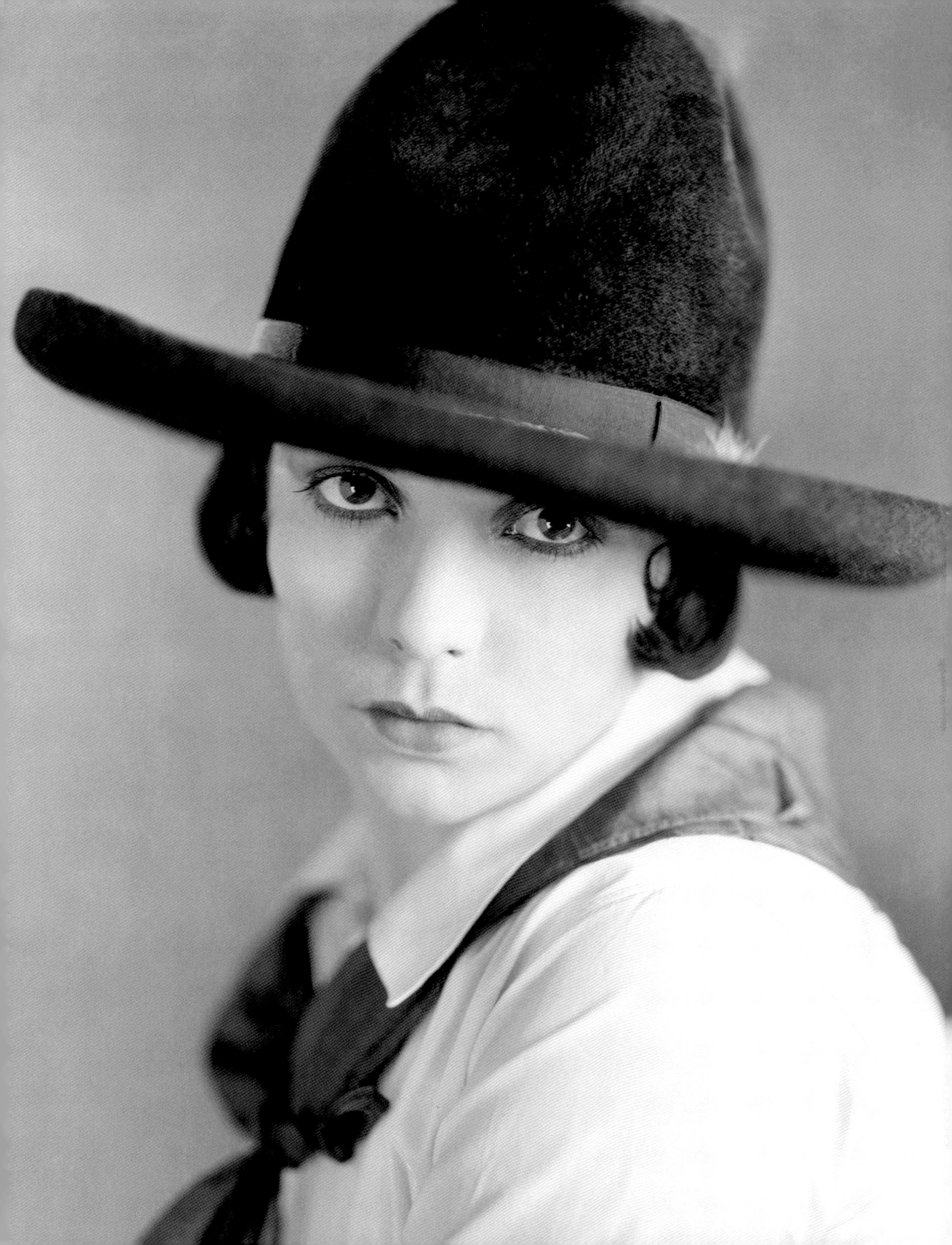

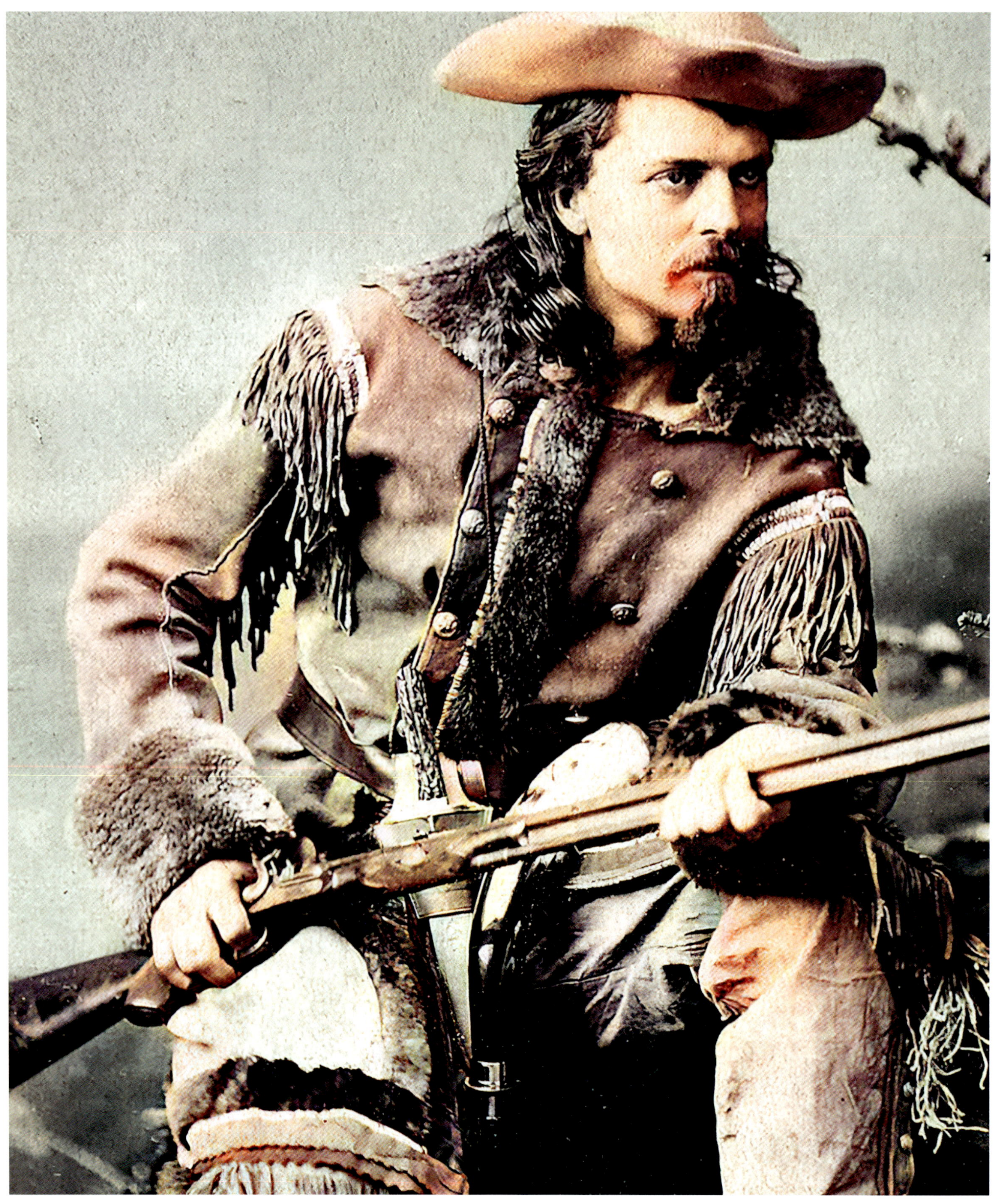

Page 70: *Advertisement for BUFFALO BILL'S WILD WEST CONGRESS ROUGH RIDERS OF THE WORLD, featuring Annie Oakley with caption 'The Peerless Lady Wing-Shot,' 1900s.*

This page: *Three-quarter-length portrait of Buffalo Bill holding a rifle, 1880.*

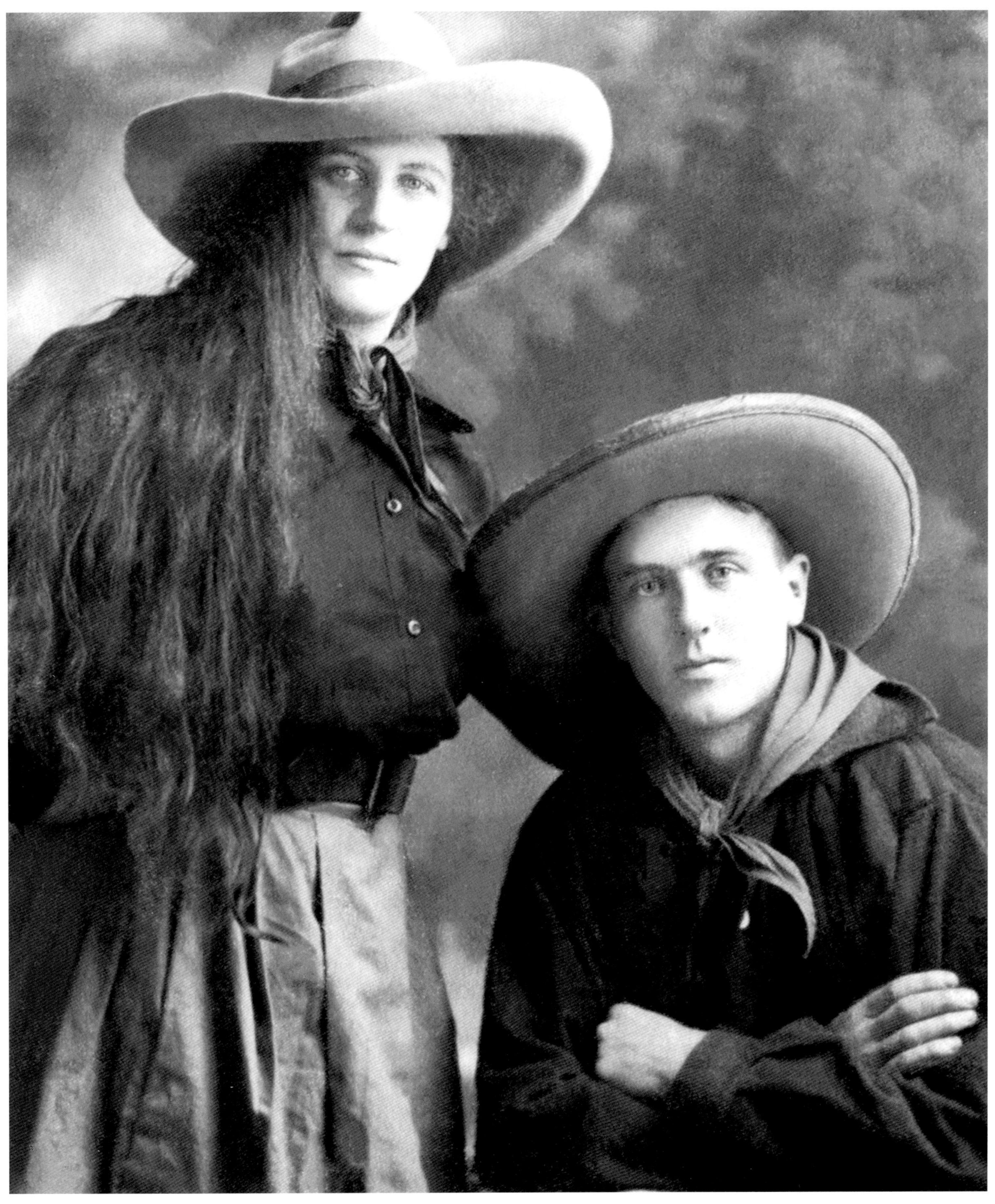

This page: *A 1915 portrait of a handsome young couple dressing up as cowgirl and cowboy for a masquerade ball in Amsterdam, the Netherlands.*

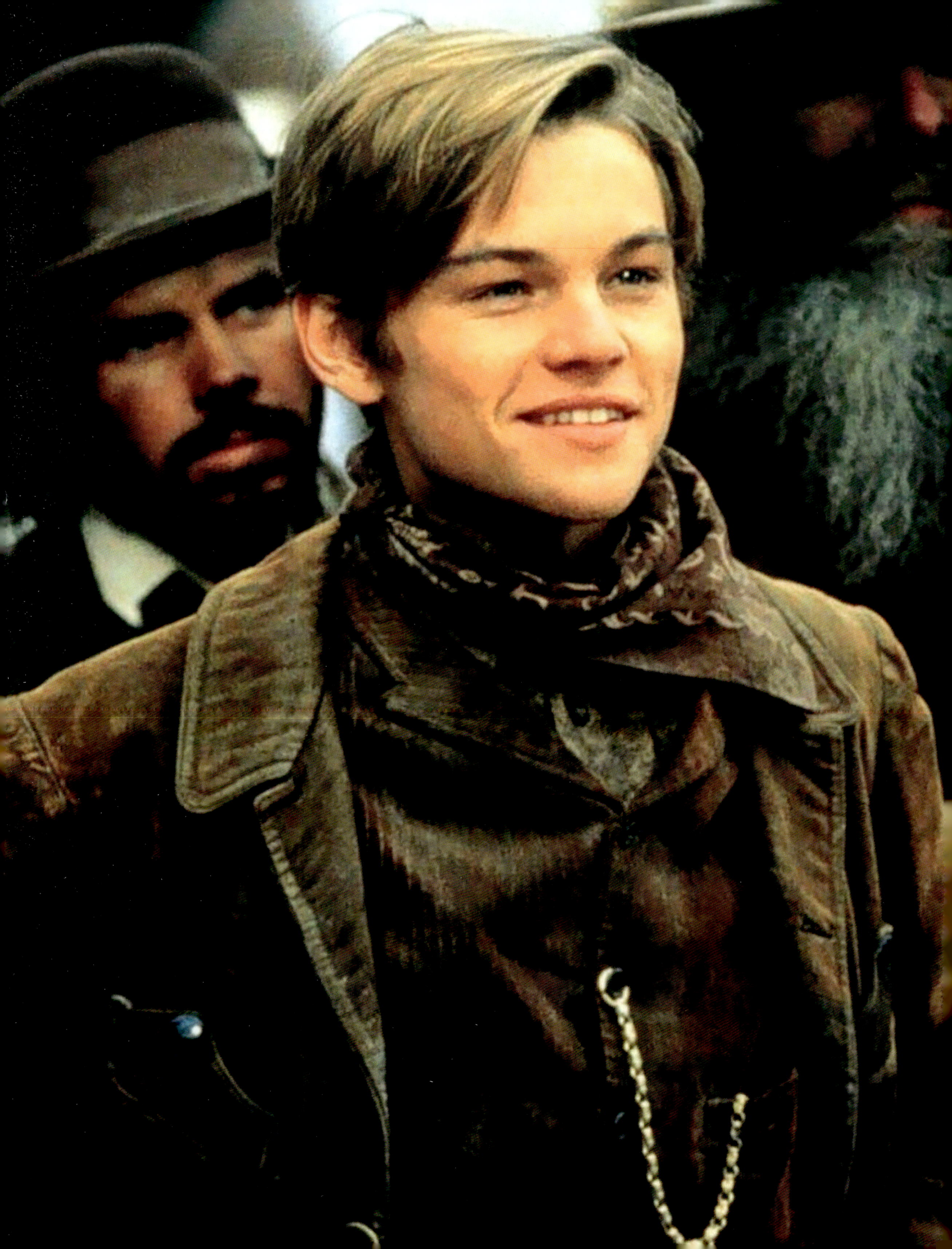

THE WILD WEST IN POPULAR CULTURE

By the turn of the twentieth century, the Wild West of Buffalo Bill, Calamity Jane, Billy the Kid and the rest was no more: with all the frontier land settled and divided into the states and Canadian provinces we know today, that world had disappeared. Something like the cowboy life continued in sparsely populated ranching regions like Wyoming, Montana, Alberta and Arizona, and continues to this day. But the lawless, wild frontier that had so gripped the national and international imagination now became the province of fiction: novels, comic books, traveling shows such as Buffalo Bill's, and above all the new media of film and television.

Of course, fictional versions of the West were nothing new. James Fenimore Cooper's *The Last of the Mohicans* was published in 1826, and books known as "dime novels" were popular from the 1850s onwards, cashing-in on public interest in the sensational aspects of life on the frontier. In 1869 Ned Buntline published *Buffalo Bill, the King of the Border Men*, apparently having encountered the real-life Bill Cody on a train; before long the book was adapted for the stage, and not long after that Buffalo Bill's own theatrical spectacle appeared, presenting reenactments of famous events that in some cases featured the original protagonists. And while the popularity of such productions waned after a few decades, the literature of the Wild West only grew in popularity, flourishing well into the 1960s.

Opposite: *Leonardo DiCaprio in THE QUICK AND THE DEAD (Raimi, 1995).*

There can be little doubt, though, that the West's real cultural monument—the form which above all others has helped Western style survive down to the present as a vital force in pop culture—is the cinematic genre of the Western. While not in fact the first example of the genre, *The Great Train Robbery* (1903) was the massive hit that boosted it to prominence, and it didn't take long before tales of the frontier became a staple of the new movie industry's release schedules. Just as the real Wild West had its stars, moreover, so did the cinematic version that immortalized it—icons who played a crucial role in creating the indelible images of cowboy style that still dominate our imaginations today.

Two of the earliest were William S. Hart and Tom Mix, who along with Broncho Billy Anderson were the pre-eminent stars of the silent Western. Hart was especially well known for the grit and realism of his films, including notably authentic costumes, and achieved tremendous success in the 1910s. But during the early 1920s public tastes shifted towards Tom Mix's less realistic and more action-heavy style, and it was probably Mix who (at least in the short-term) had the greater influence. Not only was he known as the "King of Cowboys" to future stars of the genre including Ronald Reagan and John Wayne, but it was Mix who gave Wayne his start in Hollywood. It's interesting to note that the authenticity or otherwise of costume-style was already a pivotal issue even at this very early stage.

The period usually considered the Western's "Golden Age," however, began in the late 1930s and lasted until the early '60s. This was the time of smash hits featuring stars like Errol Flynn, Gary Cooper, Gregory Peck, Tyrone Power, James Stewart and above all John Wayne, star of genre-defining John Ford-directed classics *Stagecoach* (1939) and *The Searchers* (1956). Many Westerns from this era can feel rather old-fashioned, naïve and even racist to modern viewers, yet in some cases at least they brought a new maturity and complexity to the genre—perhaps above all *The Searchers*, which stands out for its respectful attitude towards the Comanches who are ostensibly the film's "villains" and for its relatively clear-eyed view of the faults of the white settlers. And these questions aside, it's beyond question that the Western's massive profile during this period helped cement cowboy style as a force in global culture.

As we've already noted, a curious feature of the Western—and of the cowboy who is its emblem—is the ability to change with and reflect the times. The genre's peak had come and gone by the early 1960s, but gritty new styles such as the "spaghetti Western" tradition that grew out of Sergio Leone's *Dollars Trilogy* continued to draw audiences and produce iconic stars—in this case Clint Eastwood. Another noteworthy example, though a very different one, is *Midnight Cowboy* (1969), which takes cowboy style and transplants it to the grimy streets of 1960s New York City. The tale of a naïve Texan who comes north to become a gigolo, and of his friendship with a terminally ill hustler, the film turns the preeminent icon of American history and culture inside-out, using the image of the cowboy to think critically about contemporary America—and in the process bringing a new sort of resonance to traditional Western style.

Similarly, the Western felt very different when it returned to box office success in the 1990s with films such as *Dances with Wolves* (1990) and *Unforgiven* (1992): now the emphasis was upon historical brutality, racism and misogyny, and the genre seemed to have become a way for American culture to reckon with the sins of the country's past. The recent example of the various *Yellowstone* television series, which take a less overwhelmingly grim view of the West and its history, provides something of a counterexample. Nevertheless, revisionism of various kinds has been the cultural trend in recent decades, as also exemplified by "feminist" Westerns such as *The Quick and the Dead* (1995) and *Meek's Cutoff* (2010), the "gay cowboy movie" *Brokeback Mountain* (2005), or even blockbuster mash-ups like *Wild Wild West* (1999) or *Cowboys & Aliens* (2011).

Throughout all these changes and shifts, an essential through-line has been the distinctive style of clothing that's one of the key ways we know we're watching a "Western" in the first place. Theatrical productions such as Buffalo Bill's imprinted the Wild West on the global imagination, but big-screen depictions of the era have played a pivotal role in keeping it there, whether by glamorizing it, by stressing its savage realities, or by repurposing it for fun or to think about new cultural developments. When we see a catwalk model in Stetson and chaps, or an Instagram influencer flaunting a designer buckskin coat or rhinestone-studded boots, it's just another chapter in the long and shifting story of cowboy style.

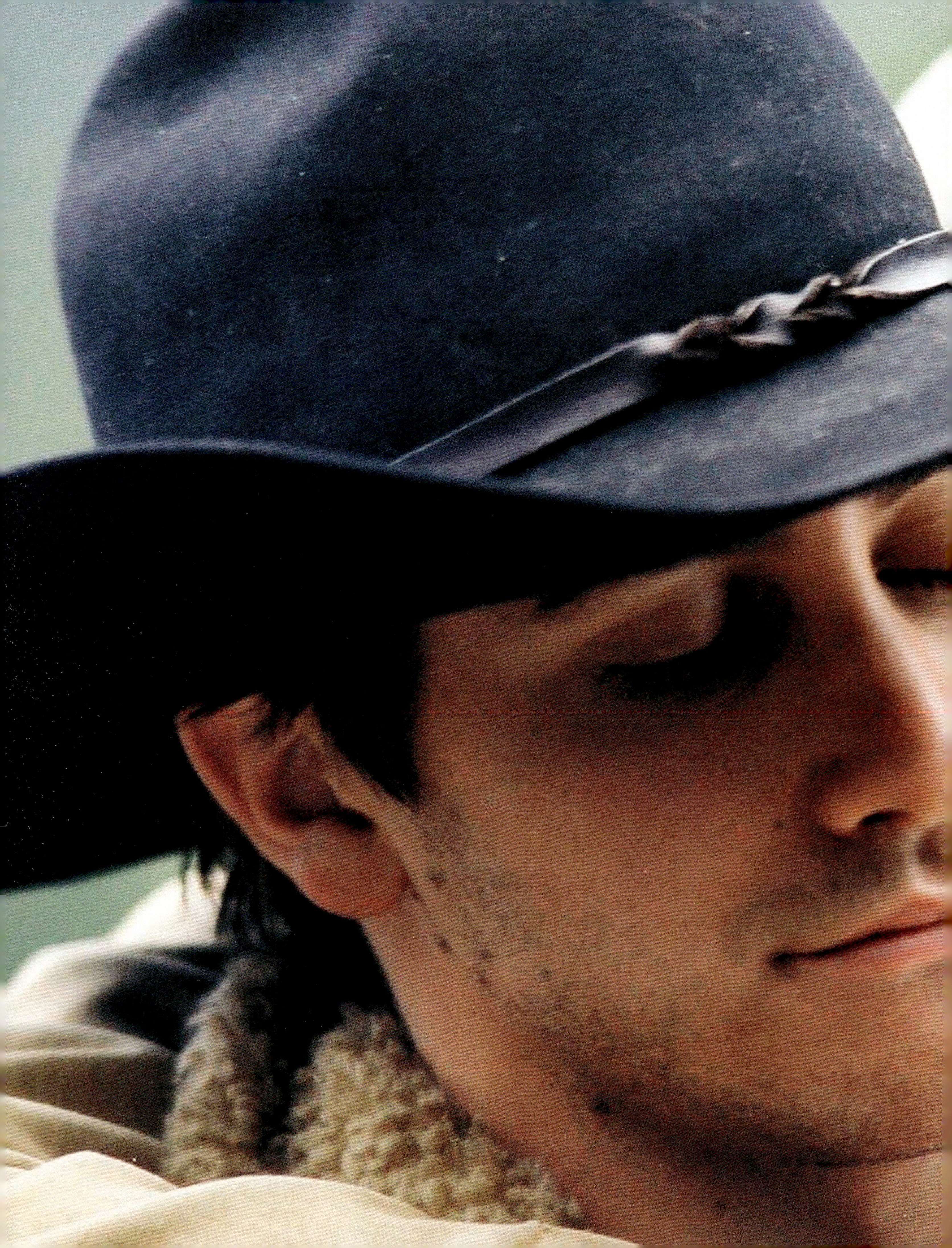

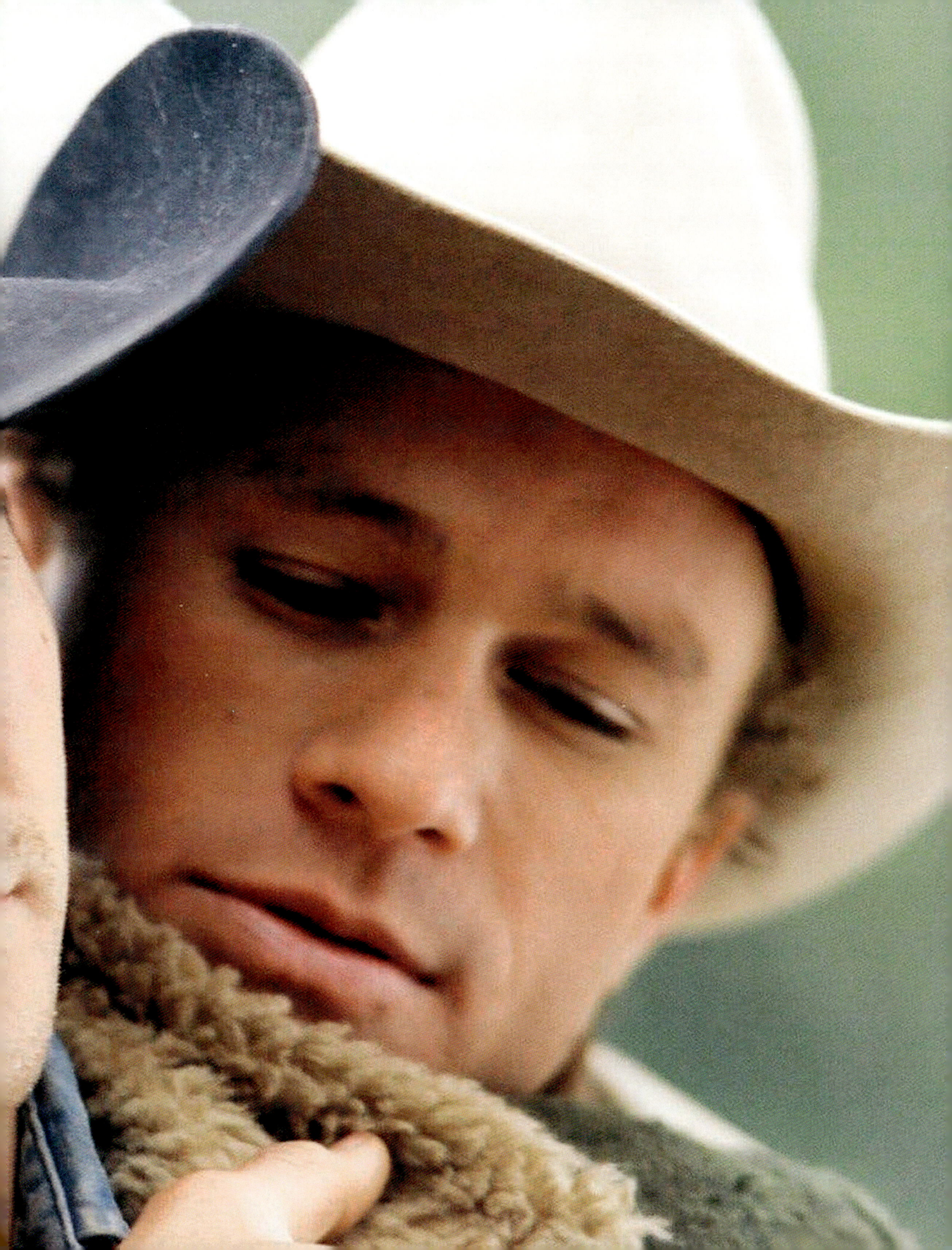

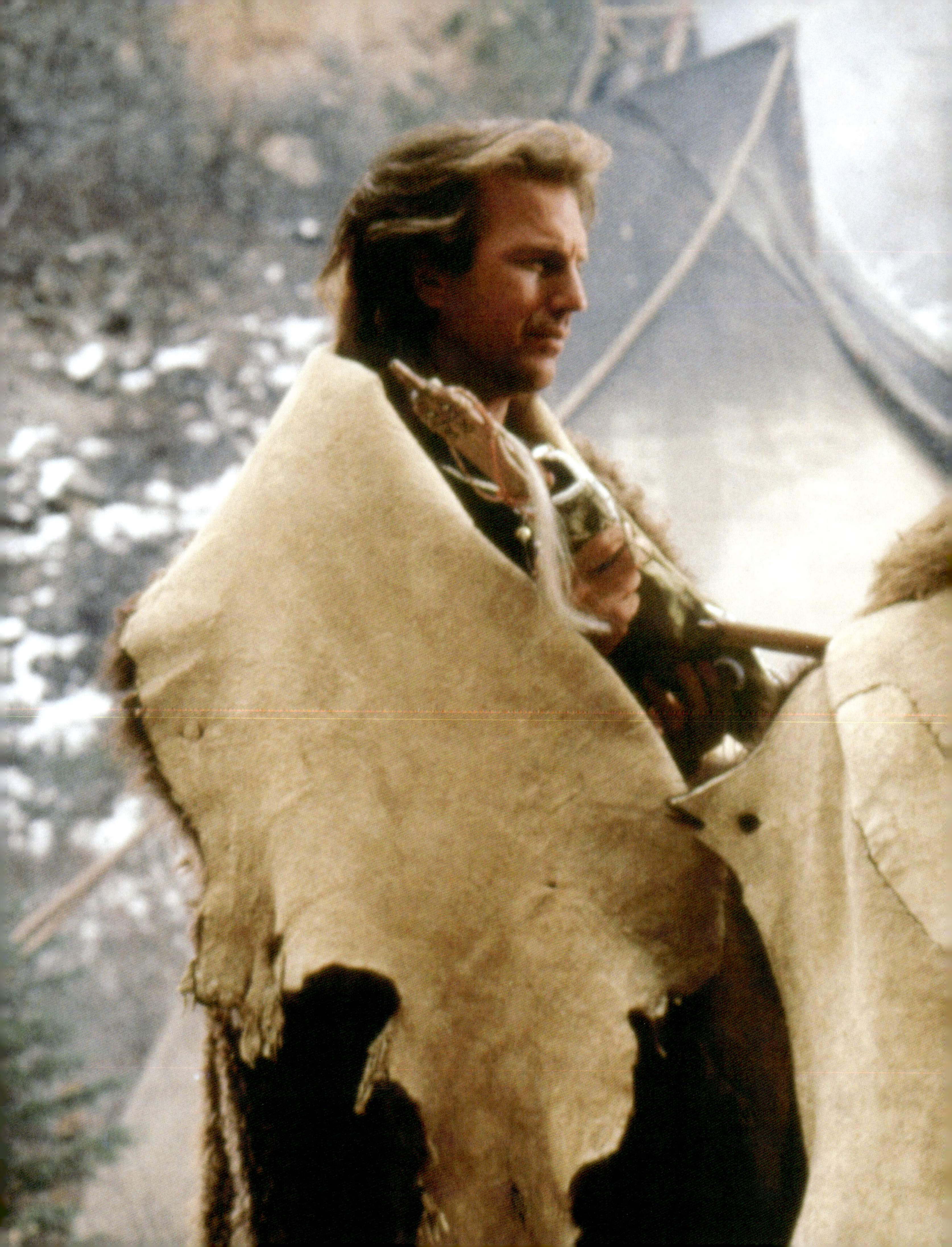

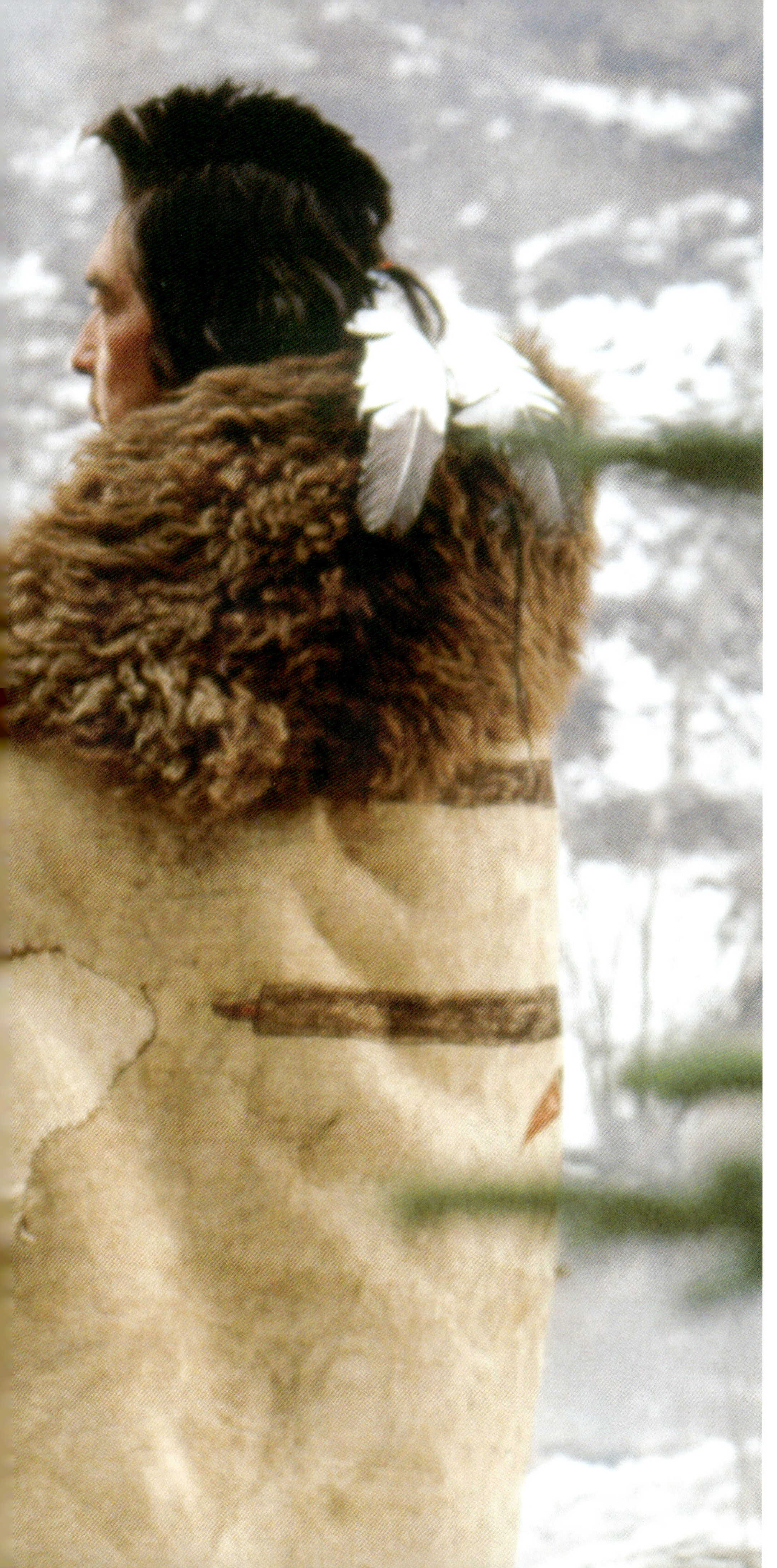

Pages 78/79: *Heath Ledger (right) and Jake Gyllenhaal in BROKEBACK MOUNTAIN (Lee, 2005).*

These pages: *Kevin Costner (left) and Graham Greene in DANCES WITH WOLVES (Costner, 1990).*

Pages 82/83: *Kevin Kostner as Lt. John J. Dunbar in DANCES WITH WOLVES.*

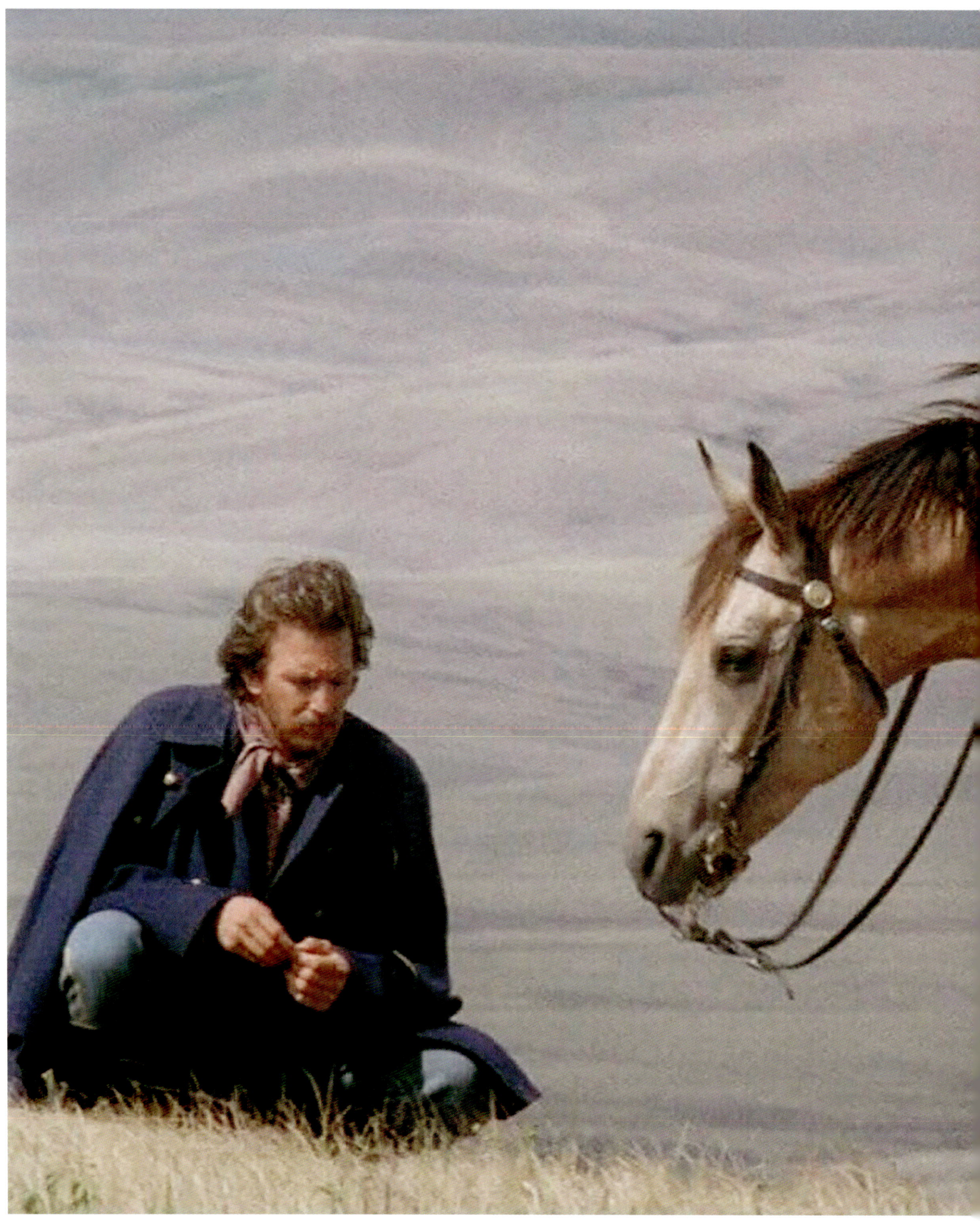

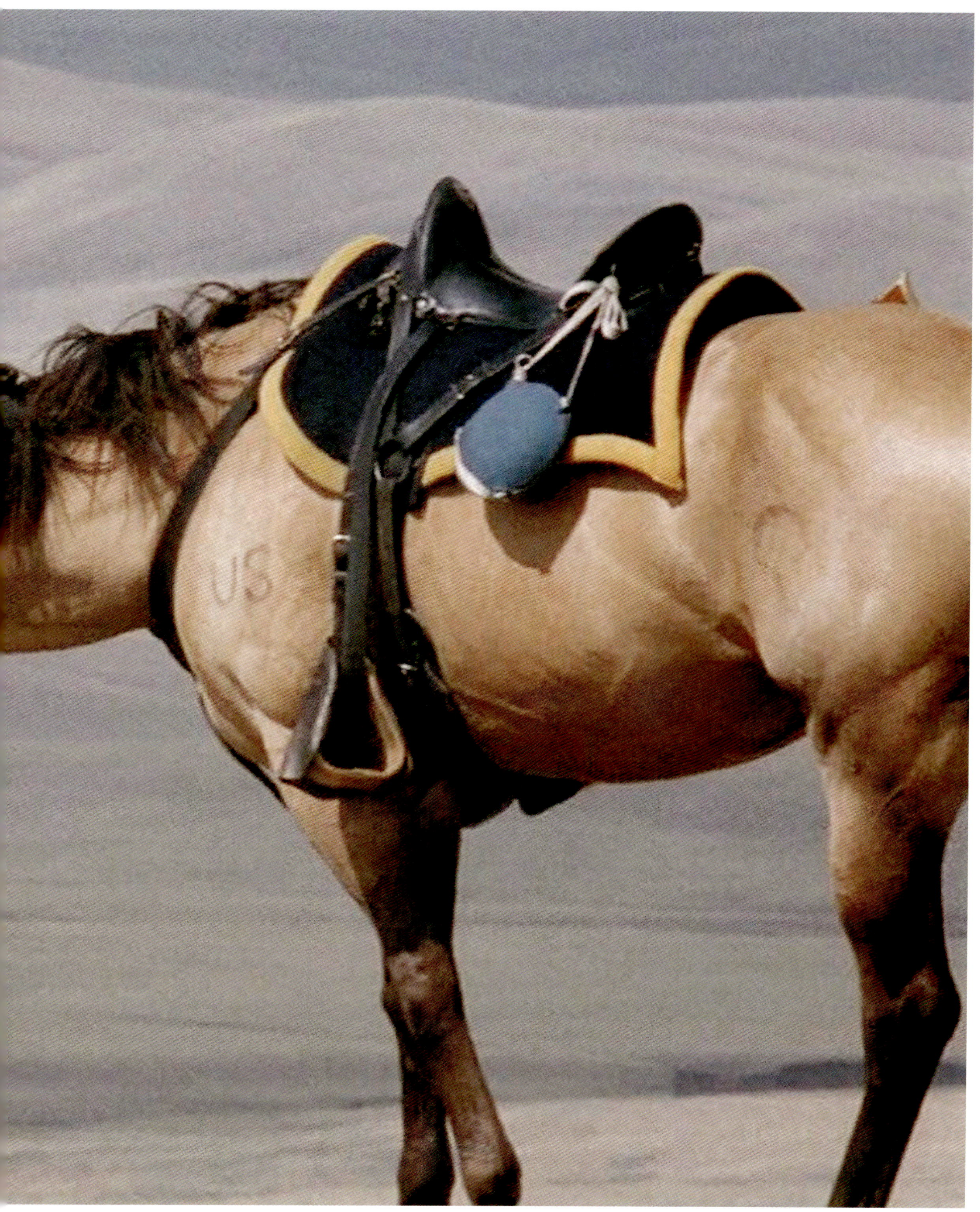

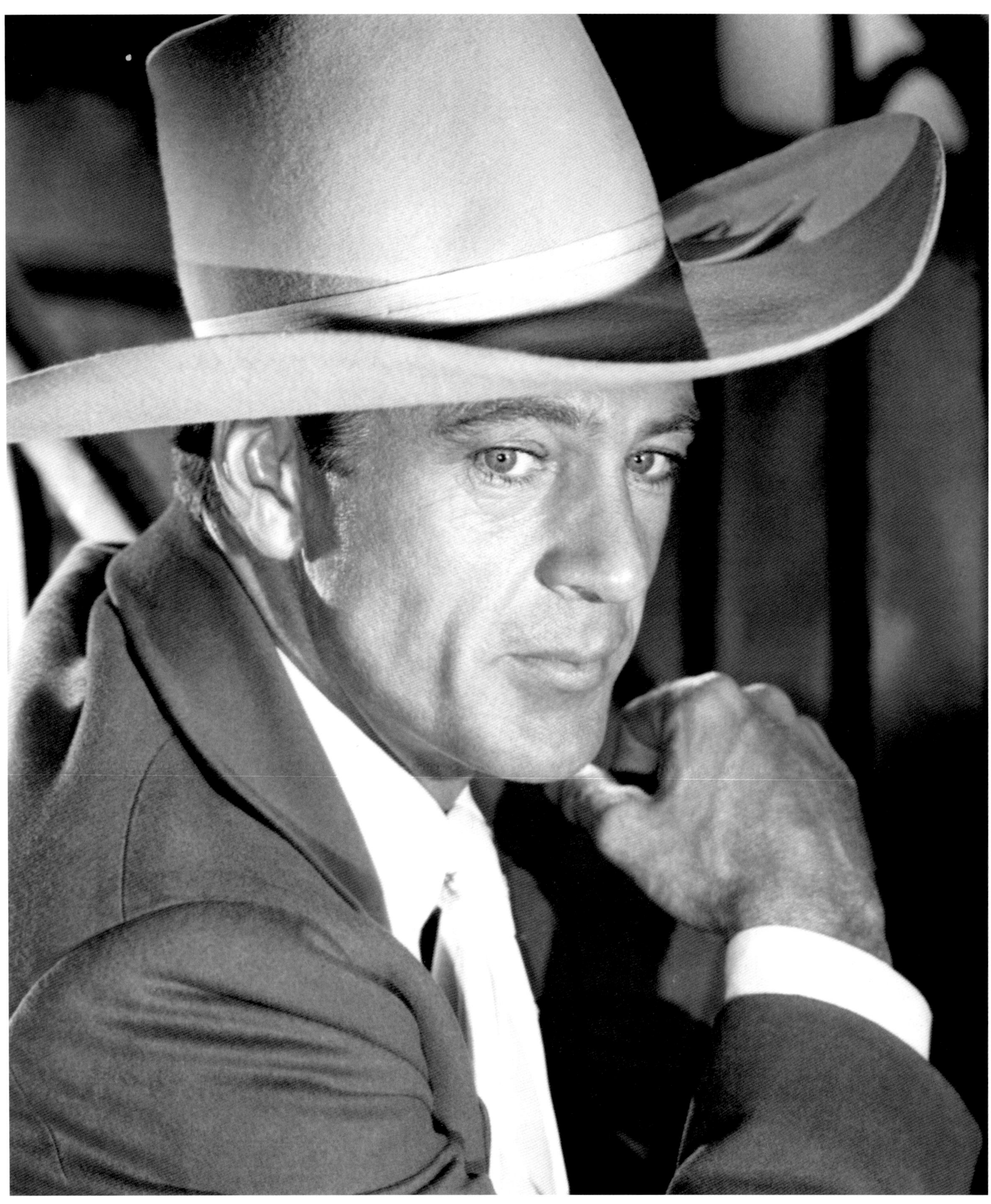

This page: *Gary Cooper in SARATOGA TRUNK (Wood, 1945).*

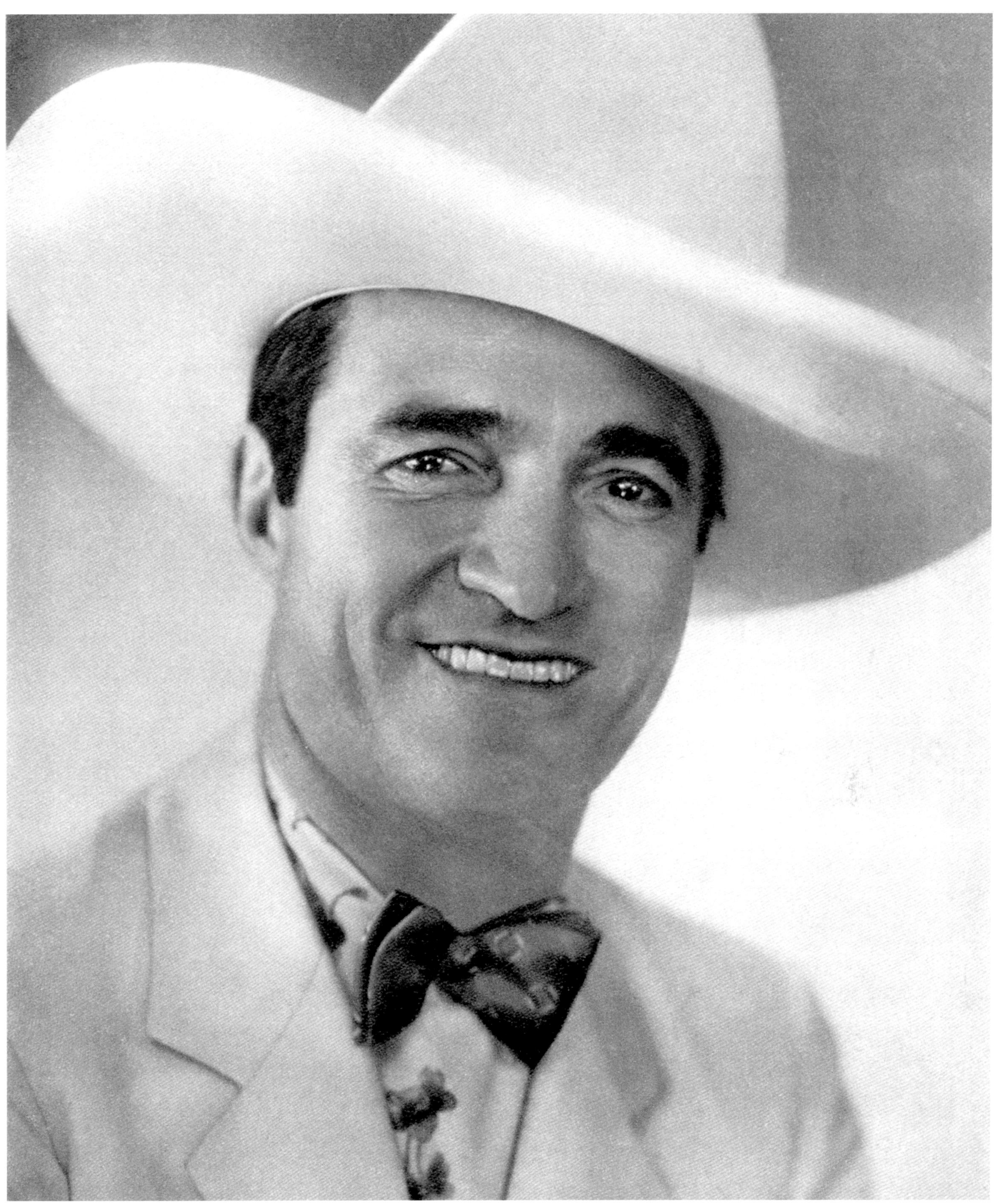

This page: *Thomas Edwin Mix was an American actor and the star of many early Western films between 1909 and 1935. Appearong in 291 pictures, all but nine of which were silent, he was one of Hollywood's first Western stars and helped define the genre as it emerged in the early days of the cinema.*

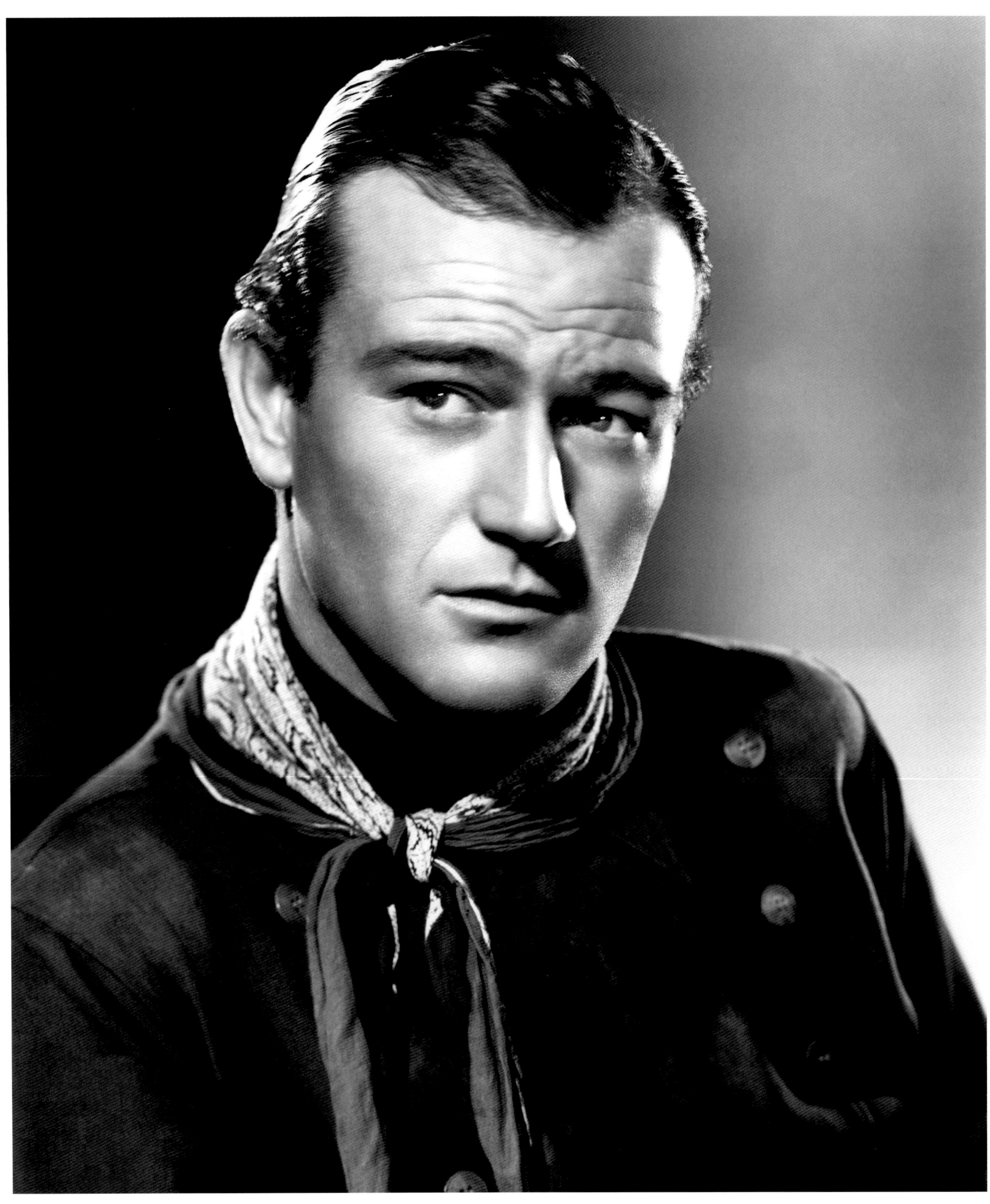

This page: *John Wayne in STAGECOACH (Ford, 1939).*

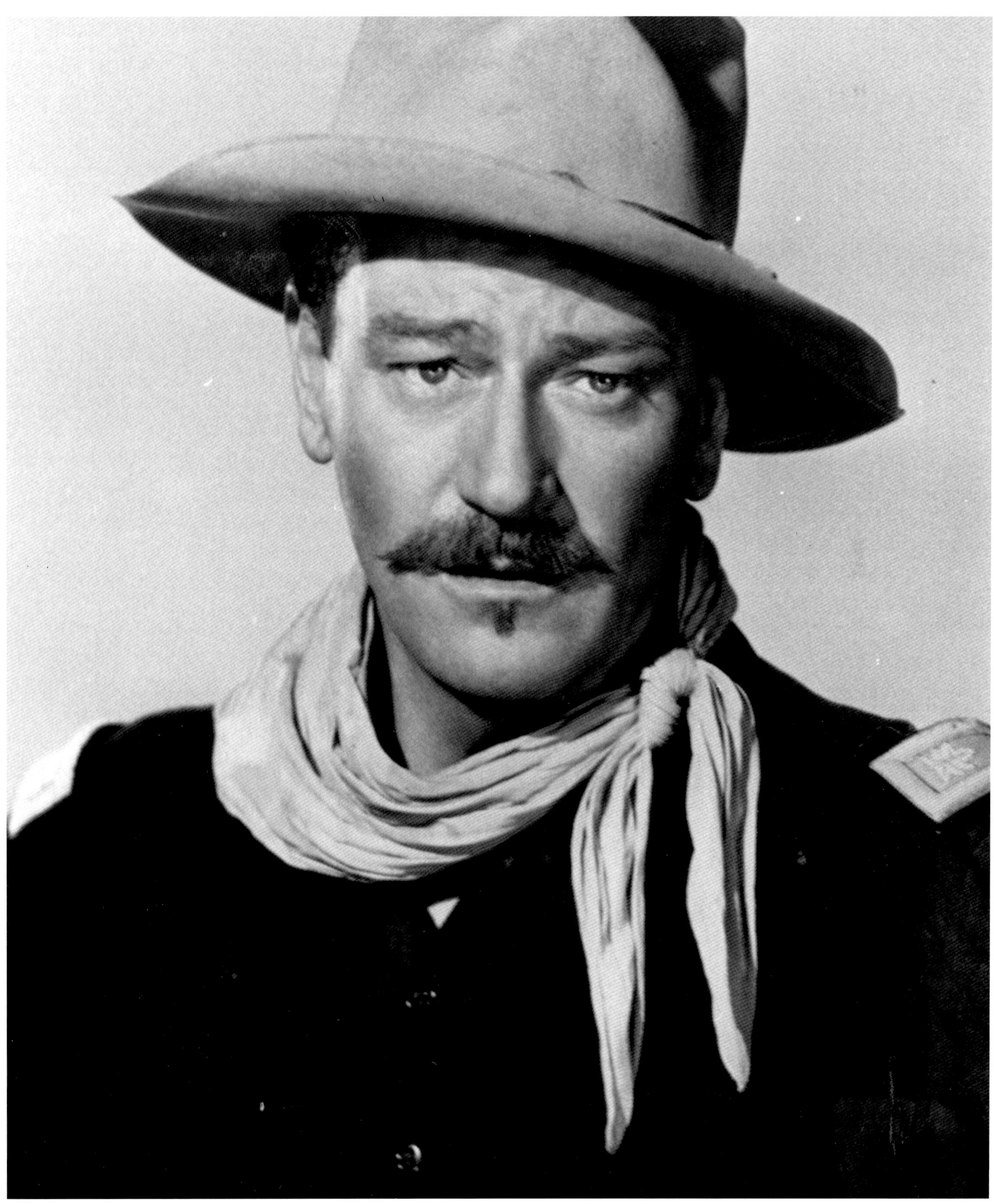

This page: *John Wayne in RIO GRANDE (Ford, 1950).*

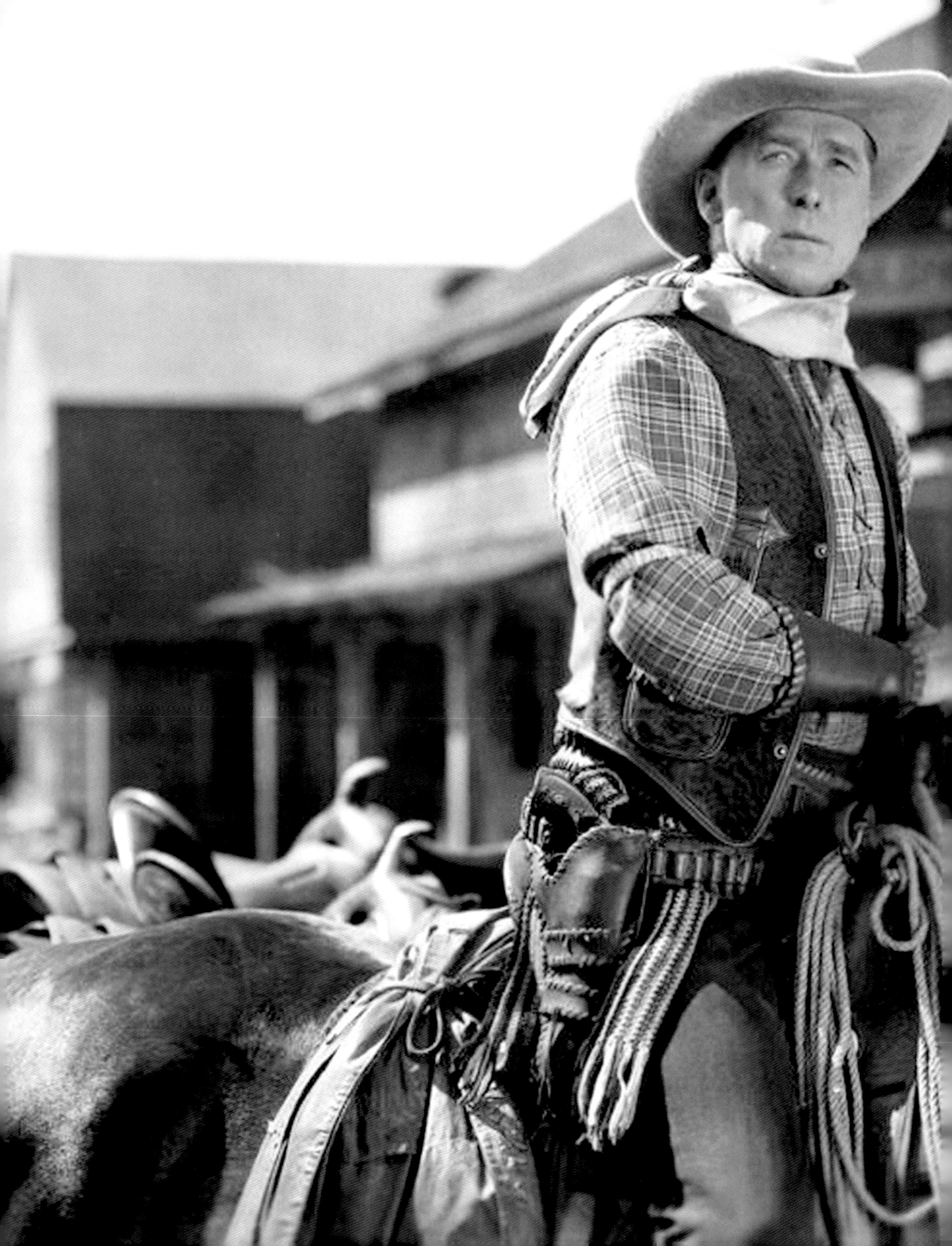

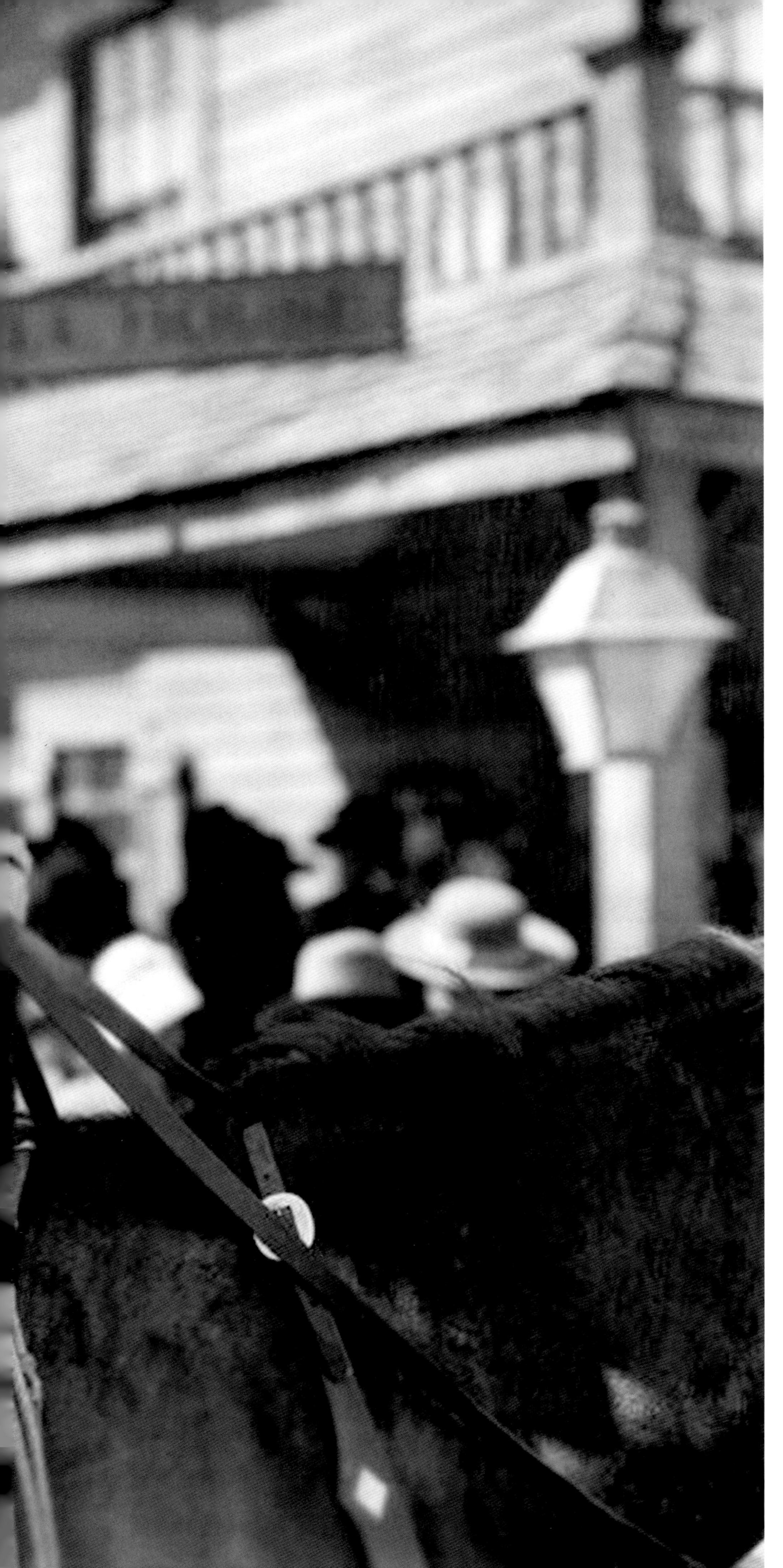

These pages: *William S. Hart in a scene from TUMBLEWEEDS (Baggot, 1926).*

Following pages: *Clint Eastwood in UNFORGIVEN (Eastwood, 1992).*

Page 92: *Poster for THE HEART OF TEXAS RYAN (Martin, 1917), an American silent Western with Tom Mix and Bessie Eyton.*

Page 93: *Poster for STAGECOACH featuring illustrations of Claire Trevor and John Wayne.*

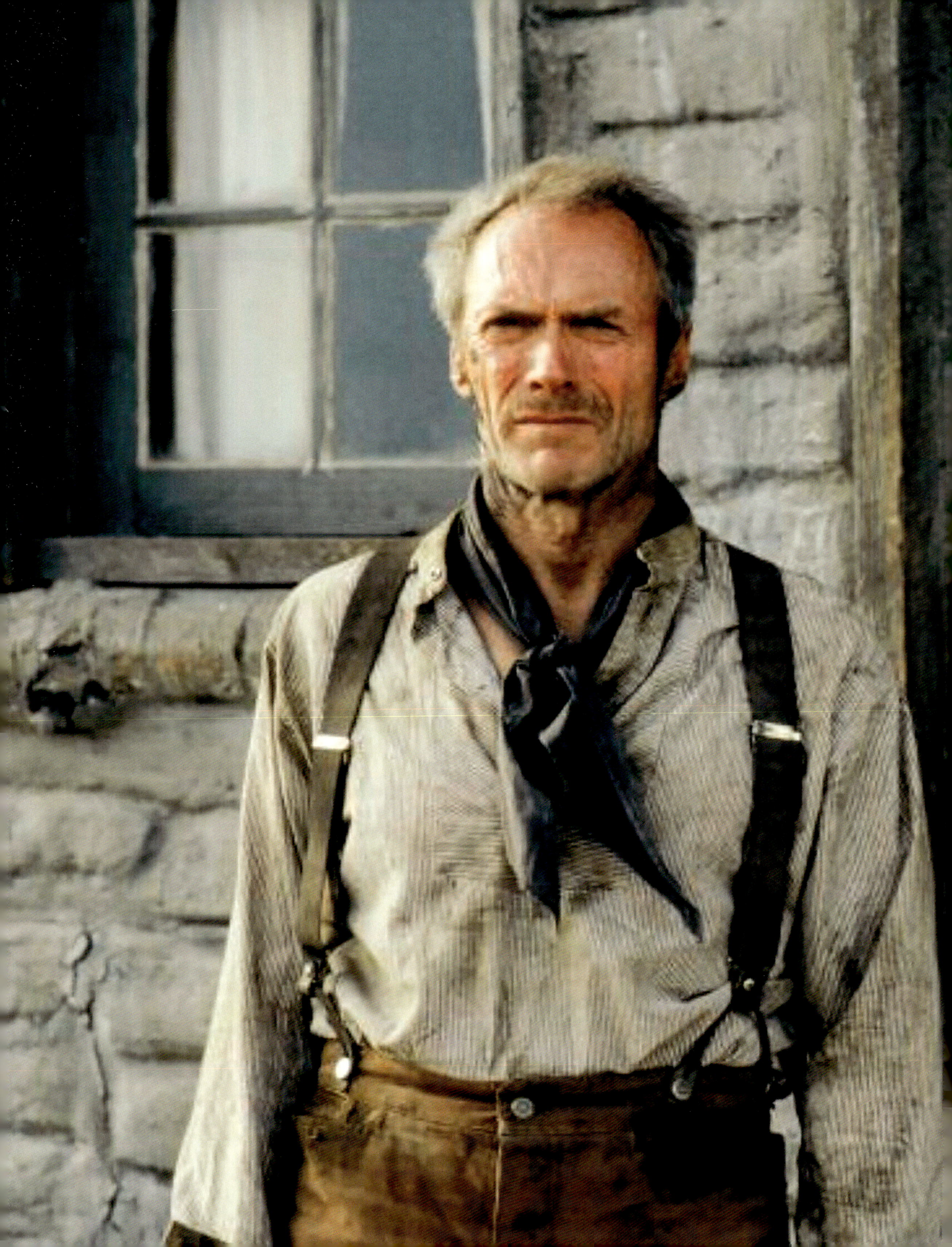

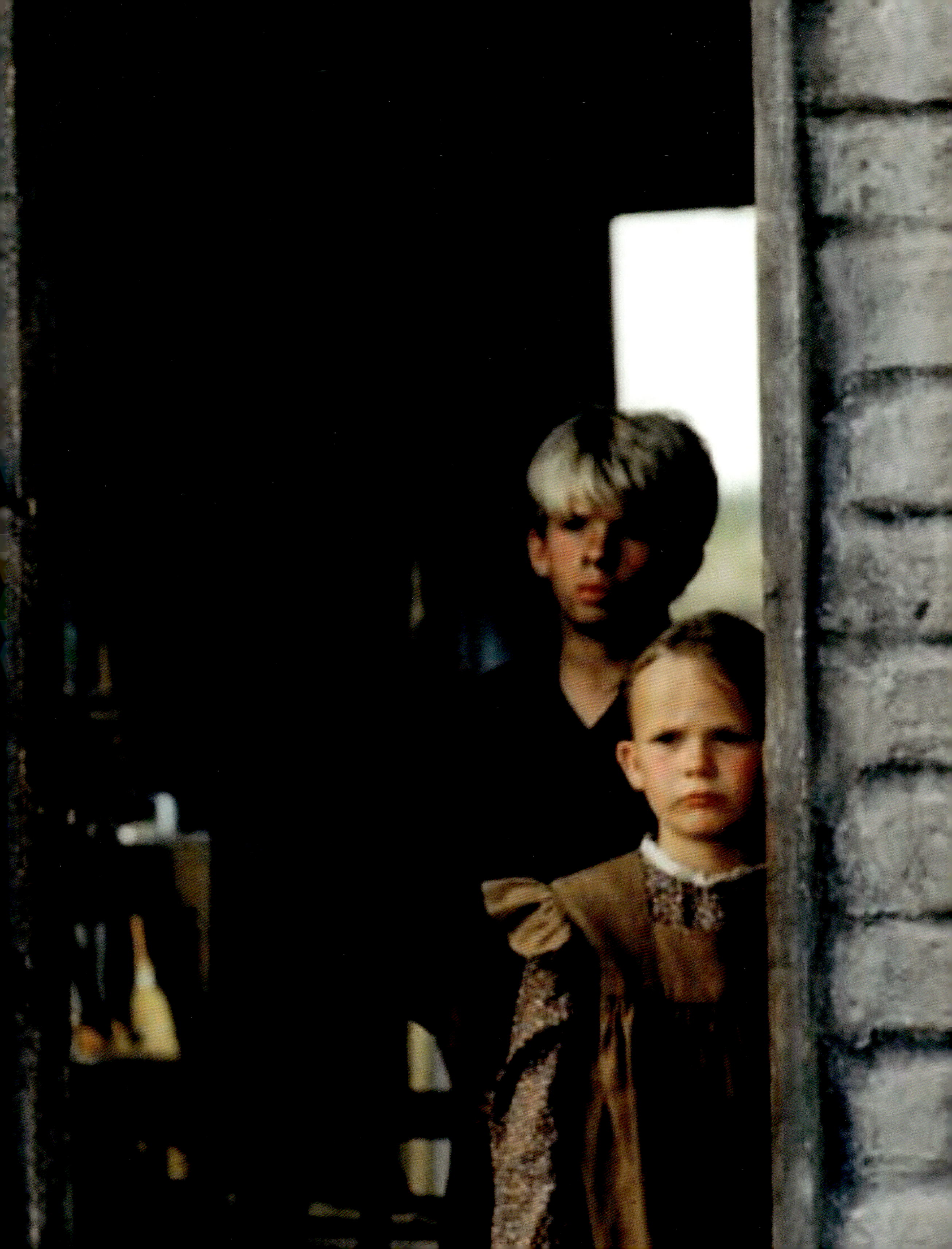

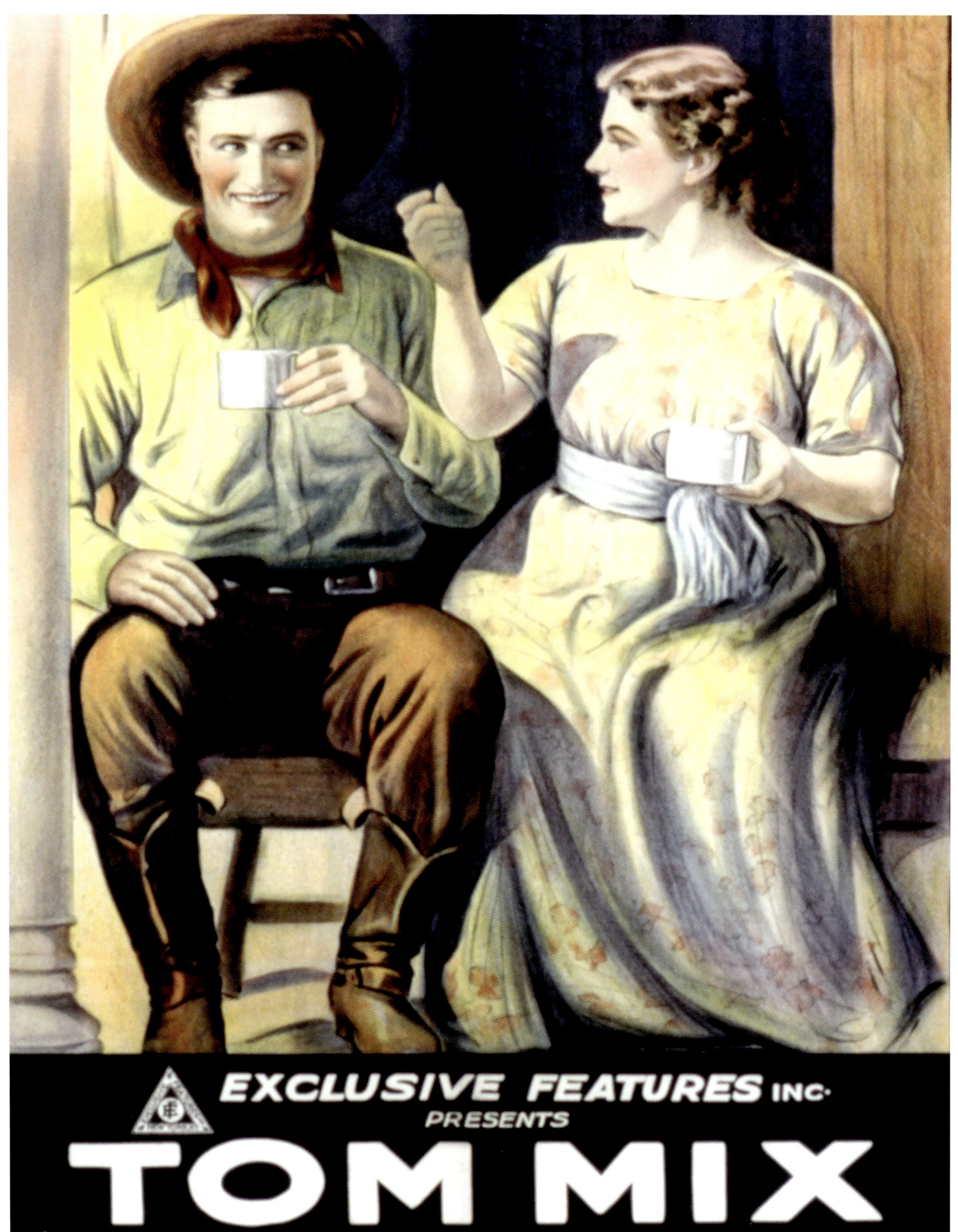
EXCLUSIVE FEATURES INC.
PRESENTS
TOM MIX

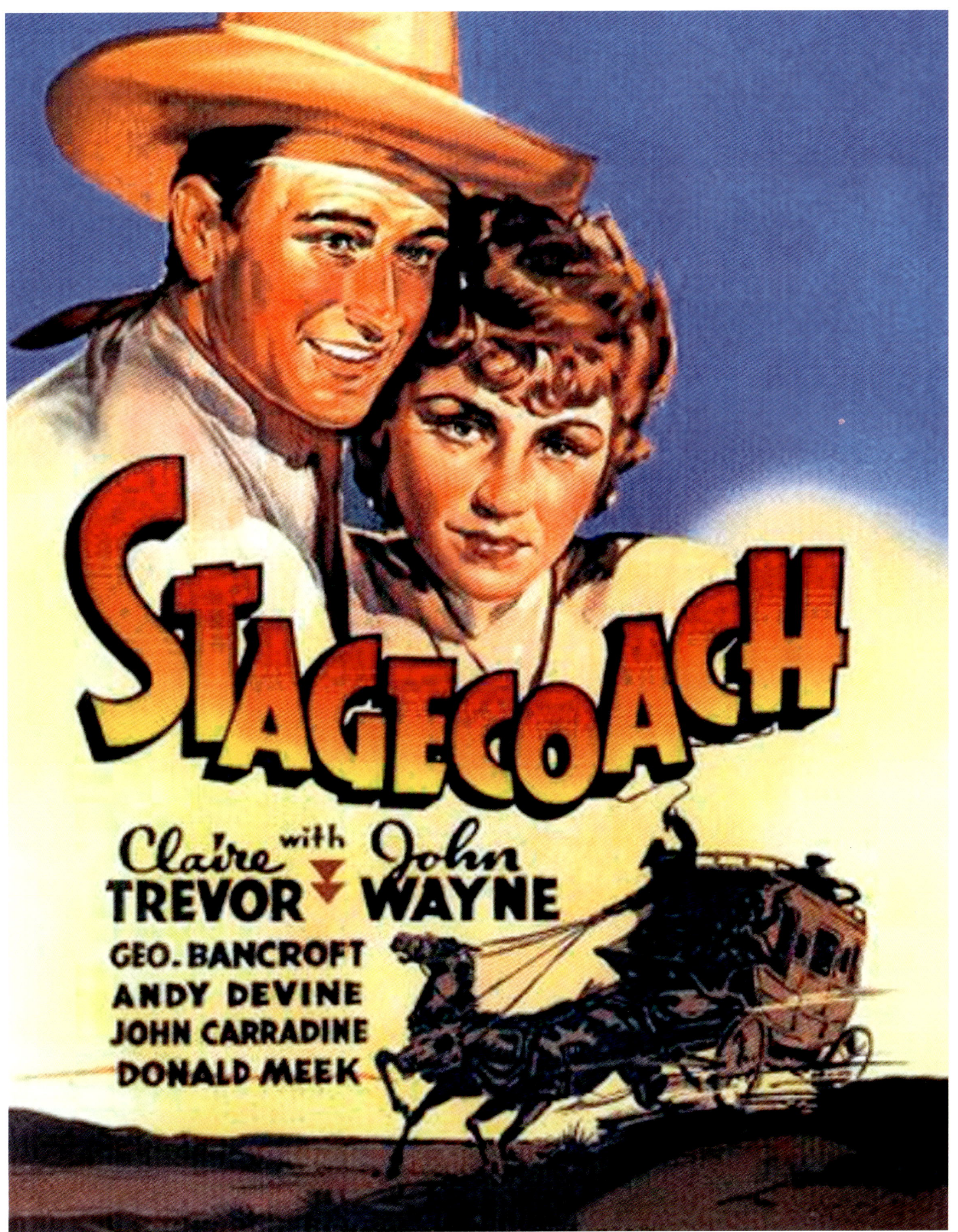
STAGECOACH
Claire with John
TREVOR WAYNE
GEO. BANCROFT
ANDY DEVINE
JOHN CARRADINE
DONALD MEEK

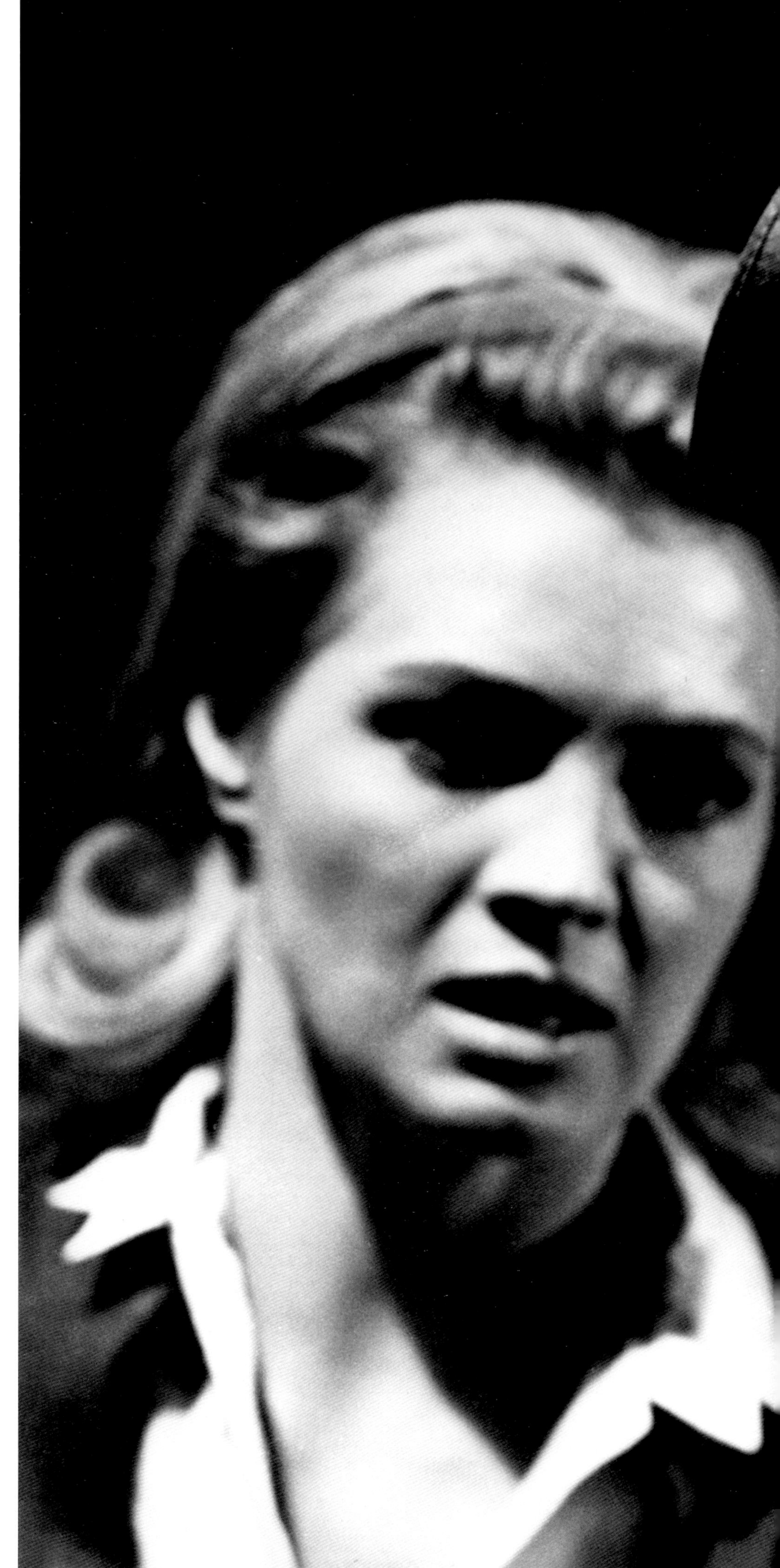

These pages: *Marlon Brando and Angie Dickinson as Sheriff Calder and Ruby Calder, respectively, in THE CHASE (Penn, 1966).*

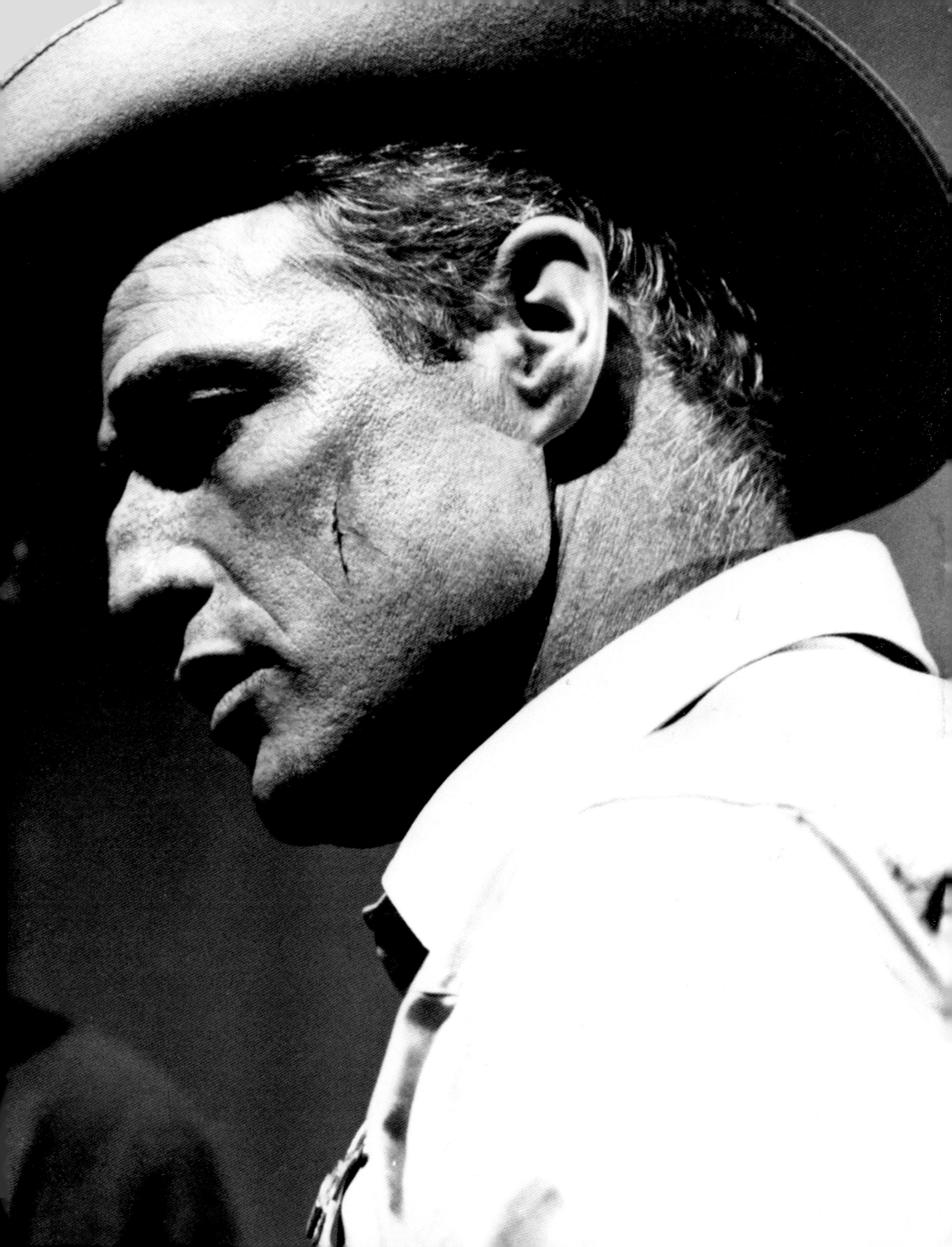

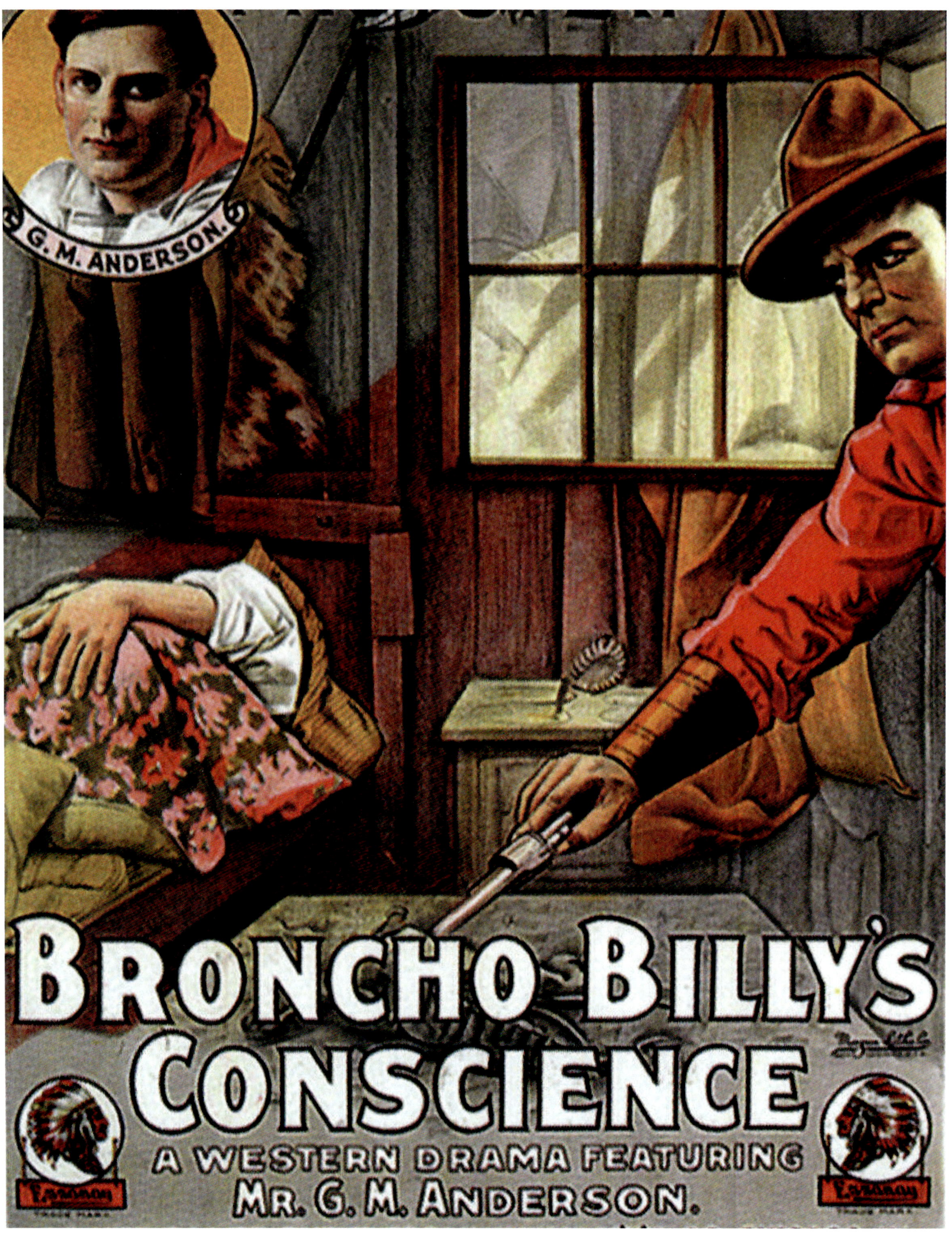
G. M. ANDERSON.
BRONCHO BILLY'S
CONSCIENCE
A WESTERN DRAMA FEATURING
MR. G. M. ANDERSON.

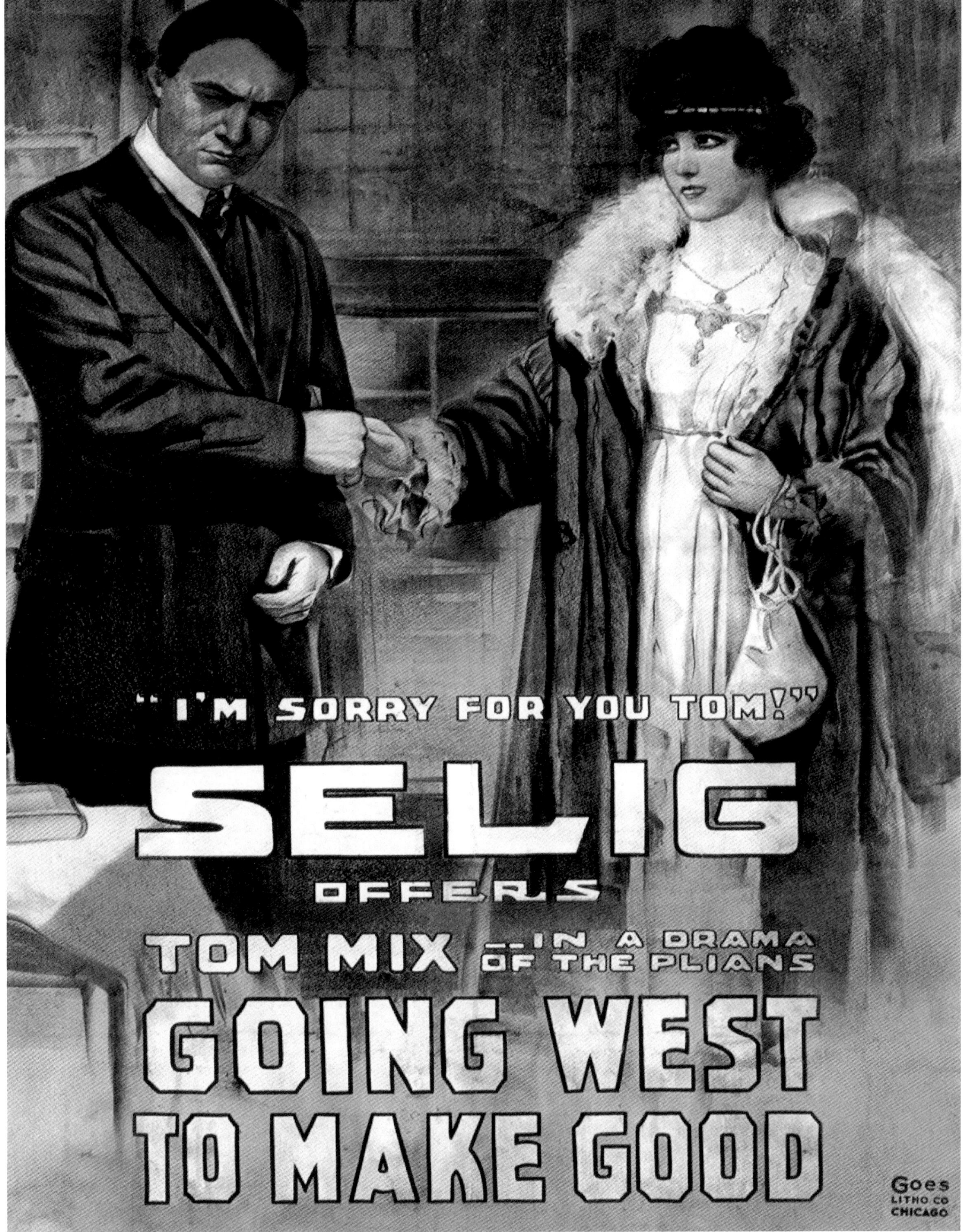

"I'M SORRY FOR YOU TOM!"
SELIG
OFFERS
TOM MIX -- IN A DRAMA OF THE PLIANS
GOING WEST
TO MAKE GOOD
Goes
LITHO.CO
CHICAGO

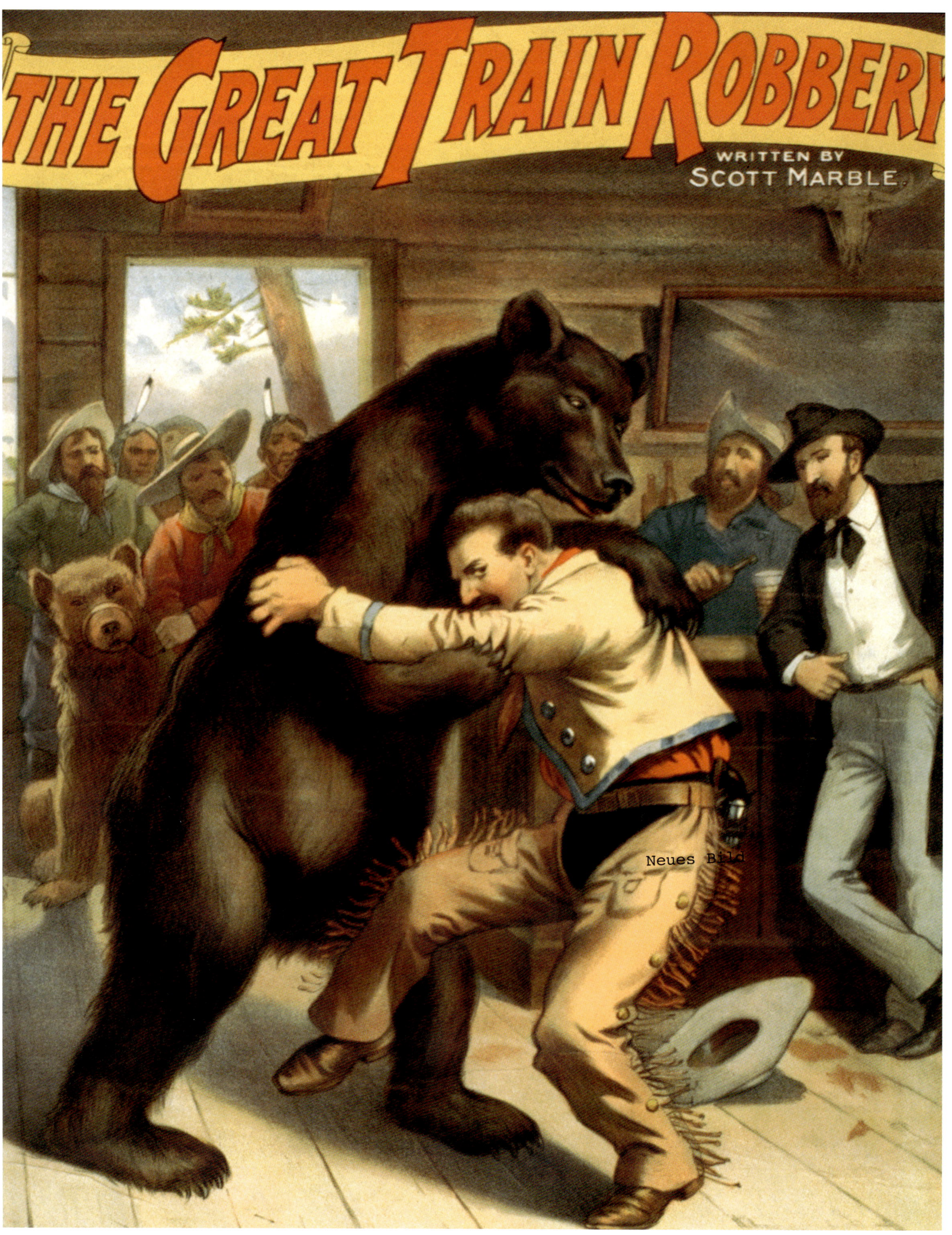

THE GREAT TRAIN ROBBERY
WRITTEN BY
SCOTT MARBLE.
Neues Bild

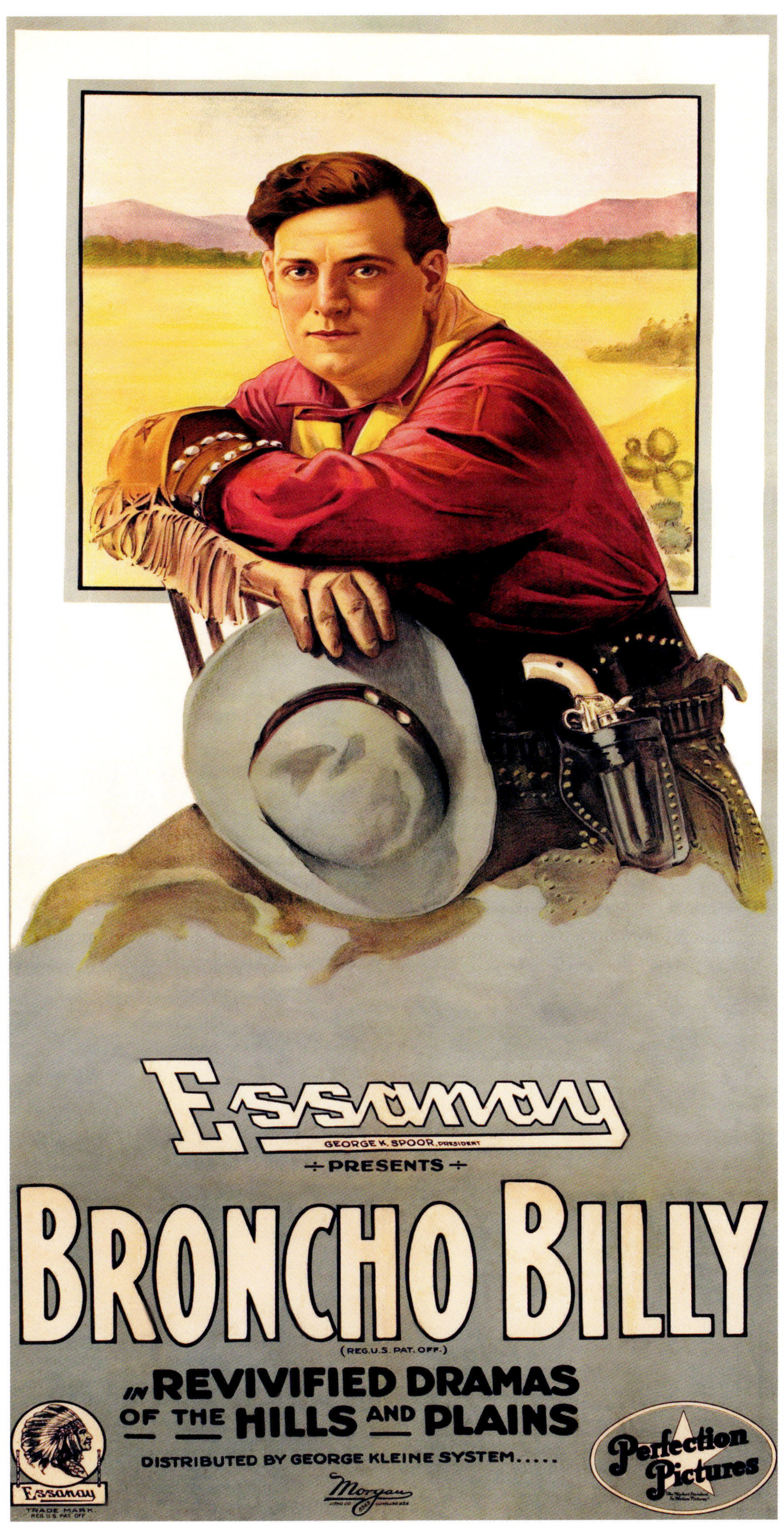

Page 96 and this page: *A poster for BRONCHO BILLY'S CONSCIENCE (Anderson, 1913), a Western short starring Gilbert M. "Broncho Billy" Anderson. Anderson played Billy a number of times between 1909 and 1915; not only the first Western film star, he co-owned the studio (Essanay) that produced most of his pictures.*

Page 97: *A poster for GOING WEST TO MAKE GOOD with Tom Mix (1916).*

Opposite: *Poster for THE GREAT TRAIN ROBBERY, an 1896 theatrical production written by Scott Marble.*

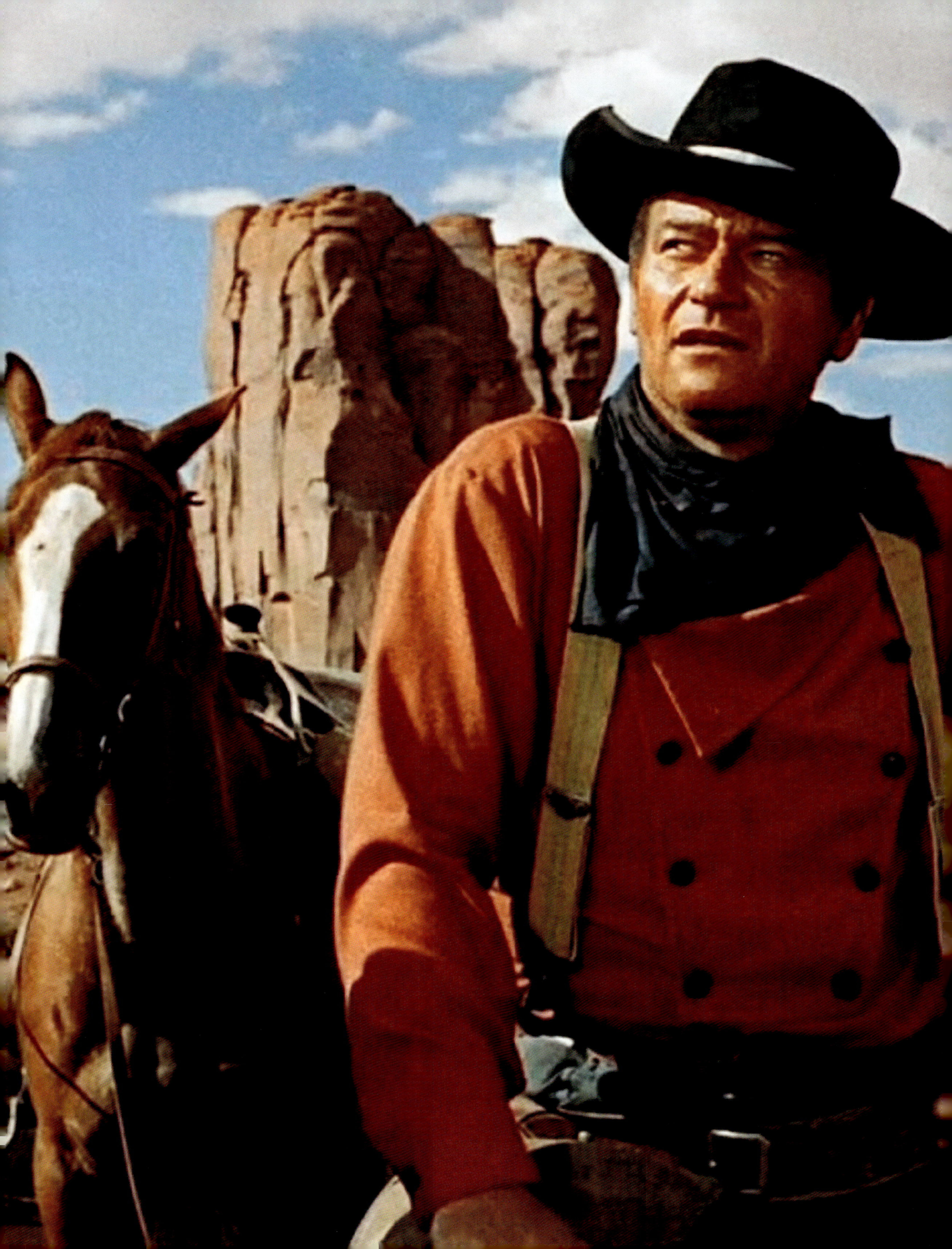

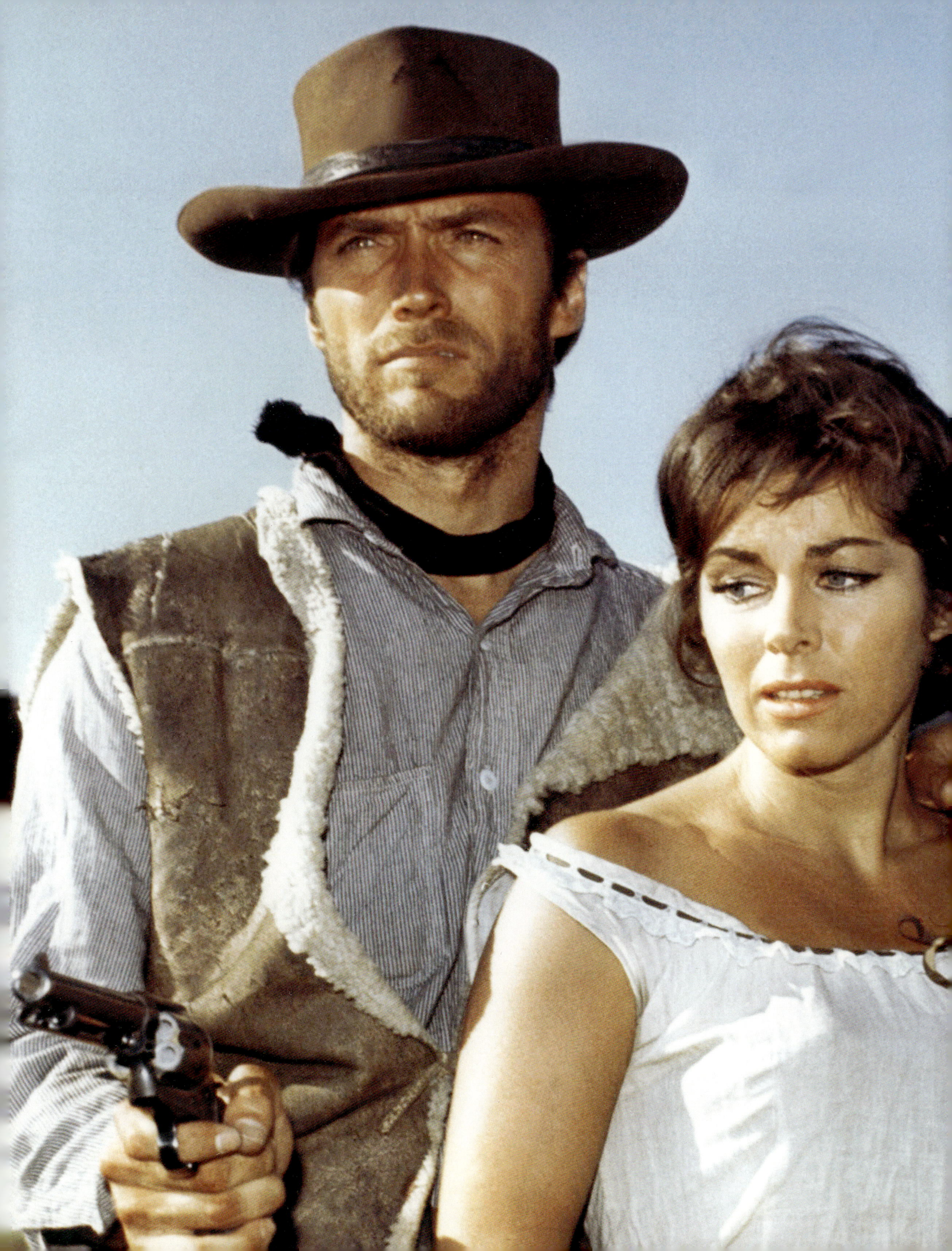

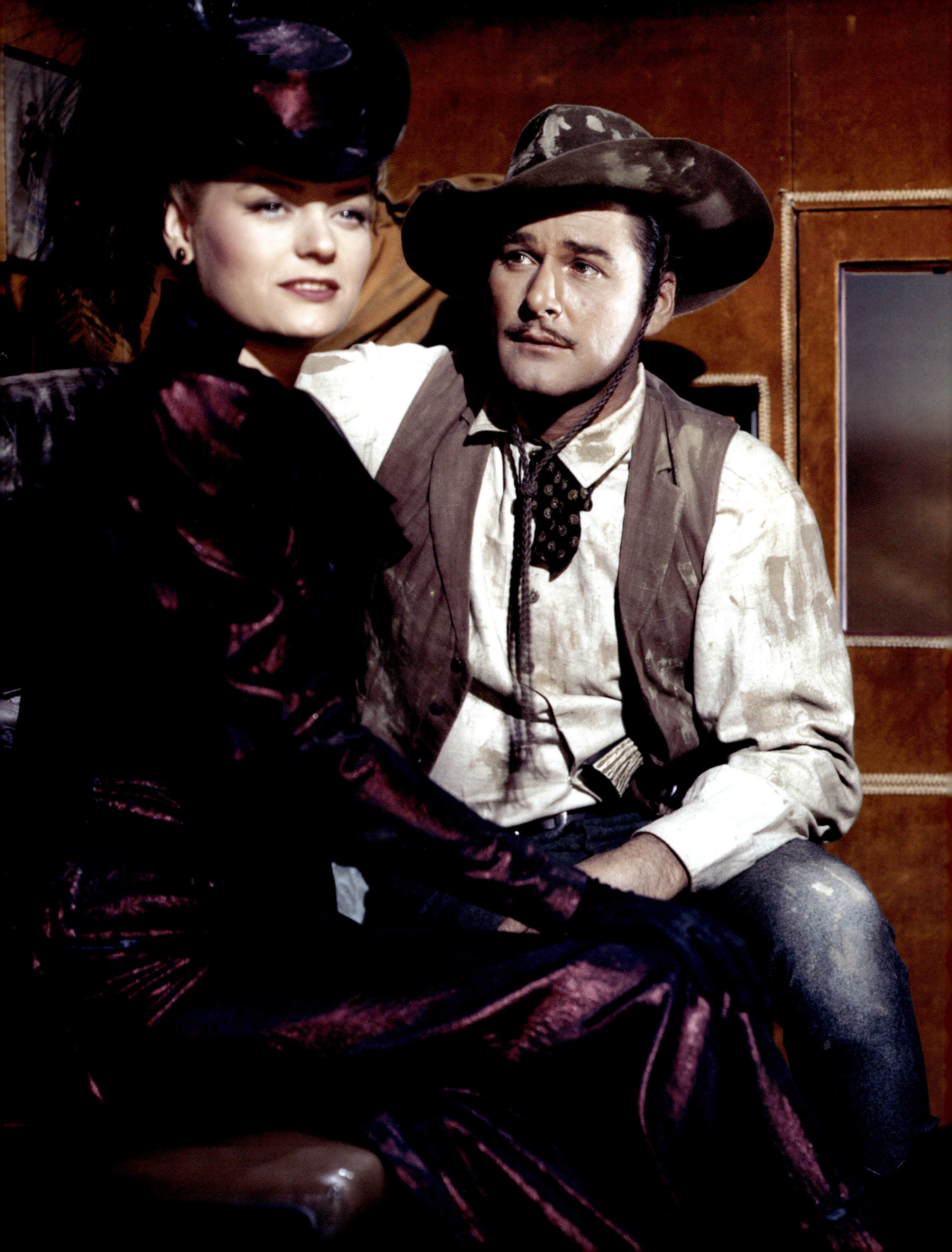

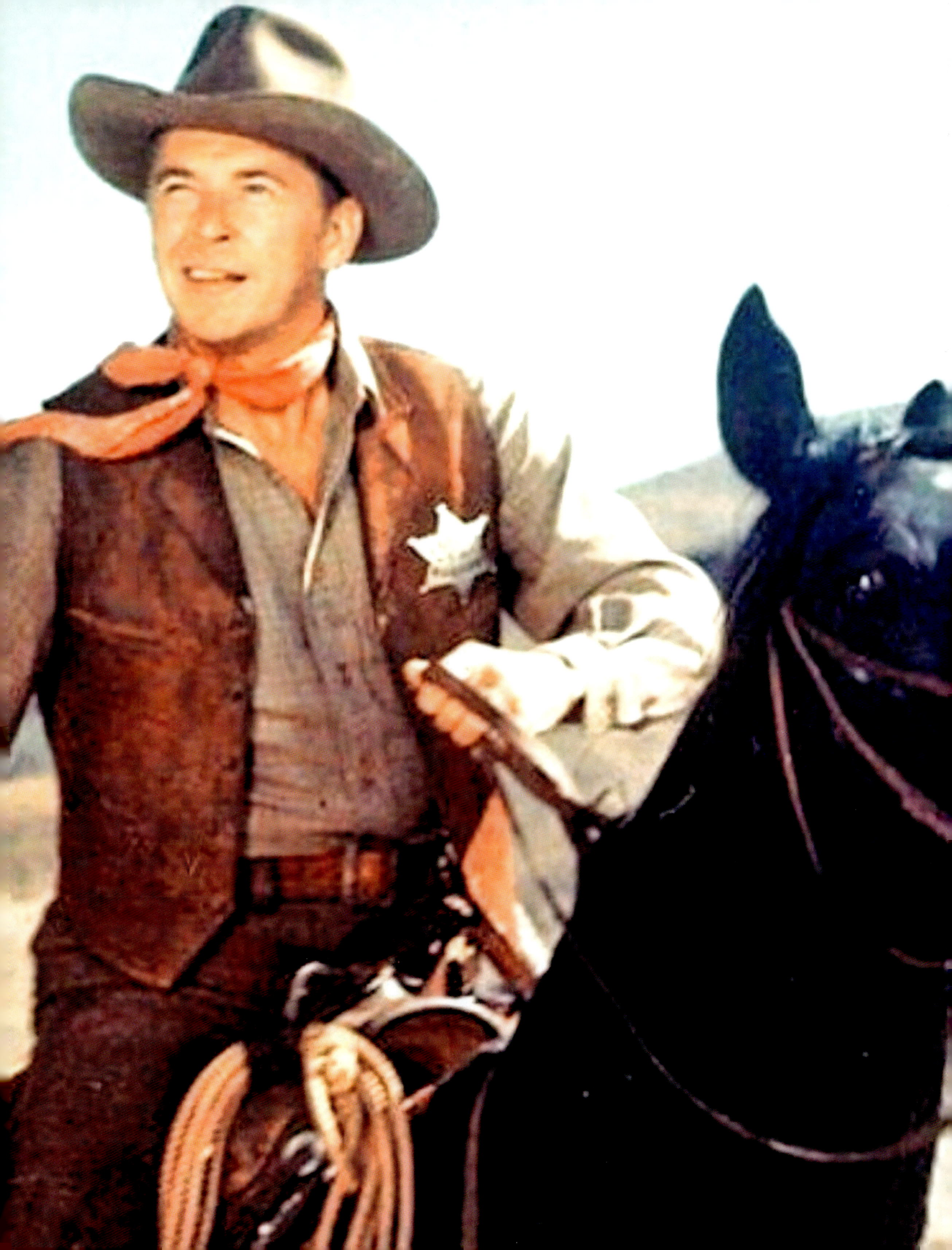

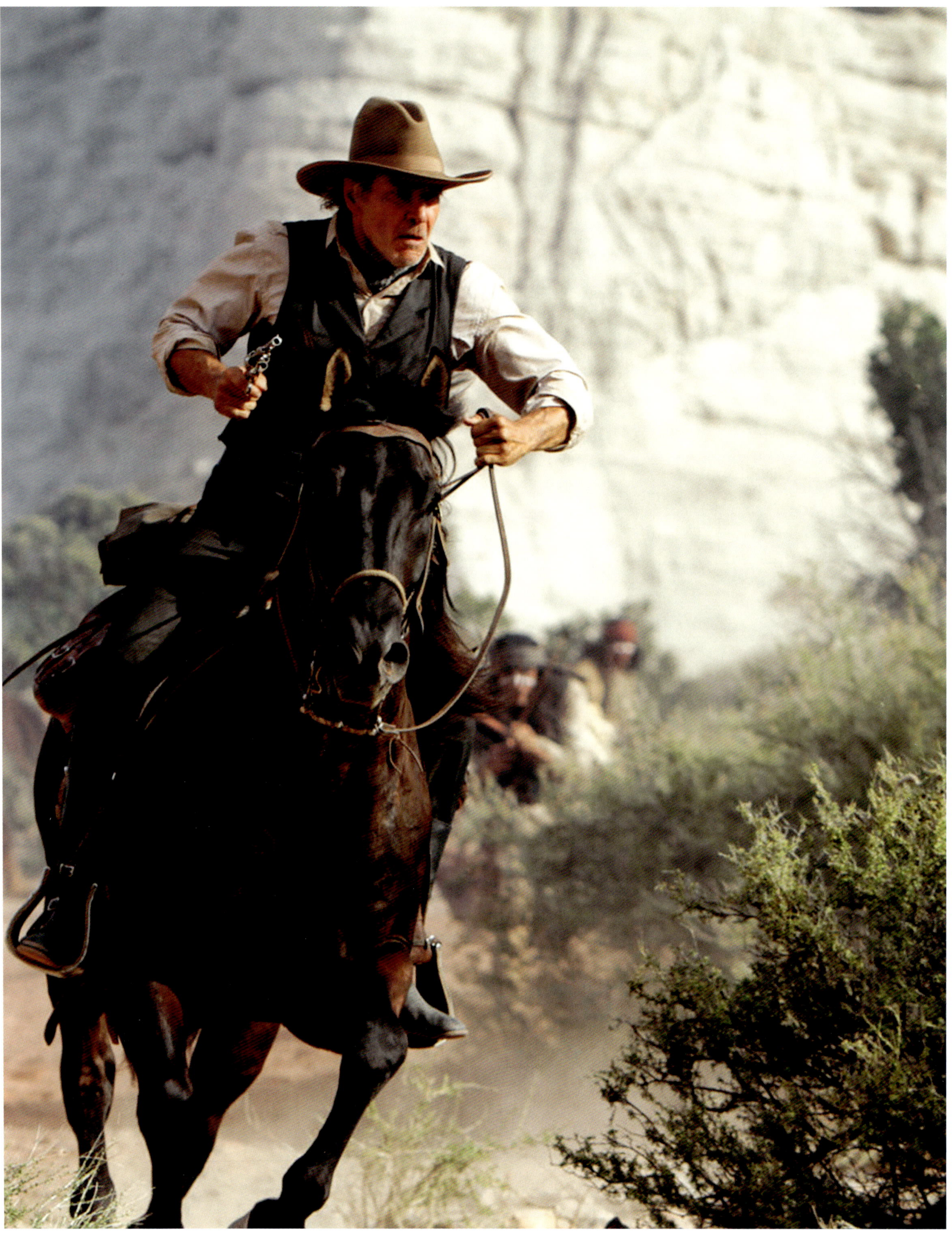

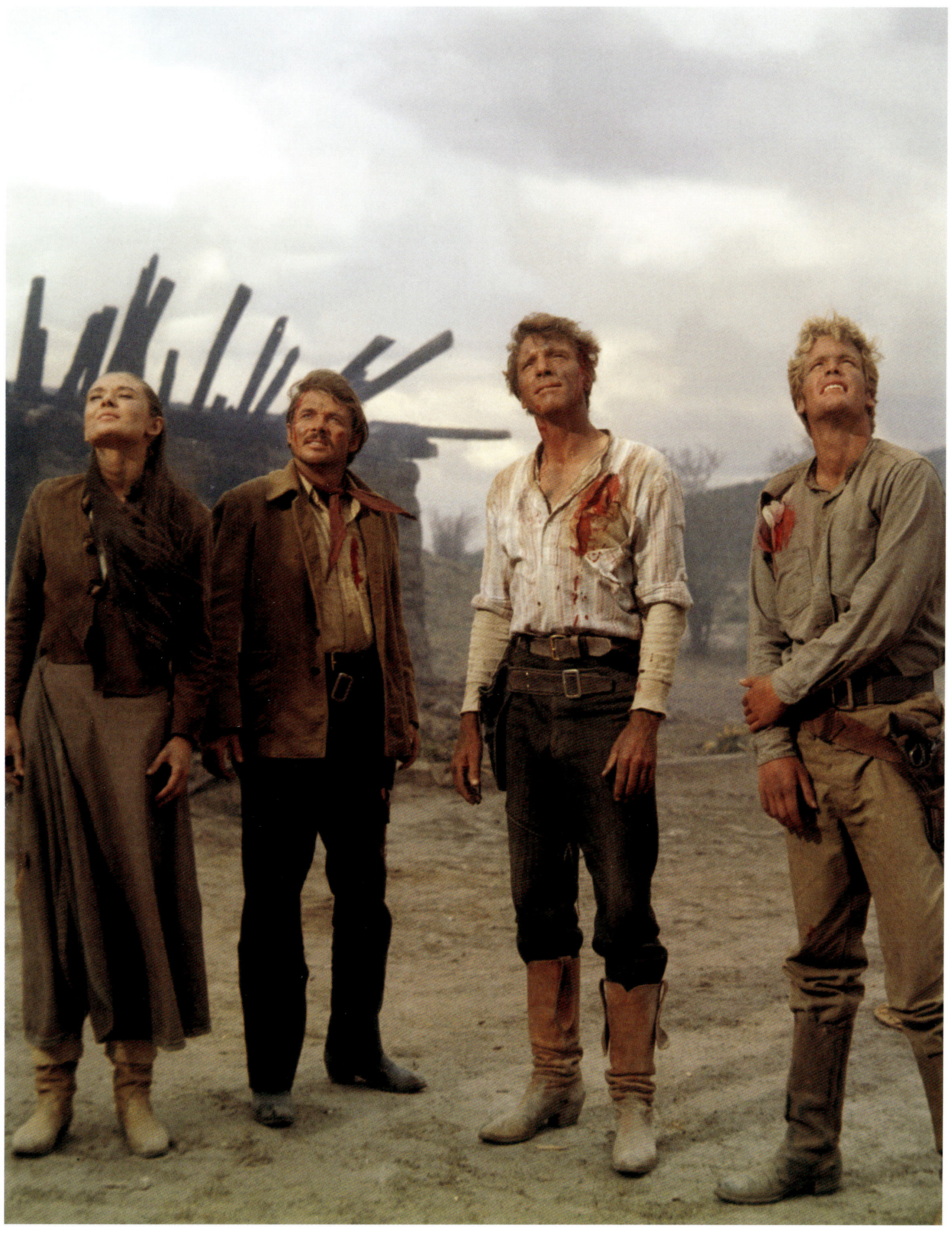

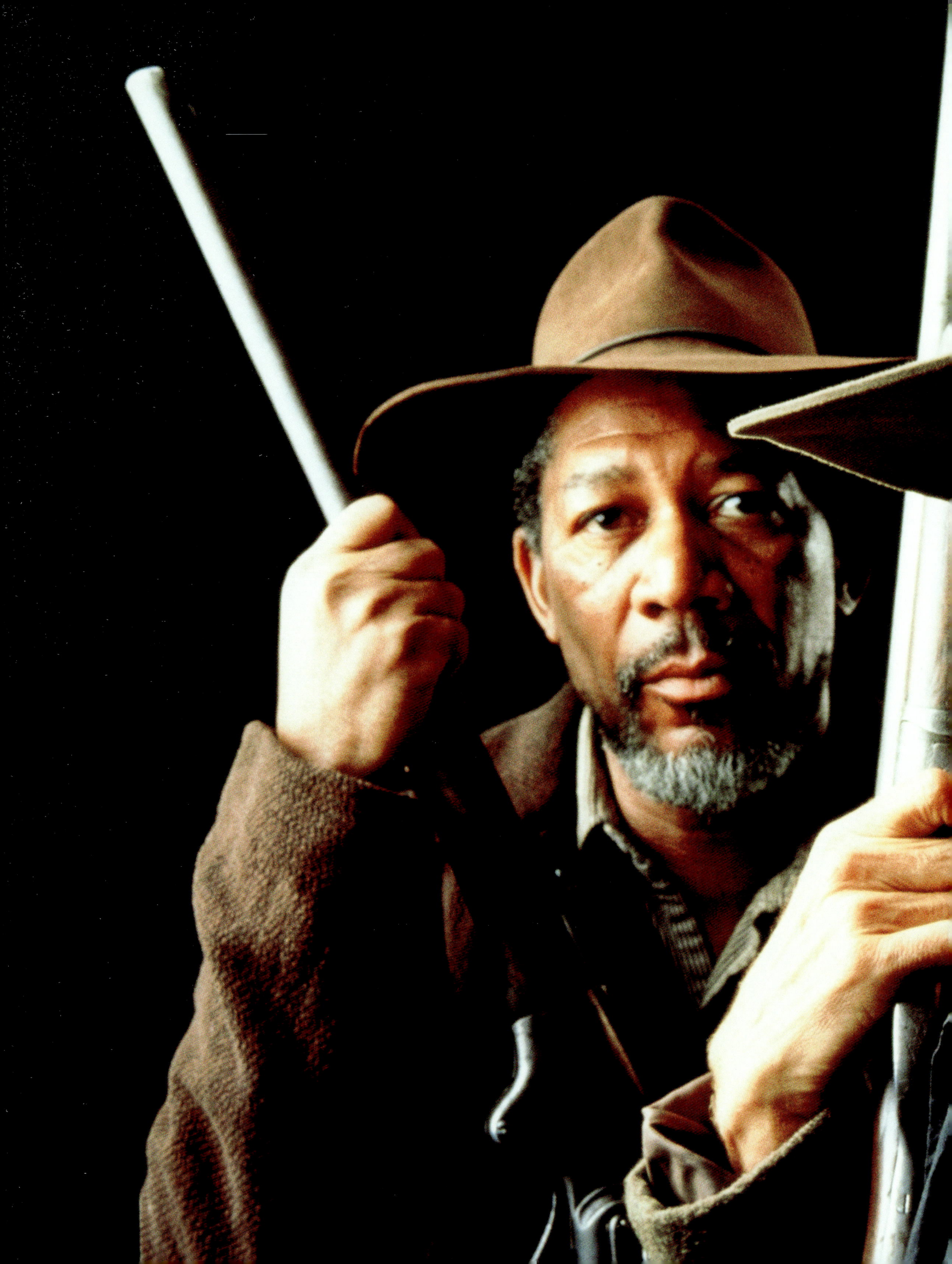

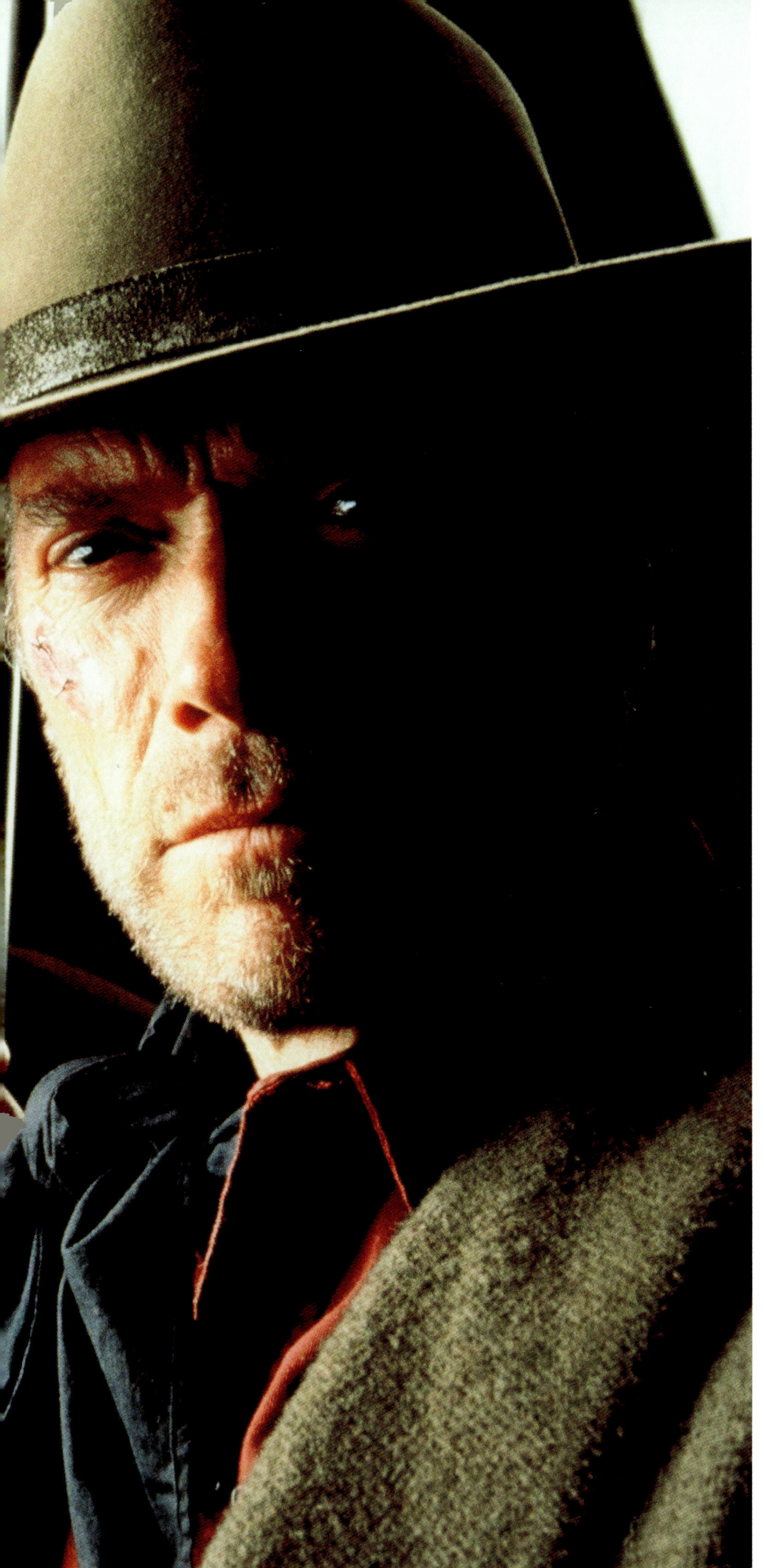

Page 100: *John Wayne in THE SEARCHERS, (Ford, 1956).*

Page 101: *Clint Eastwood and Marriane Koch in A FISTFUL OF DOLLARS (Leone, 1964).*

Page 102: *Alexis Smith and Errol Flynn in SAN ANTONIO (Butler, 1945).*

Page 103: *Ronald Reagan as US marshall Frame Johnson in LAW AND ORDER (Juran, 1953).*

Page 104, 113: *Harrison Ford in COWBOYS & ALIENS (Favreau, 2011).*

Page105: *Audrey Hepburn, Audie Murphy, Burt Lancaster and Doug McClure in THE UNFORGIVEN (Huston, 1960).*

These pages: *Morgan Freeman (left) and Clint Eastwood in UNFORGIVEN (Eastwood, 1992).*

These pages: *Sharon Stone as the gunslinger known as "The Lady" in THE QUICK AND THE DEAD (Raimi, 1995).*

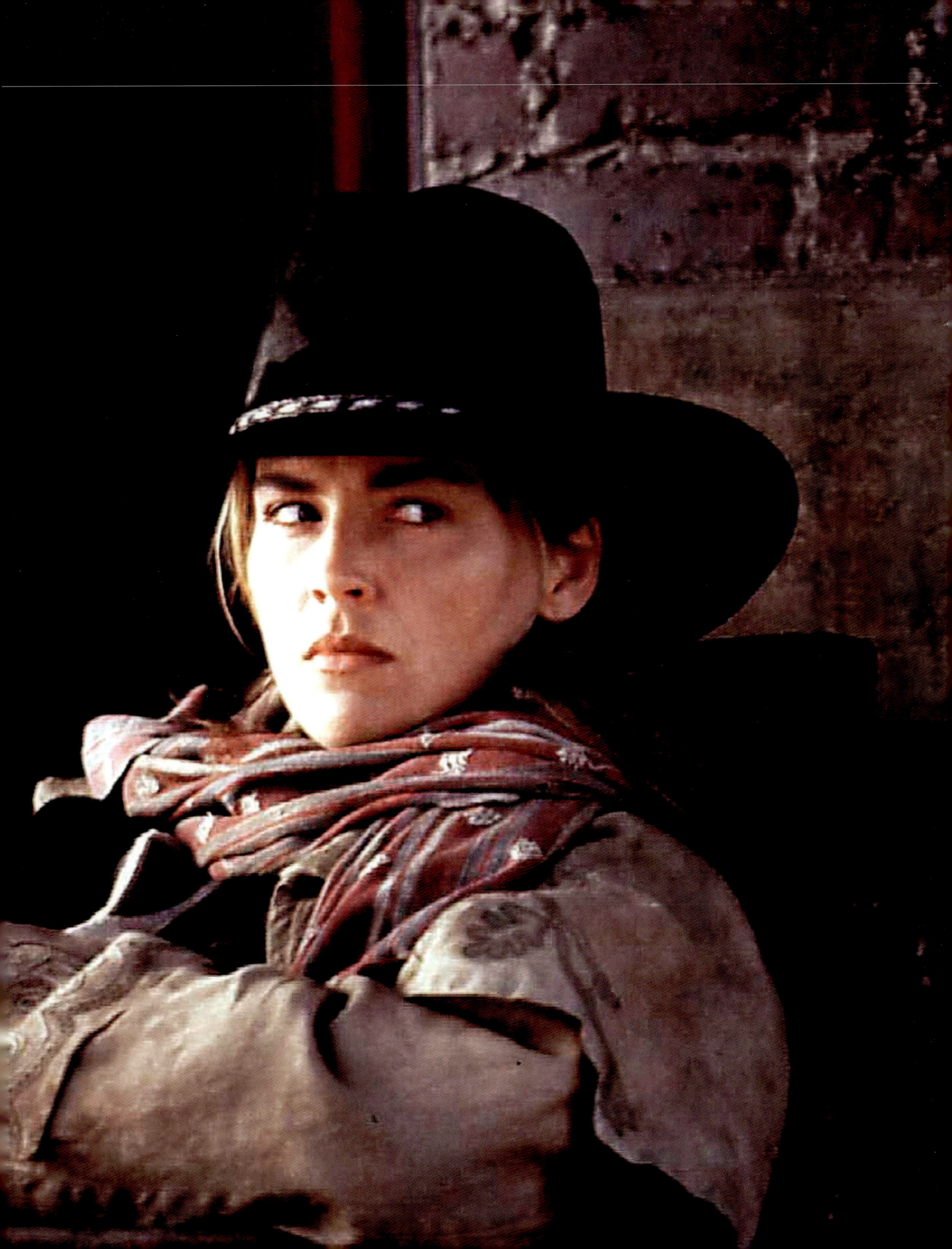

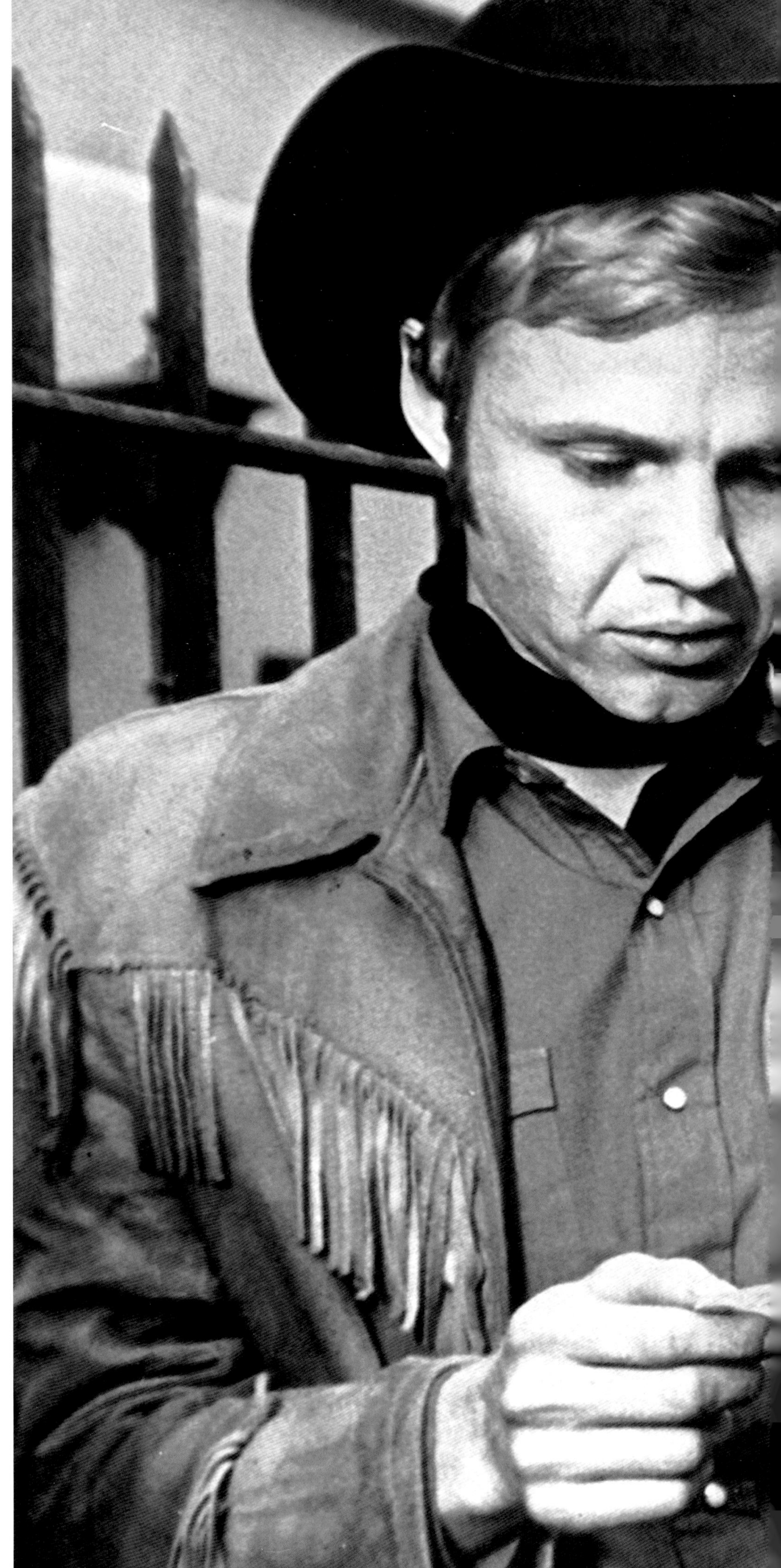

These pages: *Jon Voight (left) and Dustin Hoffman in MIDNIGHT COWBOY (Schlesinger, 1969), adapted for the screen by Waldo Salt from James Leo Herlihy's 1965 novel.*

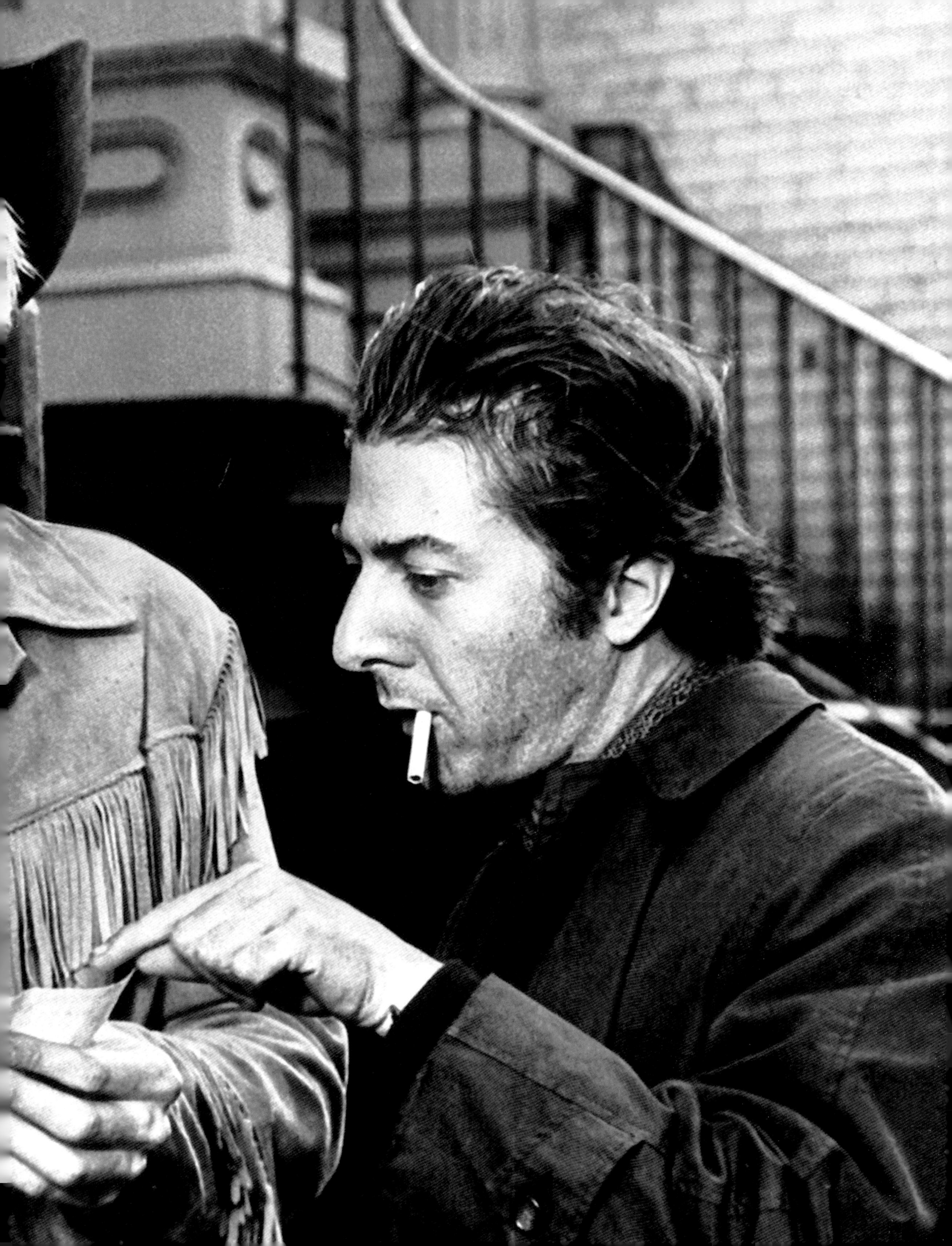

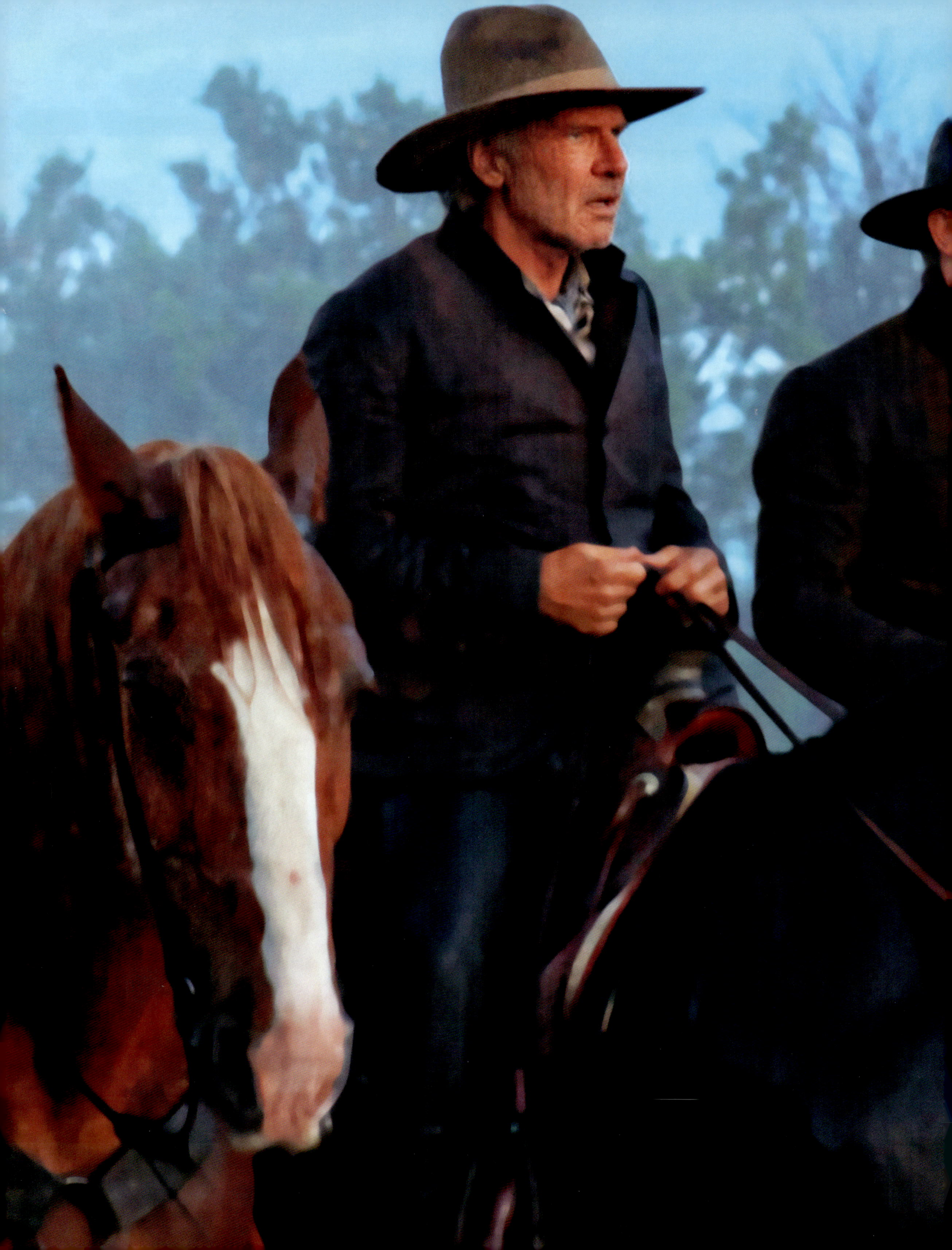

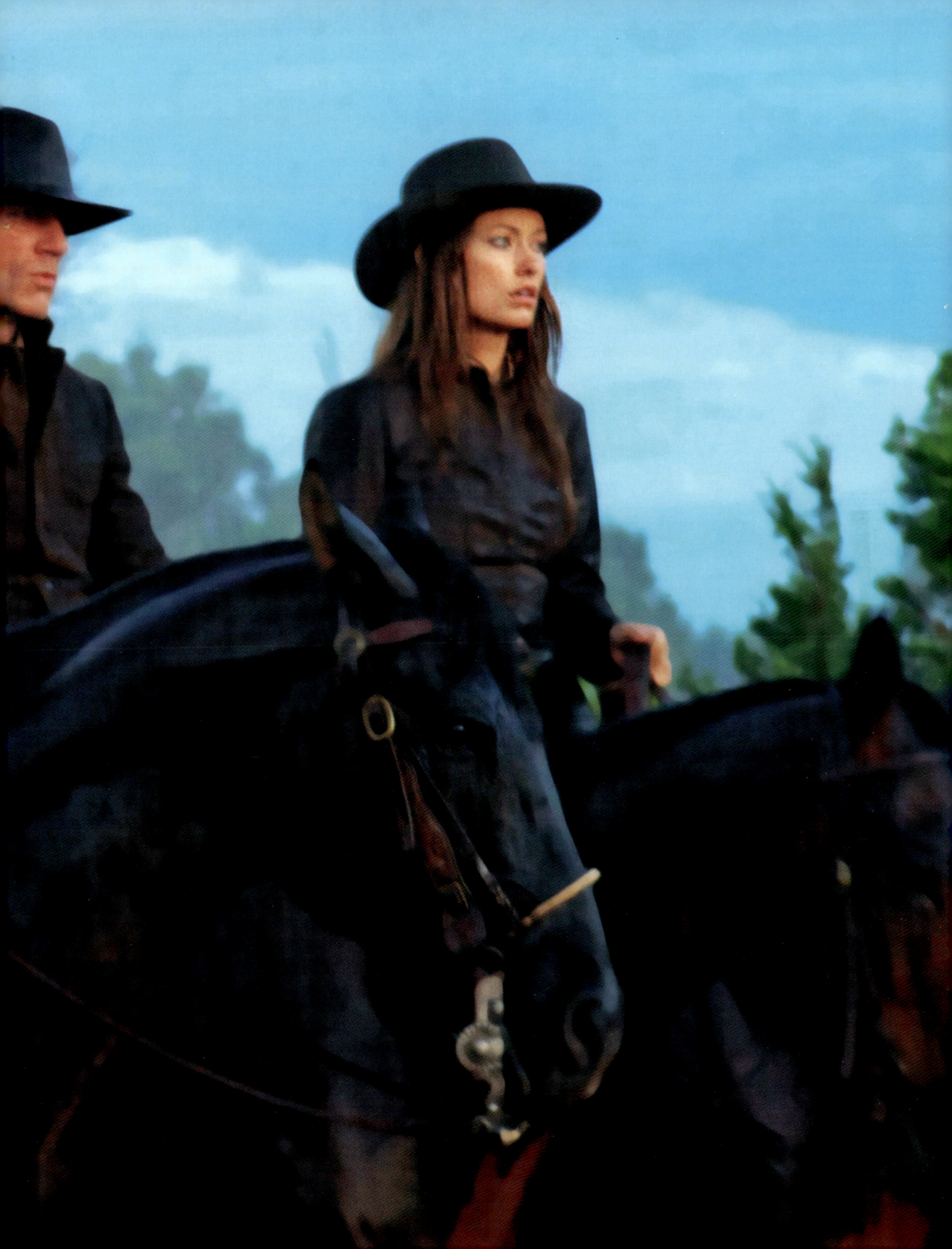

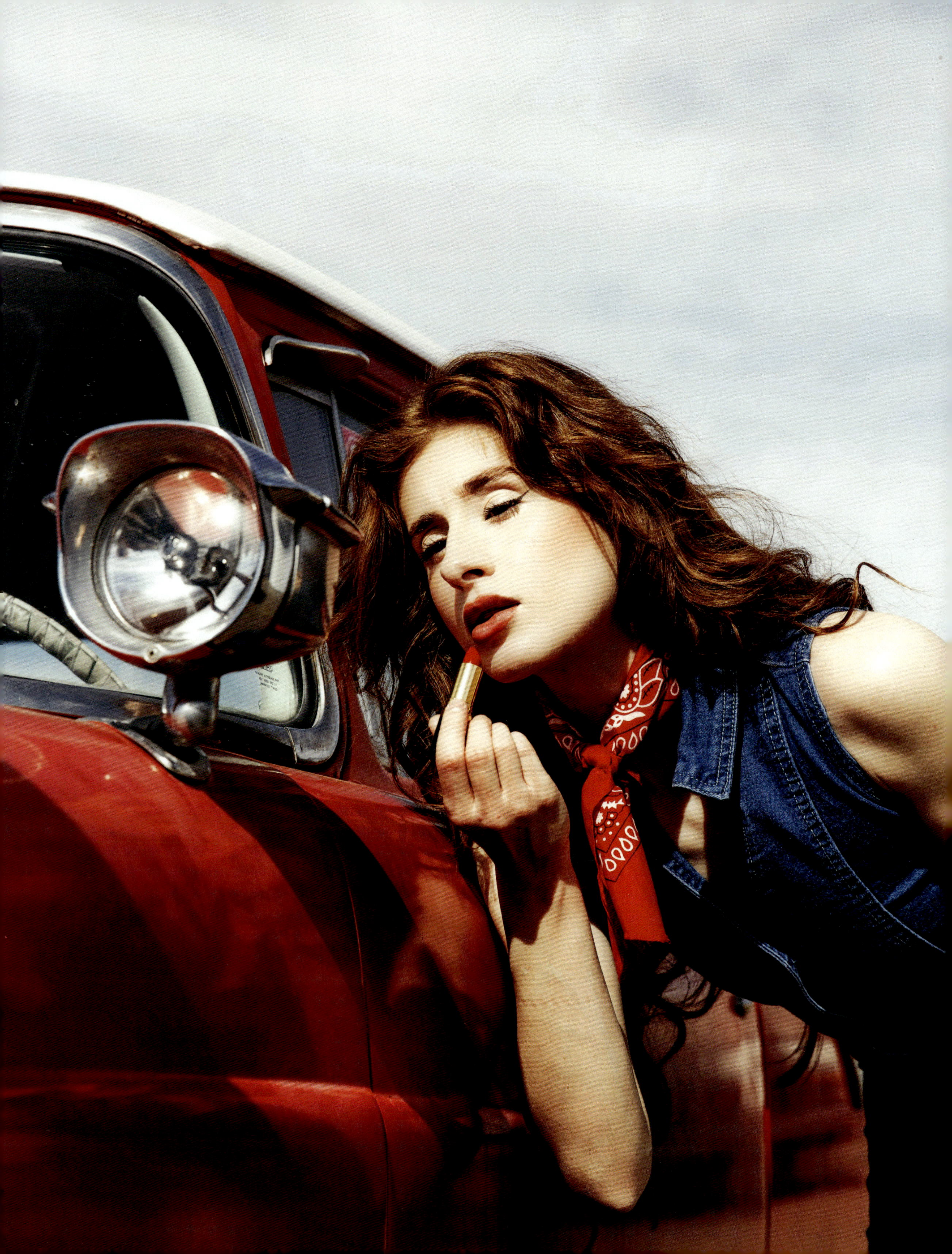

FROM RANCH TO RUNWAY

COWBOY STYLE TODAY

So what comes to mind when we think of twenty-first-century cowboy style? Do we picture Kevin Costner in *Yellowstone*, Tommy Lee Jones in the neo-Western *No Country for Old Men* (2008), Jeff Bridges in the Coen brothers' remake of *True Grit* (2010), Clint Eastwood in *Cry Macho* (2021)—all recent spins on the traditional grizzled, honorable Western hero? Or perhaps we might look to real life. As we've seen, the attire of a rancher in Wyoming or Montana has in some regards changed little over time, and anyone who's ever visited Houston or Calgary knows that a bolo tie, Stetson and cowboy boots are considered everyday business attire across large swathes of North America. Cowboy style isn't just alive and well—it continues to ride the trails (or drive them) and strut the streets.

Or for another view we could turn to a scene that's somewhere between fantasy and reality: the rodeo. Some of what we see at a rodeo, naturally, is no more "real" than a scene from a Western movie or a nineteenth-century Wild West show. Yet the rodeo has existed for nearly as long as there have been cowboys, and so in some sense is as real a part of cowboy existence as anything else. (Though we can't be certain when they began, informal rodeos were certainly taking place by the 1820s, and by the later part of the century the professional version was firmly established.)

It's also the case that the rodeo, performative as it may be, does reflect many aspects of real cowboy life. All the skills demonstrated there—calf roping, bull riding, goat tying, breakaway and team roping—reflect real-life ranch activities, and the stylish garments sported by participants are only especially fine versions of real-life ranch garb. Perhaps if true cowboy style exists anywhere in the contemporary world, it's at the rodeo.

Or maybe we picture something else entirely. Beyoncé dancing in denim chaps, or riding sidesaddle—backwards—on a white horse while brandishing an American flag. Post Malone showing off his numerous tattoos bare-chested in jeans and cowboy hat, boots and belt. The video for Lil Nas X's "Old Town Road," which follows its cowboy-appareled protagonist from a gunfight in the Old West to the streets of a modern urban American neighborhood. Queer-coded country music star Orville Peck's fringed masks. The heavily stylized Western-themed outfits modelled at Pharrell Williams' 2024 Louis Vuitton show, featuring suede hats, silk yoked shirts and carved leatherwork. Even Kendrick Lamar's bootcut jeans at the 2025 Superbowl half-time show.

There's no doubt that these sometimes outlandish adaptations of traditional cowboy style are a long way from "authentic" ranch life, and in fact they are often presented partly as a way of reclaiming and adapting cowboy style after more than a century of whitewashing. As Williams said at the Louis Vuitton show, despite the impression given by most movies, cowboys "looked like us. They looked like me. They were Black and they were Native American." But ostentatious flair and surprising diversity are nothing new in cowboy couture.

Take the famous "Nudie Suits" designed by the celebrity tailor Nudie Cohn from the 1940s onwards to capitalize on the era's craze for cowboy style. Worn by "country" icons including Elvis Presley, John Wayne, Gram Parsons, Roy Rogers and George Jones, not only would these glittering rhinestone-studded affairs have been impractical on the open plains of the 1860s—to say the least—but their designer was Ukrainian-born and of Jewish descent. In fact, all of mid-twentieth-century cowboy fashion's "big three"—Cohn as well as Bernard "Rodeo Ben" Lichtenstein and Nathan Turk—were from similar Eastern European and Jewish backgrounds. Another example is Manuel Cuevas, a Mexican national who would go on to become a major Western wear figure as Cohn's head tailor.

Western style is no doubt highly functional in origin, and its history has certainly been whitewashed. We need more shows like Pharrell Williams'. But as this book vividly shows, it's a style that is also capable of huge fun and creativity, and whose cultural origins are surprisingly diverse. It's a fashion tradition that fuses heritage and innovation, asceticism and fun, the requirements of the open plain and the flair of the catwalk, and it has stuck around this long in no small part because of that capacity for adaptation and transformation.

Following pages: *Model Angela Lindvall wearing a white sheath and cashmere cardigan by Ralph Lauren, seated on a drystone wall and flanked by three cowboys, a horse and two dogs.*

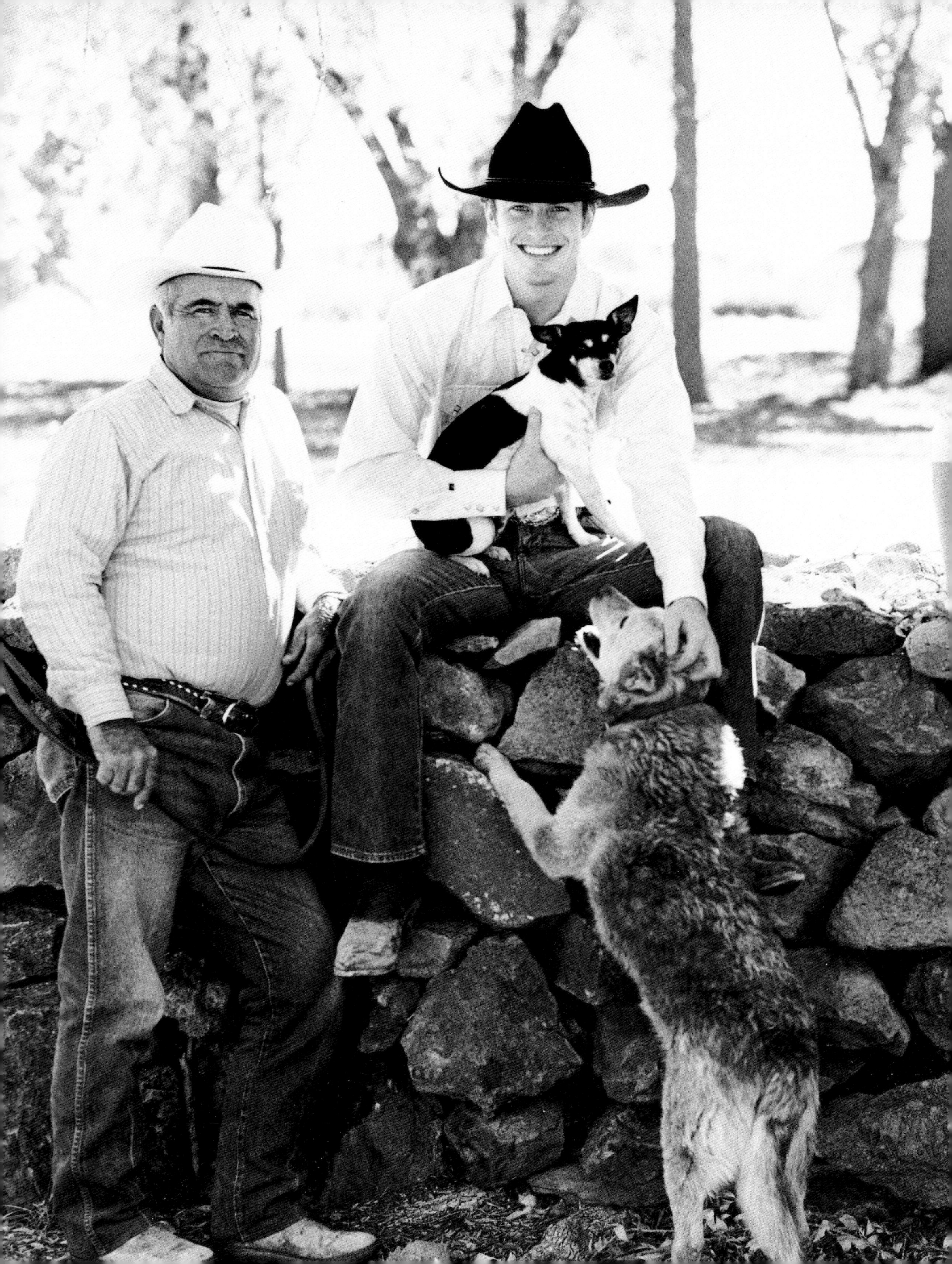

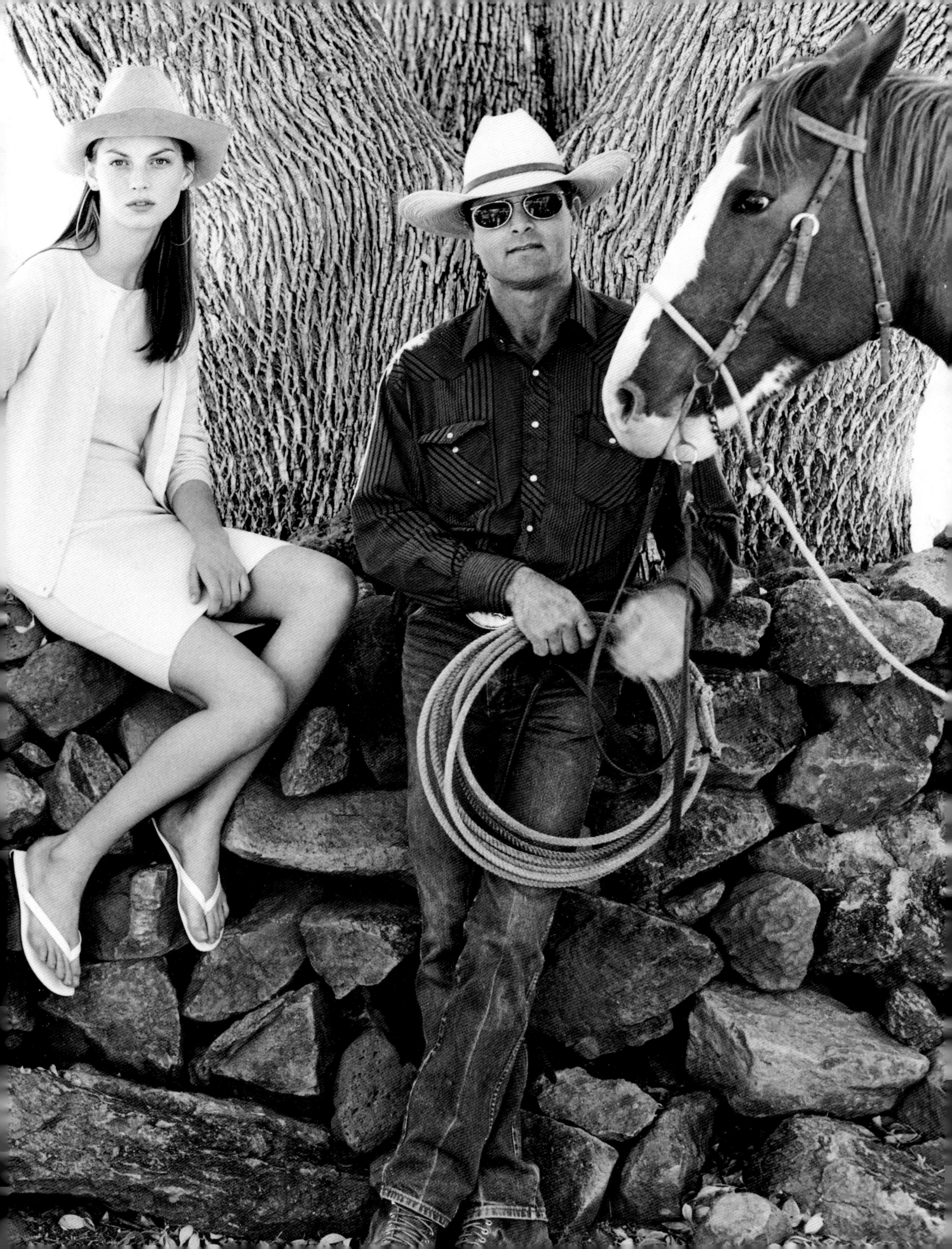

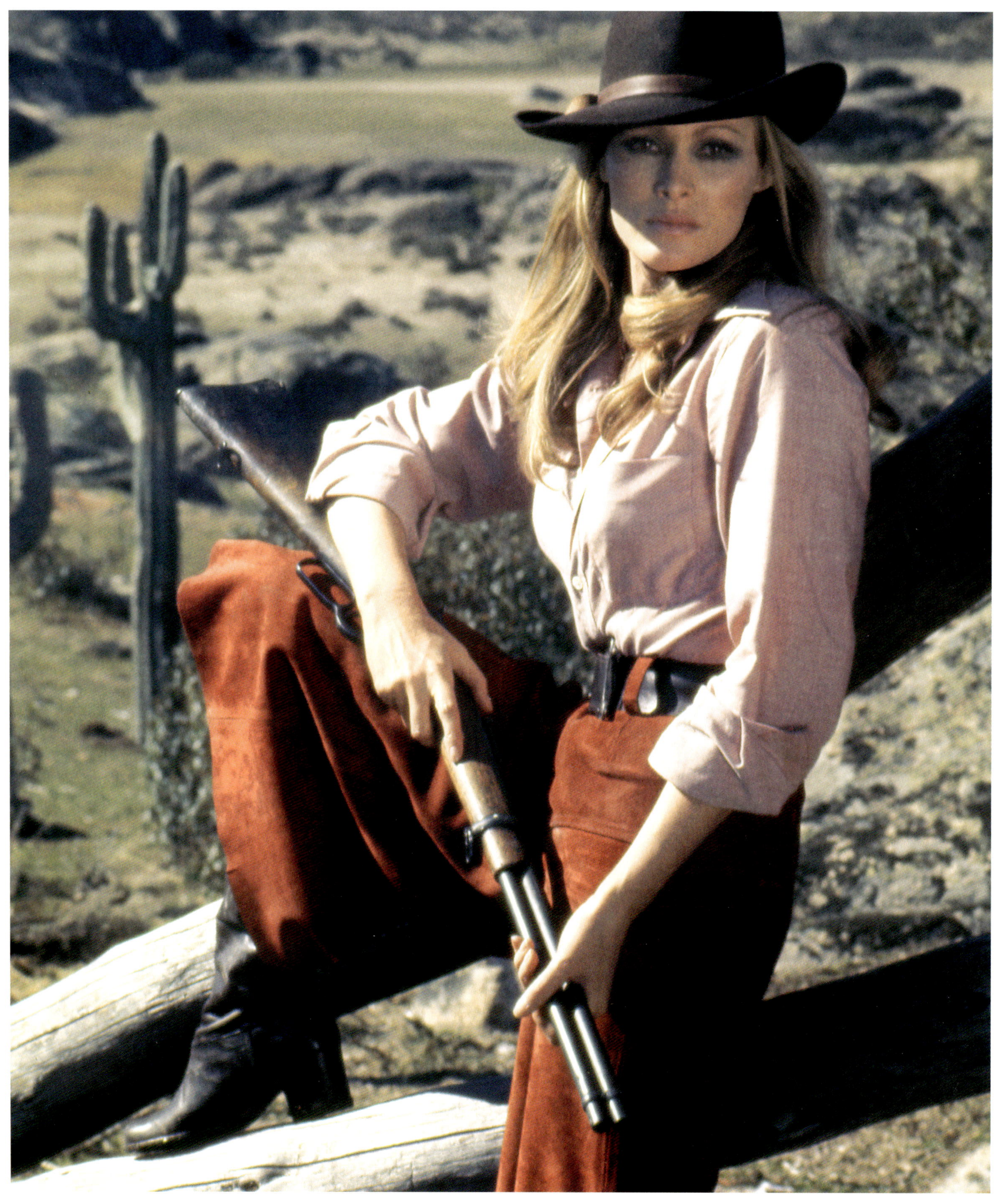

This page: *Swiss actress Ursula Andress on the set of SOLEIL ROUGE (RED SUN) (Young, 1971).*

Opposite: *Model Stella Tennant wearing a white bow-tie blouse with eyelet-ruffle sleeves, long black silk skirt, and black hat by Yves Saint Laurent Haute Couture.*

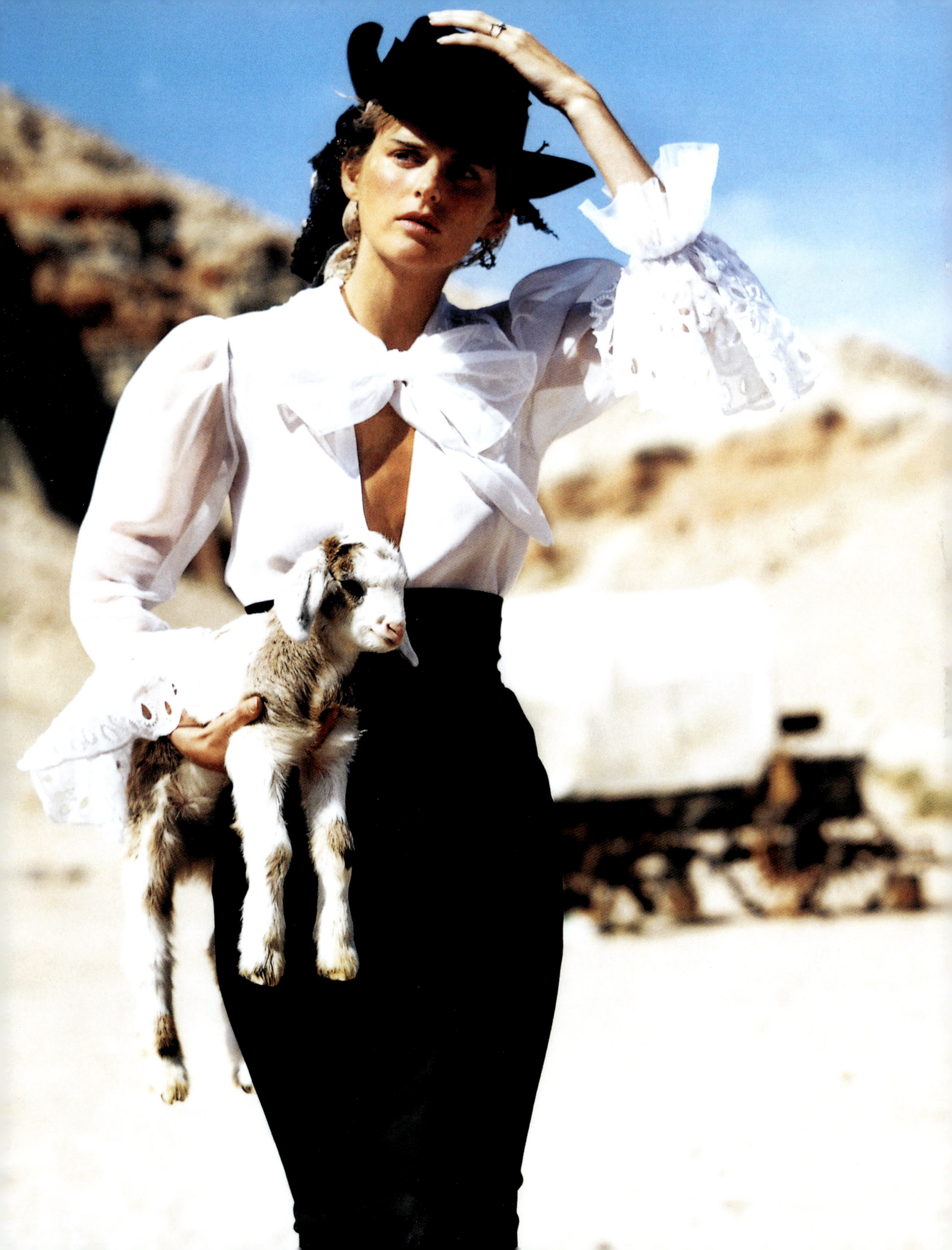

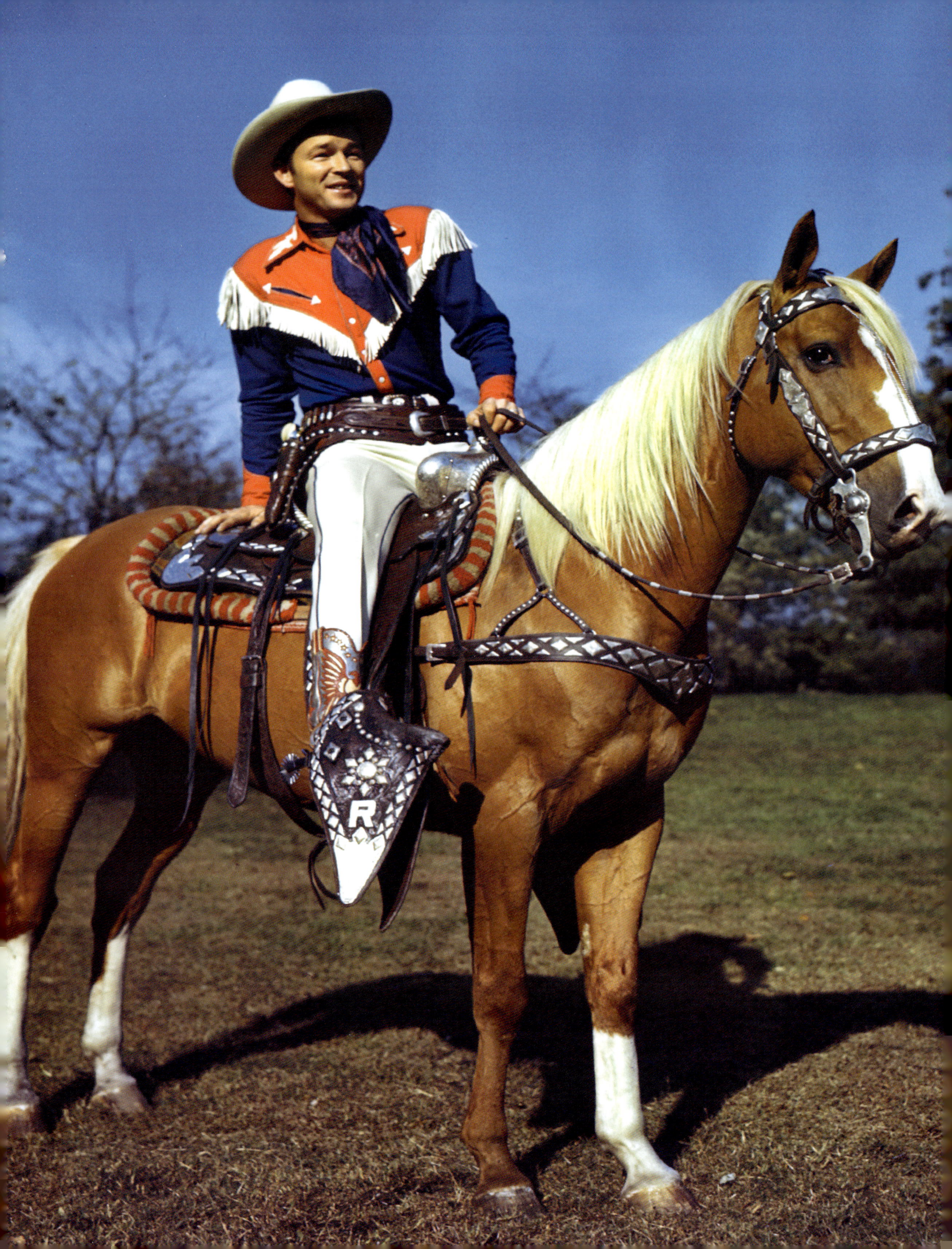
R

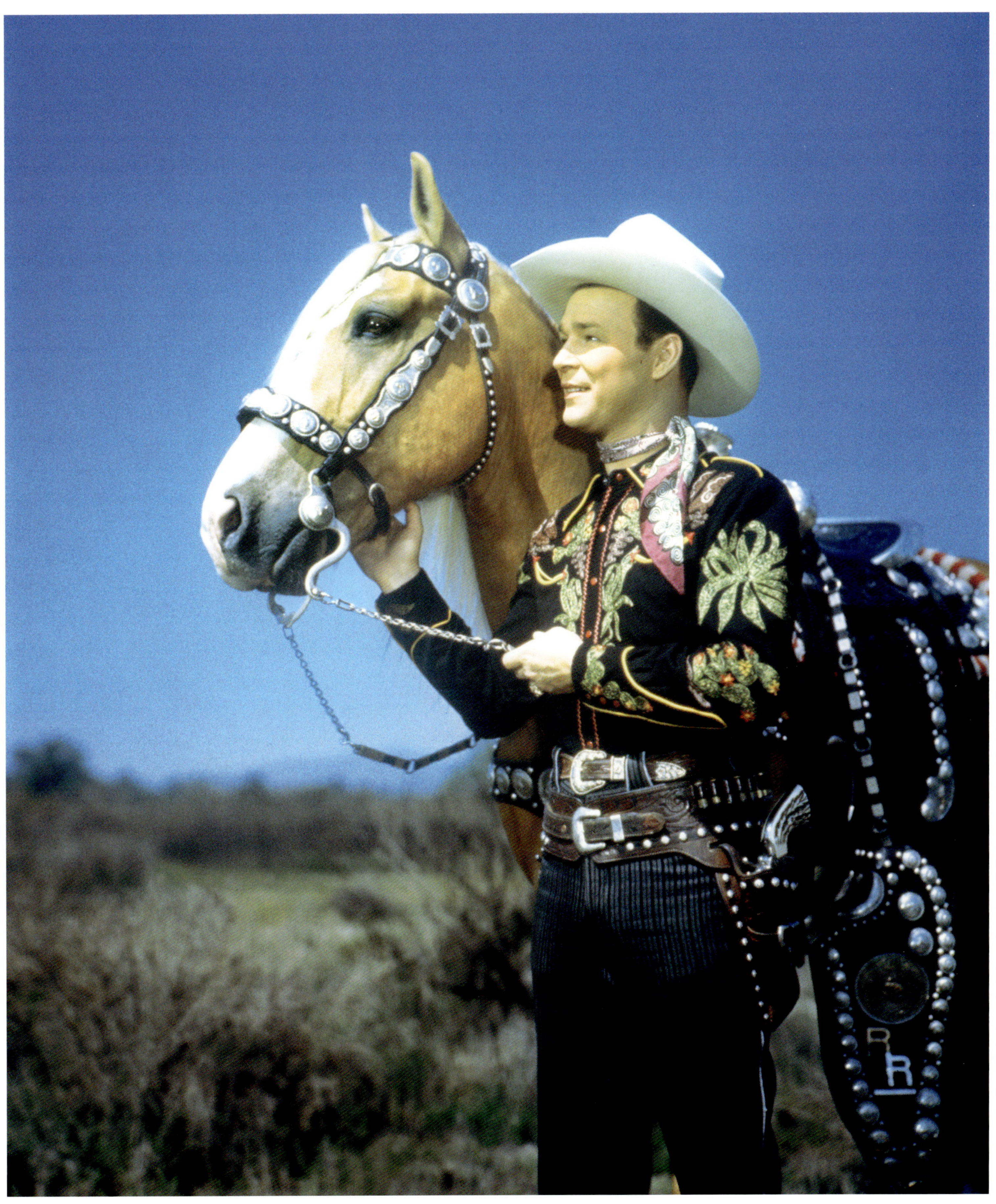

This page, opposite: *Singer and actor Roy Rogers pictured astride his palomino horse Trigger, c. 1945.*

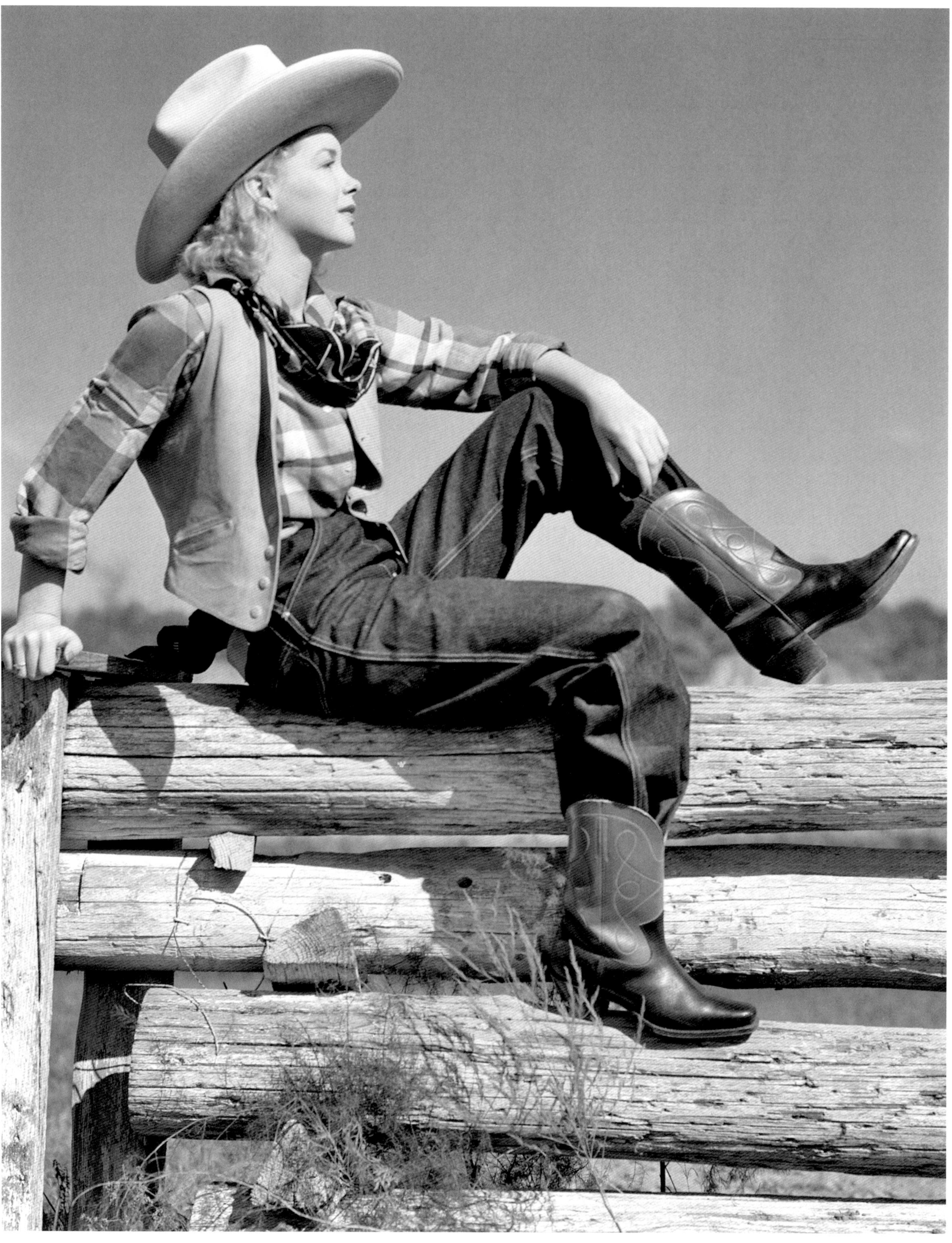

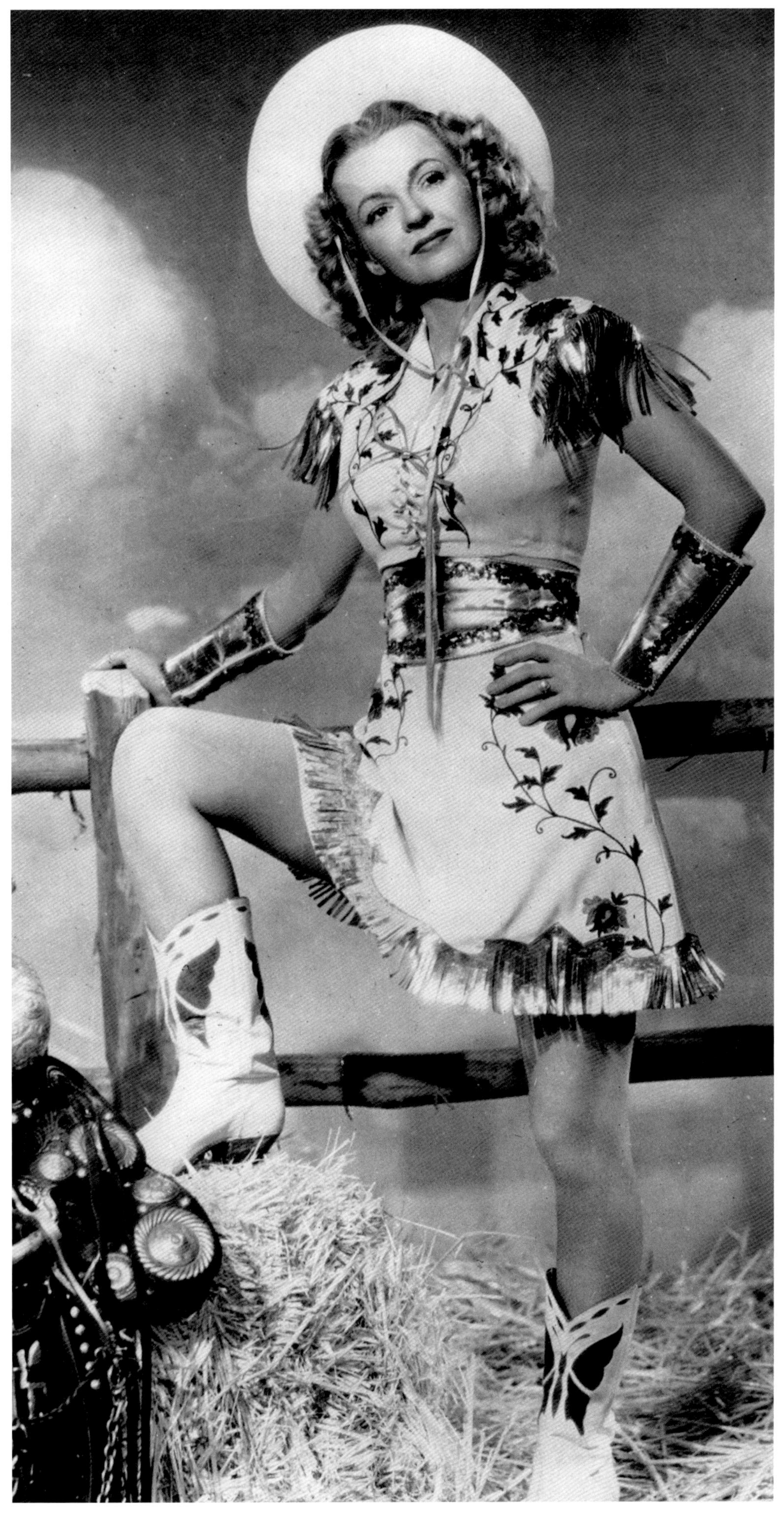

Opposite: *A blonde cowgirl in a wide-brimmed cowboy hat sits on a corral fence dressed in plaid, denim, boots and a bandana, c. 1940s.*

This page: *Dale Evans Rogers was an American actress, singer and songwriter best known as the second wife of singing cowboy film star Roy Rogers. She's shown here dressed in a Wild West outfit in 1945.*

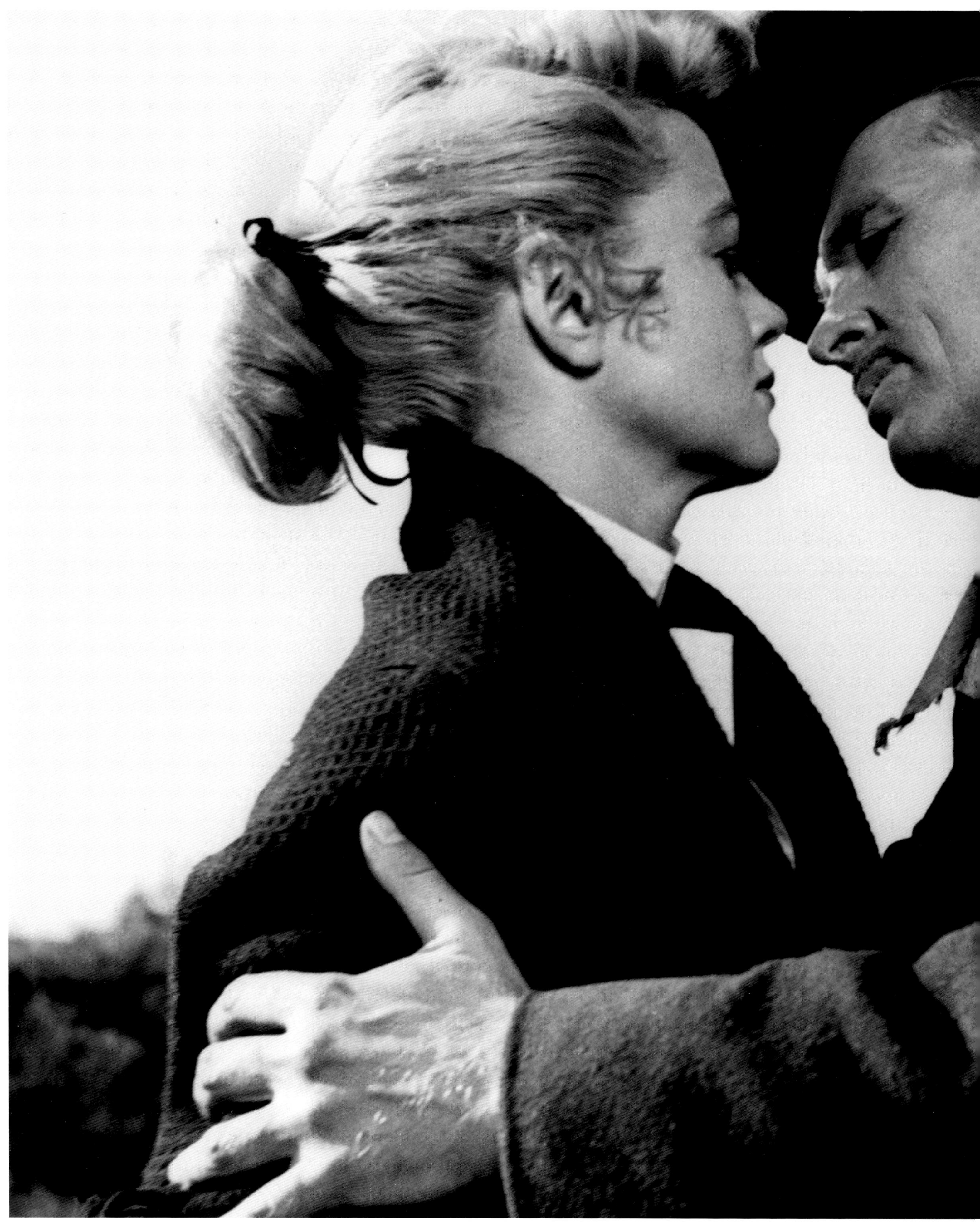

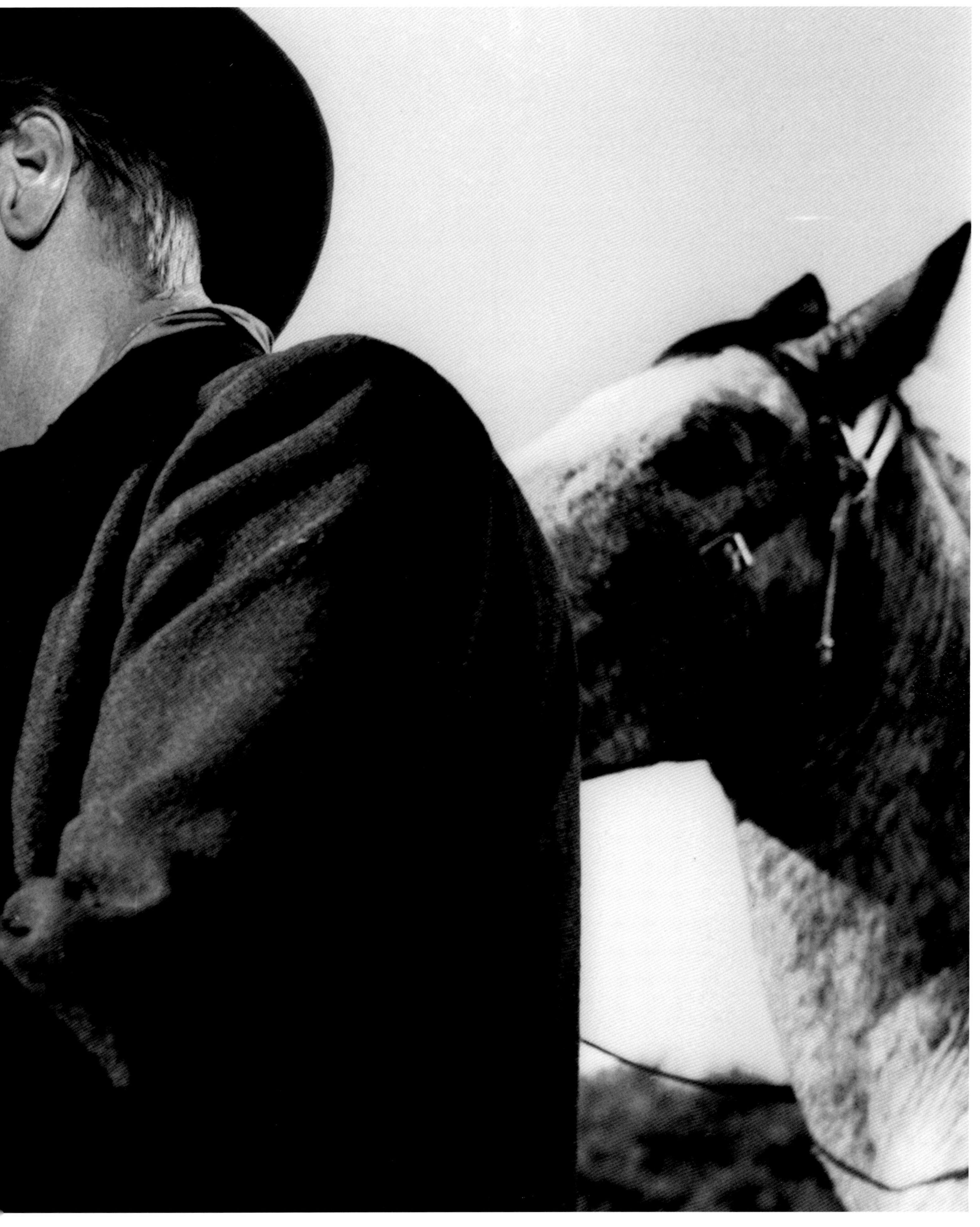

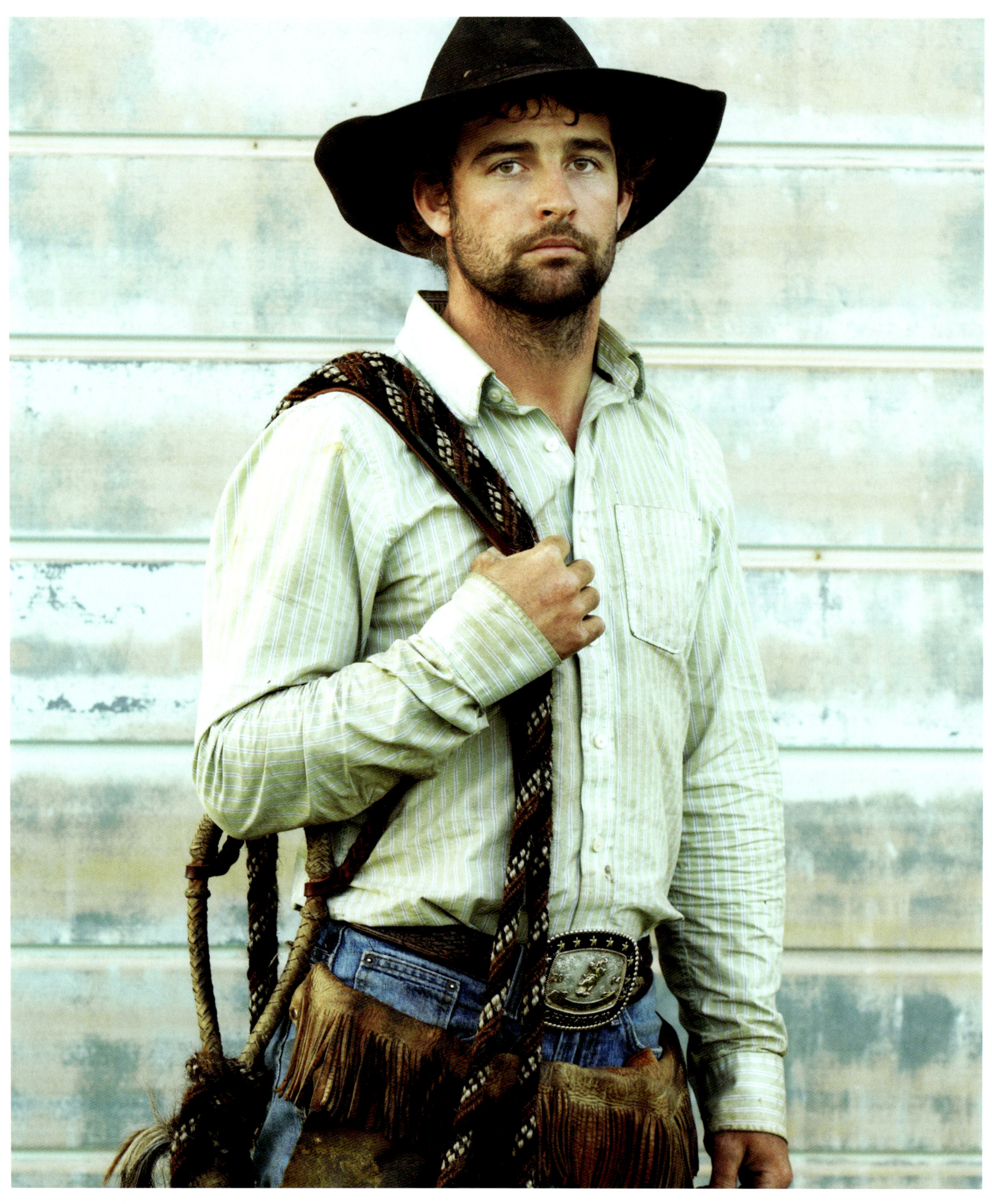

Pages 126/127: *Dorothy Malone about to kiss John Lund in a scene from FIVE GUNS WEST (Corman, 1955).*

Page 129: *Model Susan Schoenberg in VOGUE, 1969 wearing a Cerruti pant suit and white cowboy hat.*

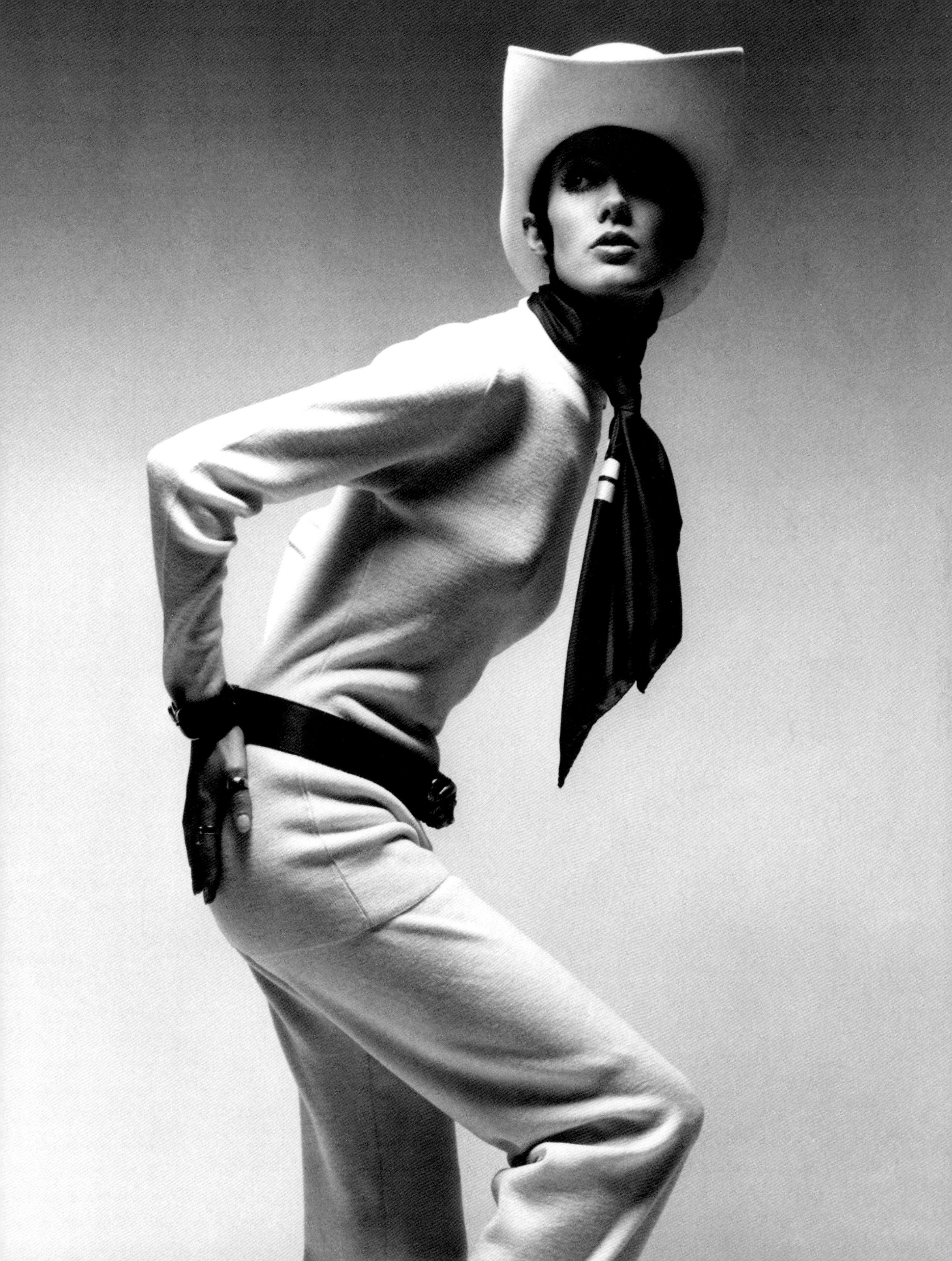

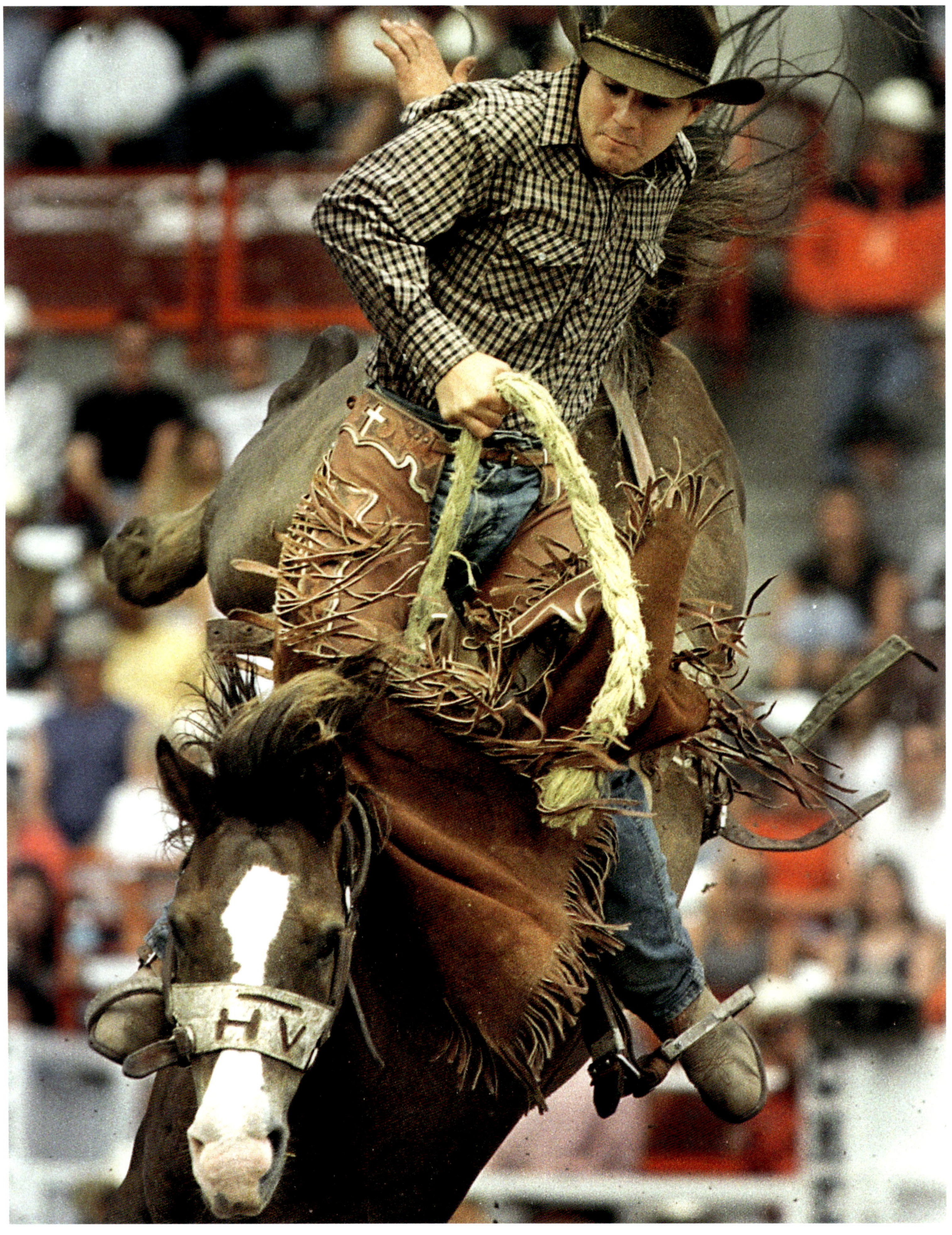

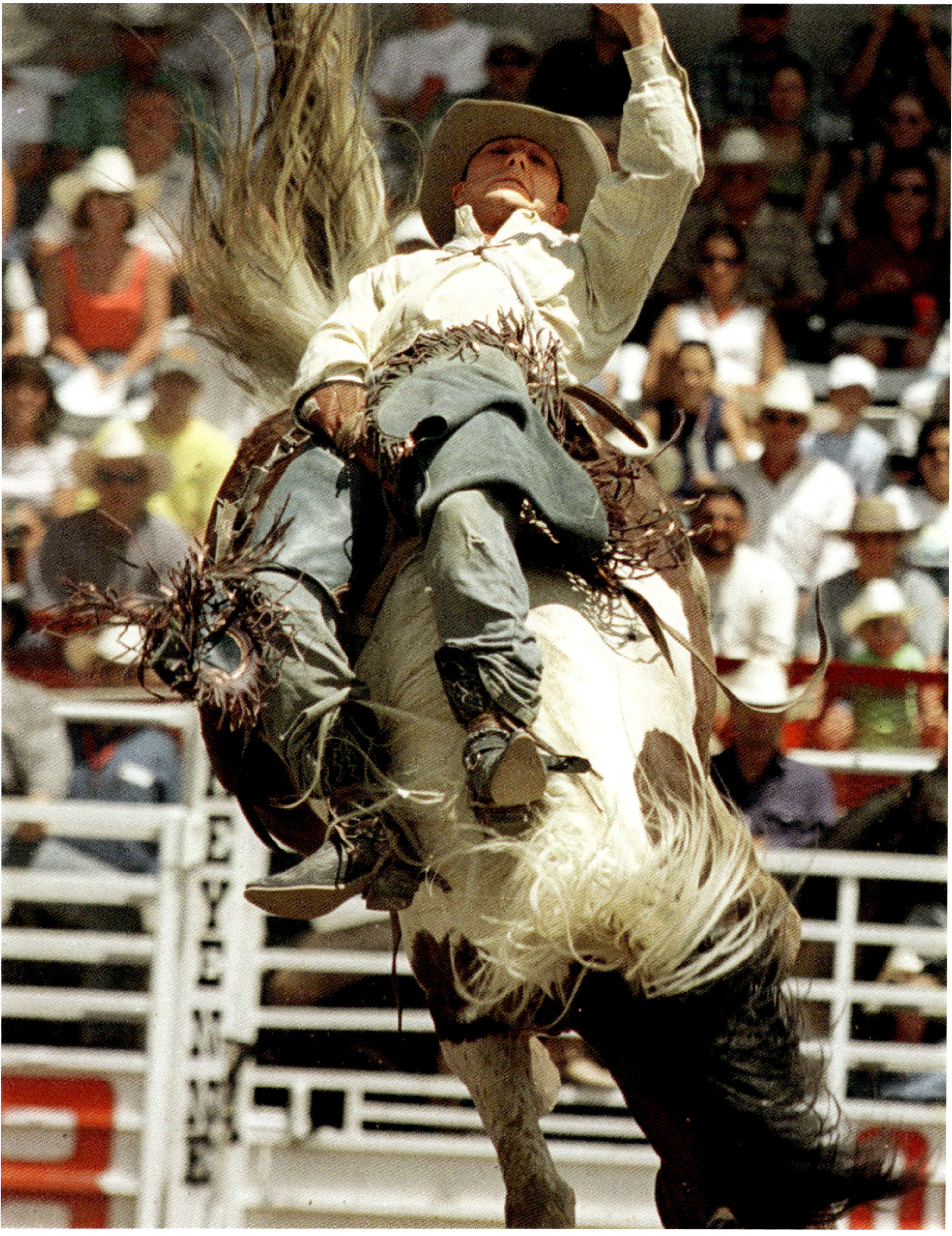
EYENNE

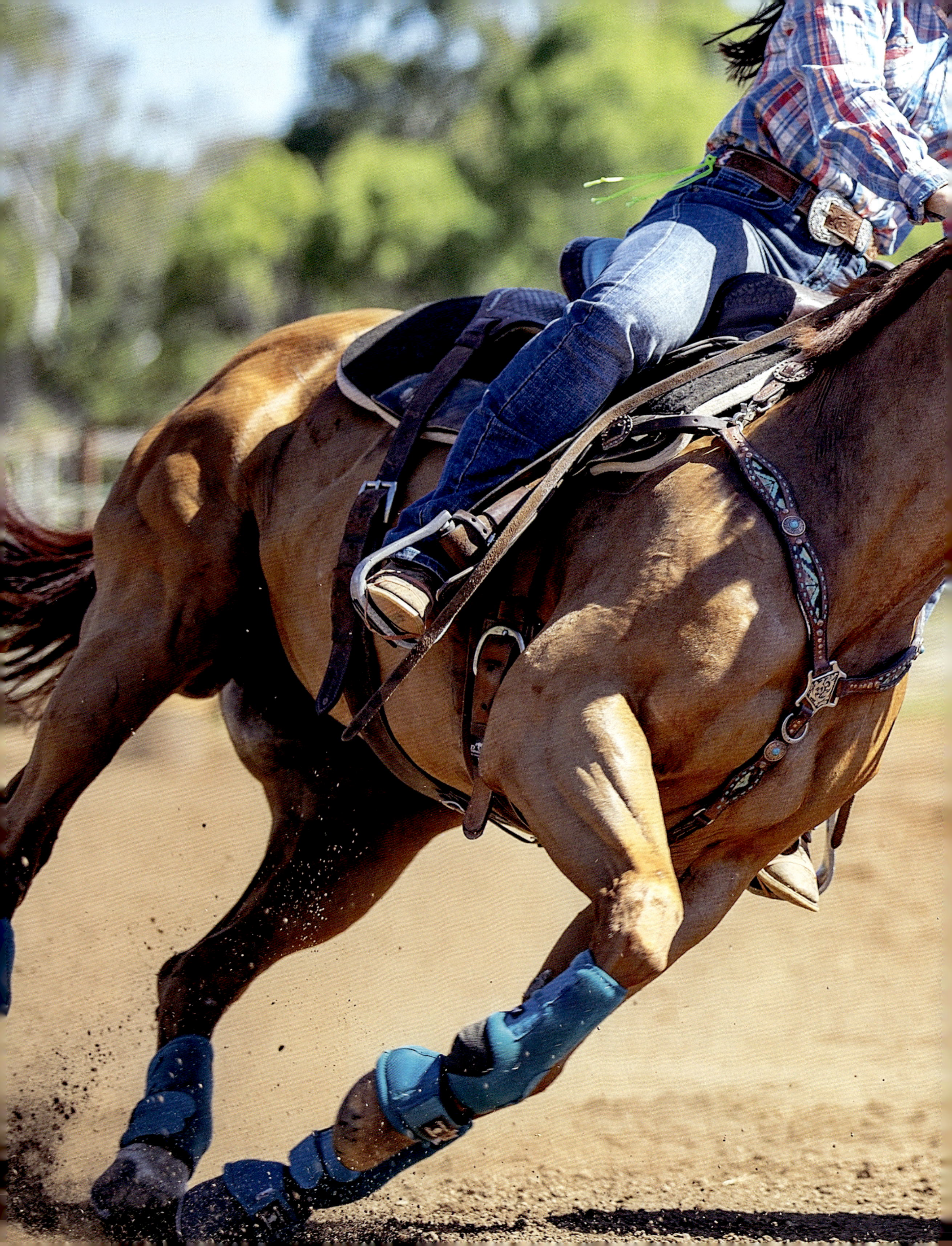

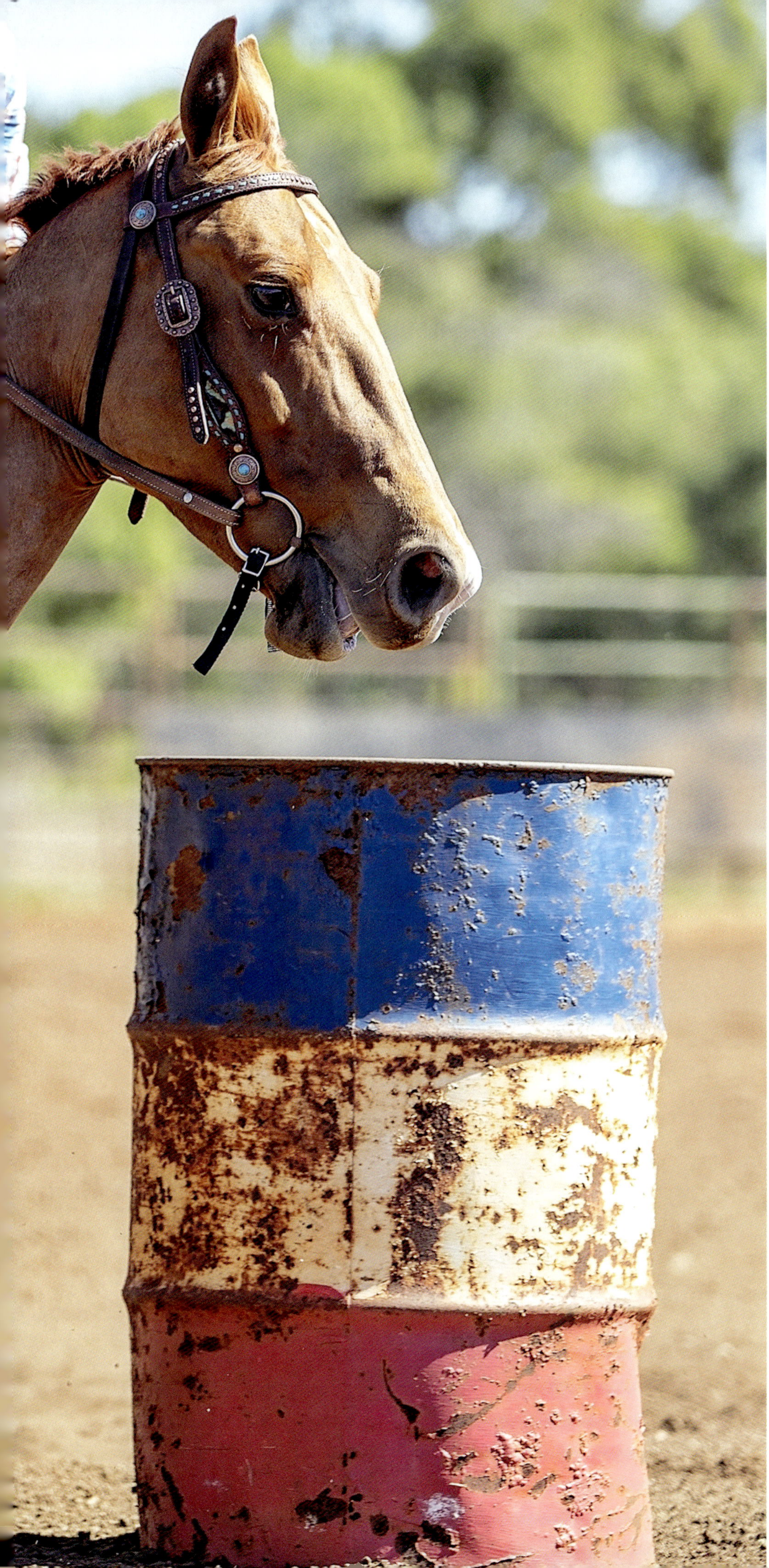

Page 130 and 131: *Cowboys during the first round of the Saddle Bronc competition at the Cheyenne Frontier Days Rodeo in Wyoming on July 24, 2001.*

These pages: *Horse and rider competing in a barrel race at Outback Country Rodeo.*

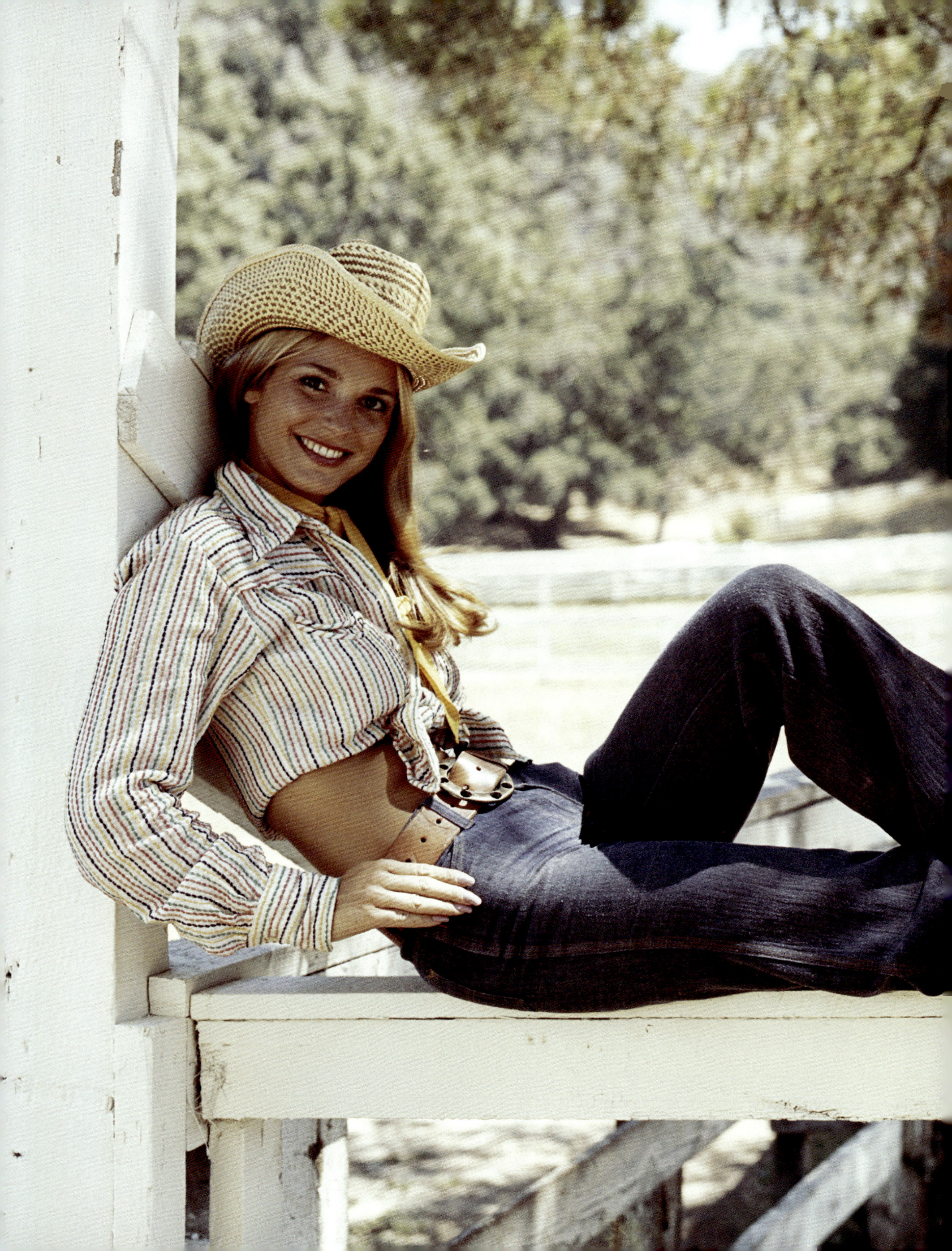

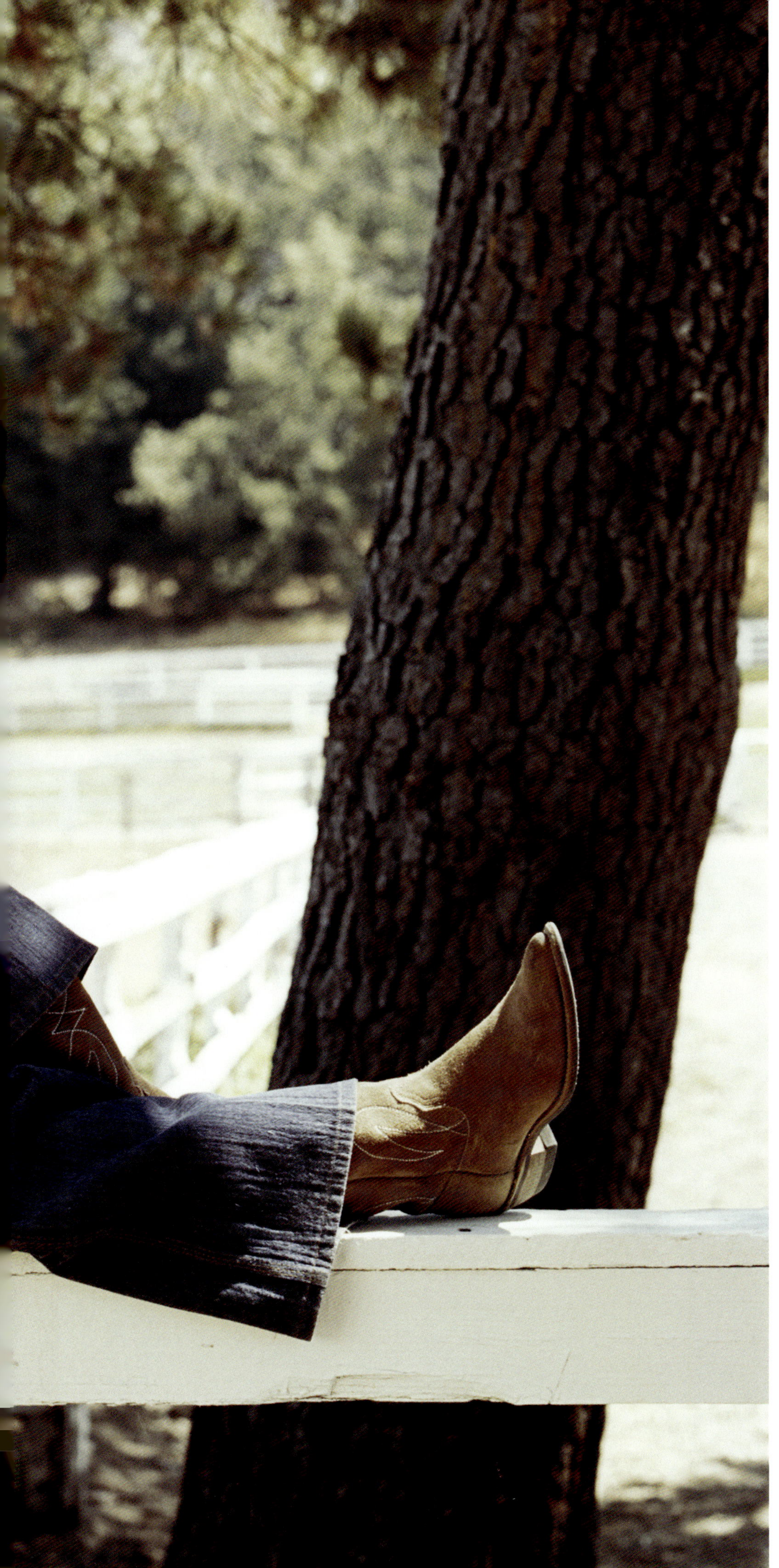

Page 135–137: *These cowgirls sport a variety of outfits that all have one element in common: jeans.*

Pages 138/139: *A cowboy being bucked off a horse during a rodeo.*

Pages 140/141: *Cowboys rounding up donkeys on a ranch in California.*

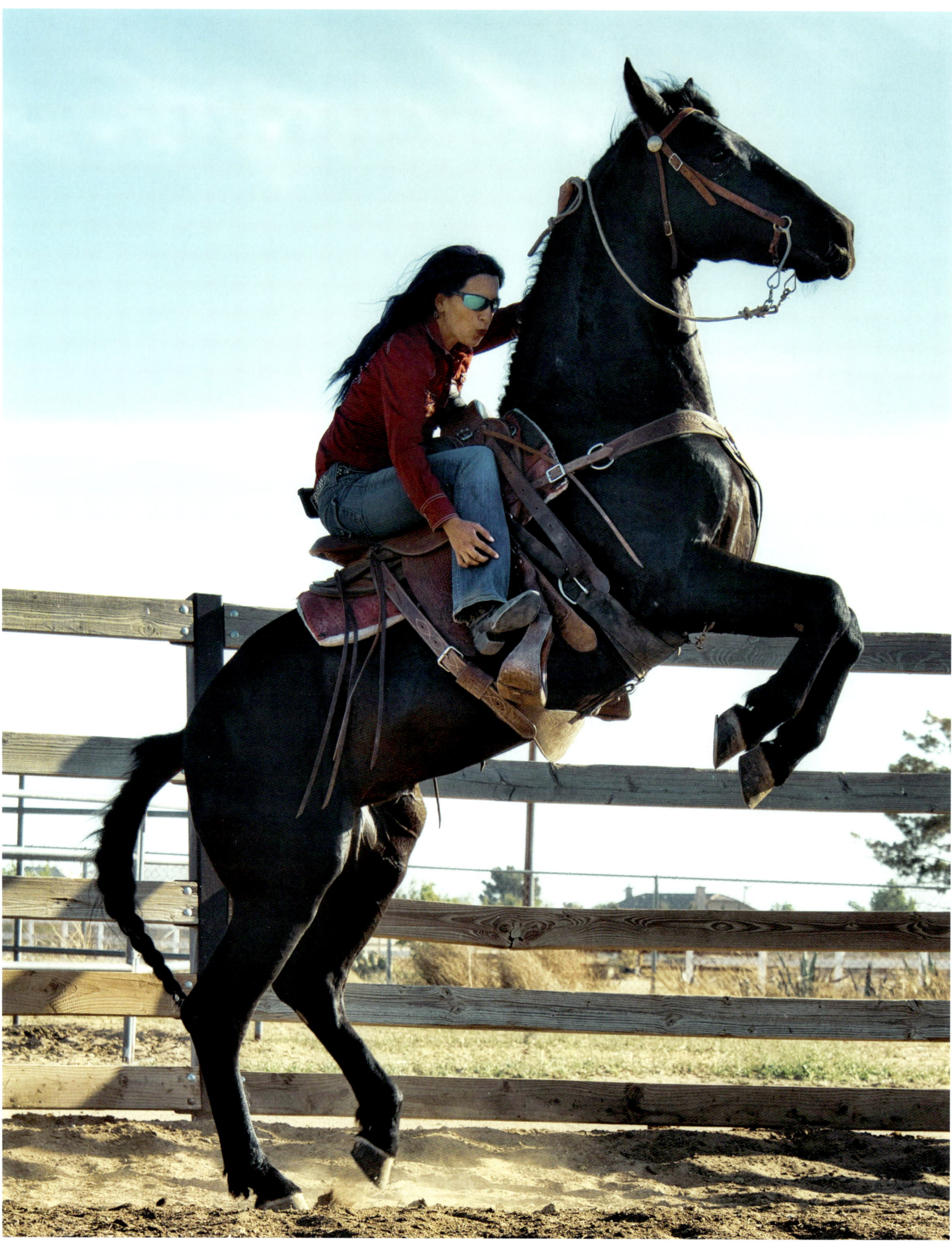

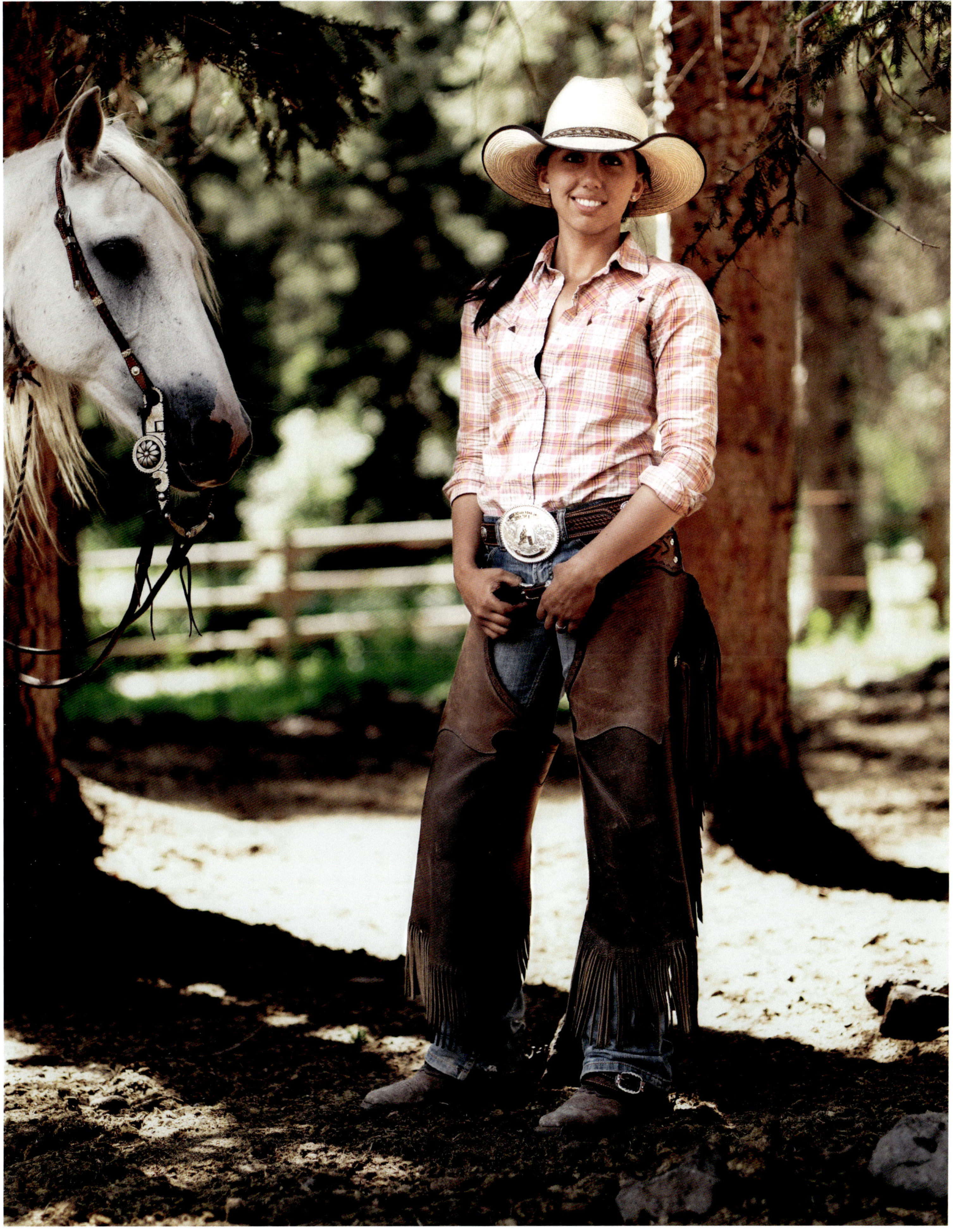

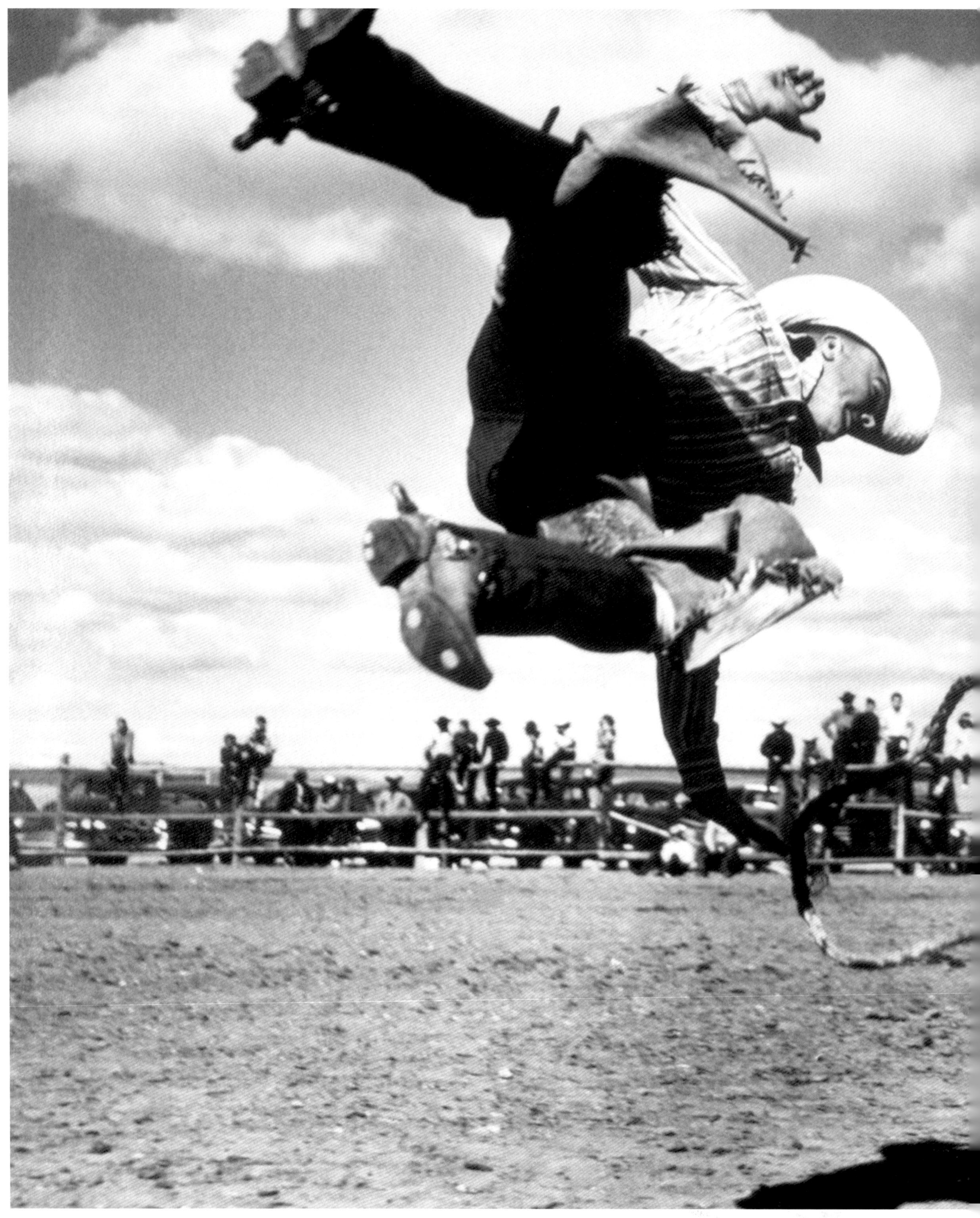

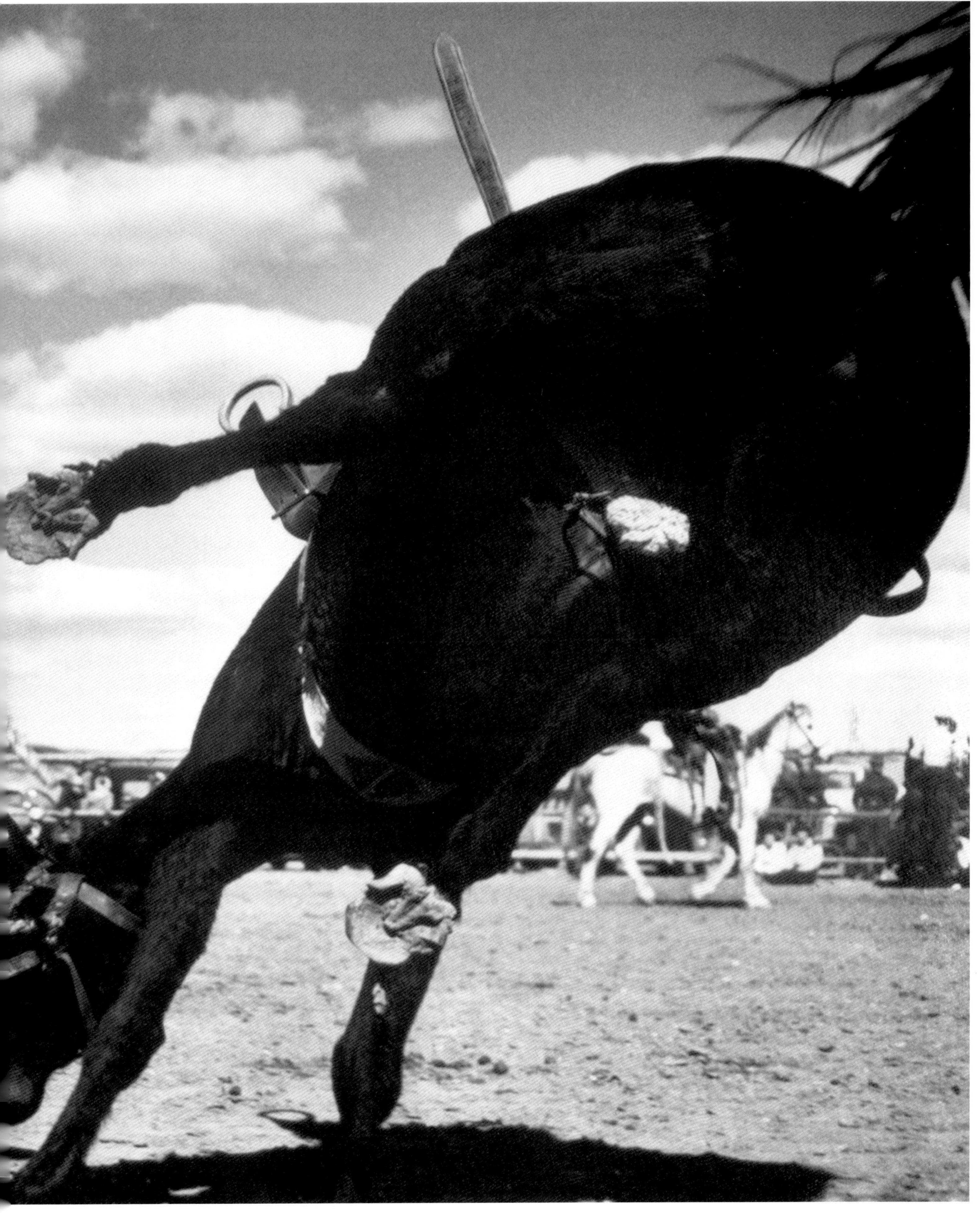

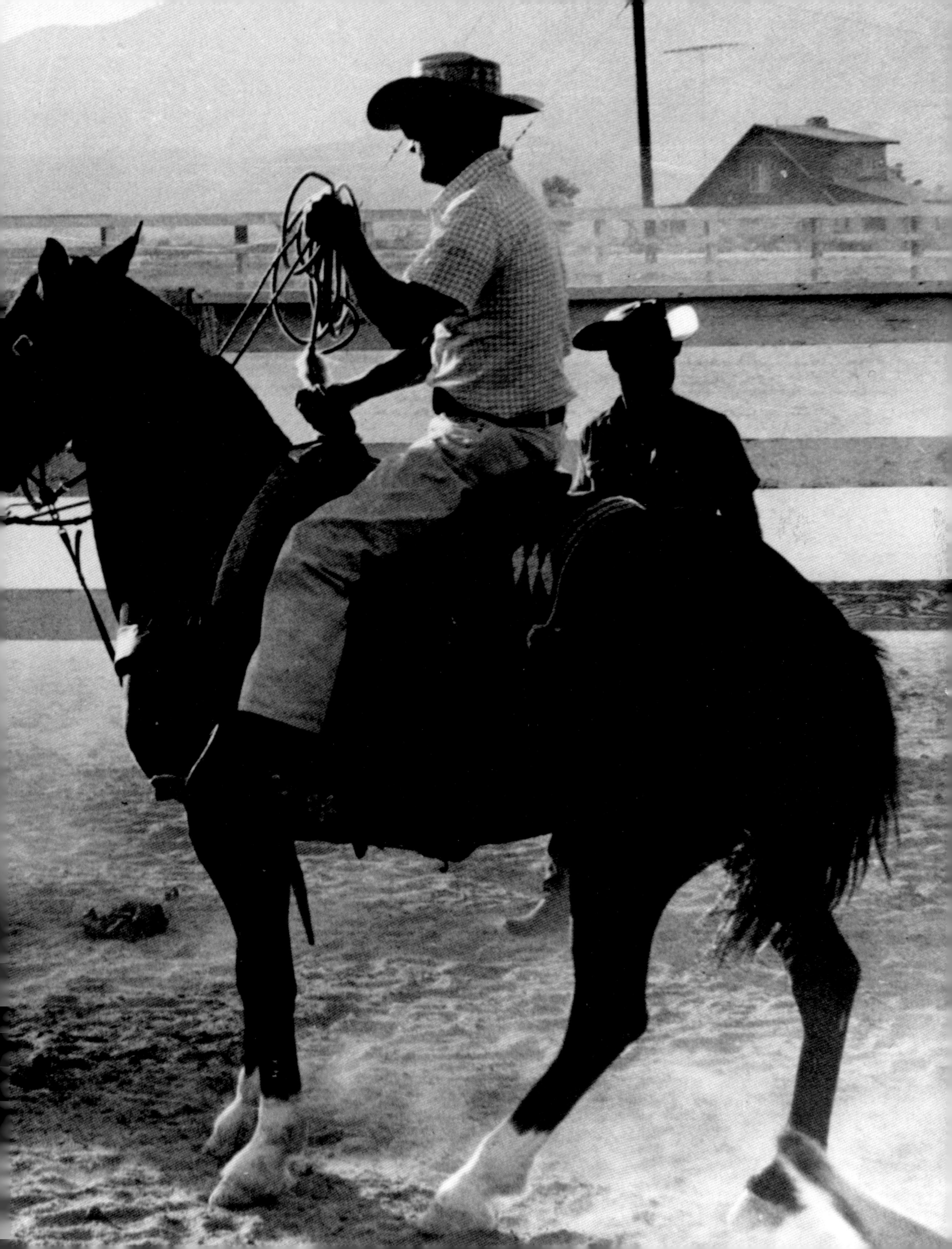

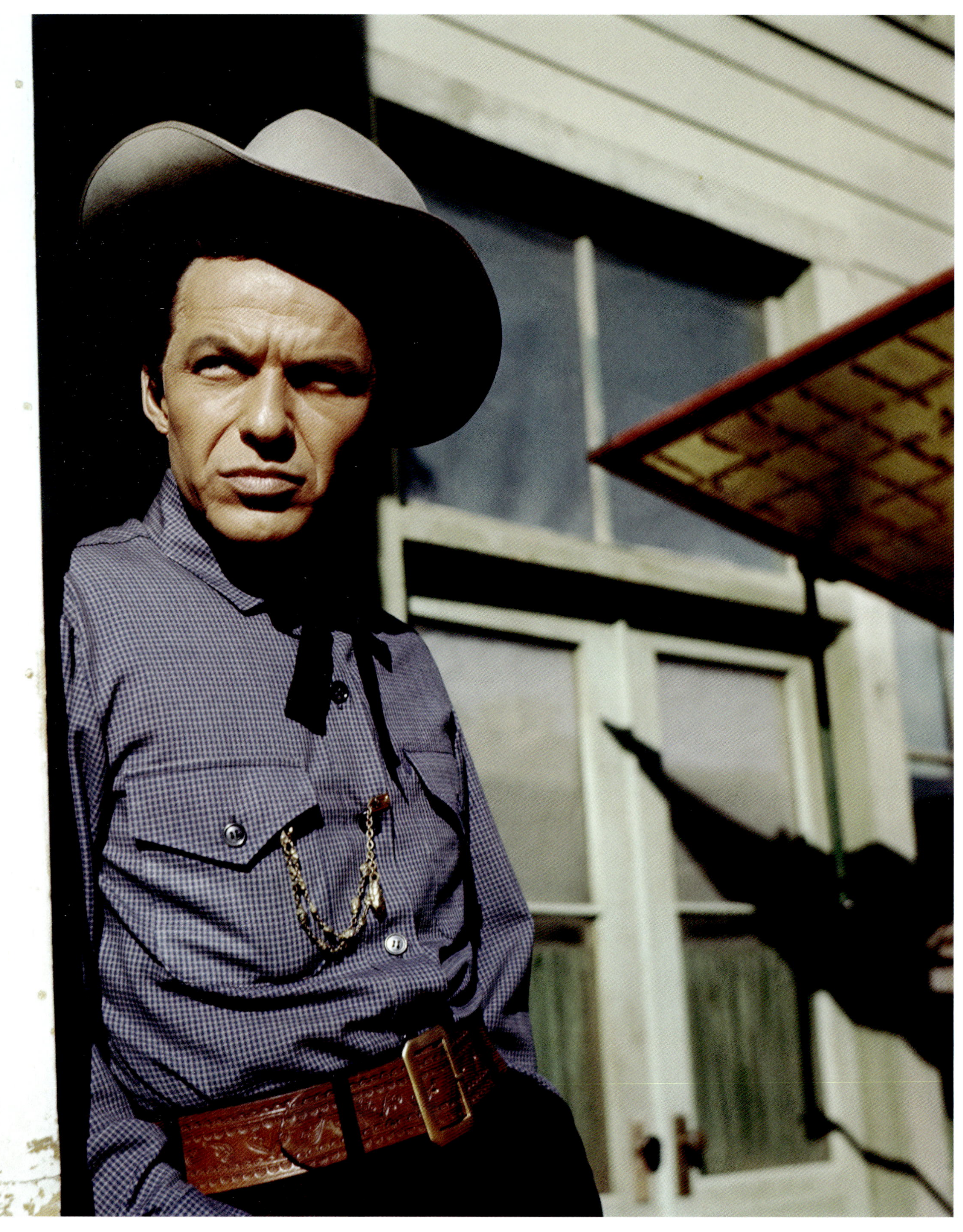

This page: *Frank Sinatra on set in a cowboy hat in the 1960s.*

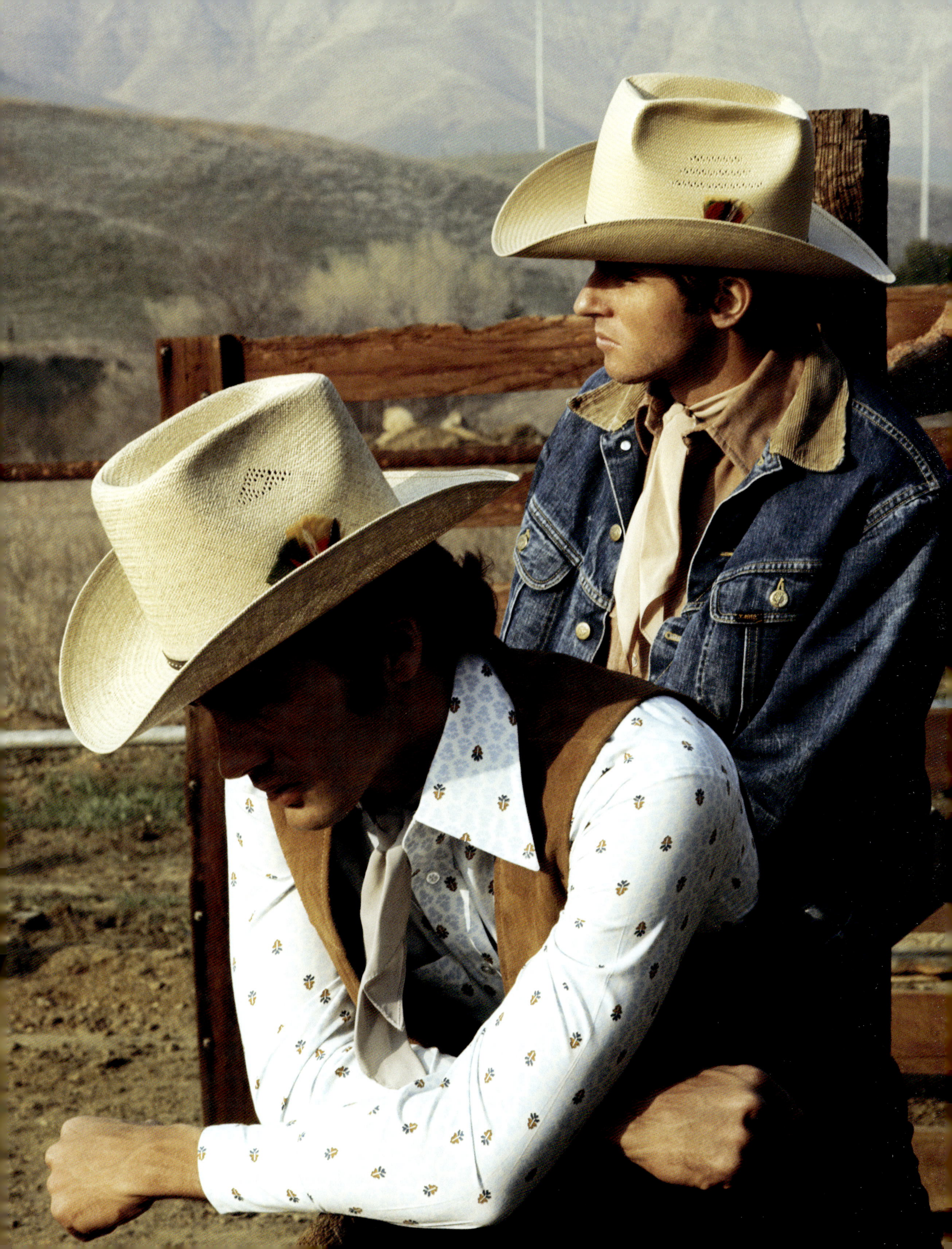

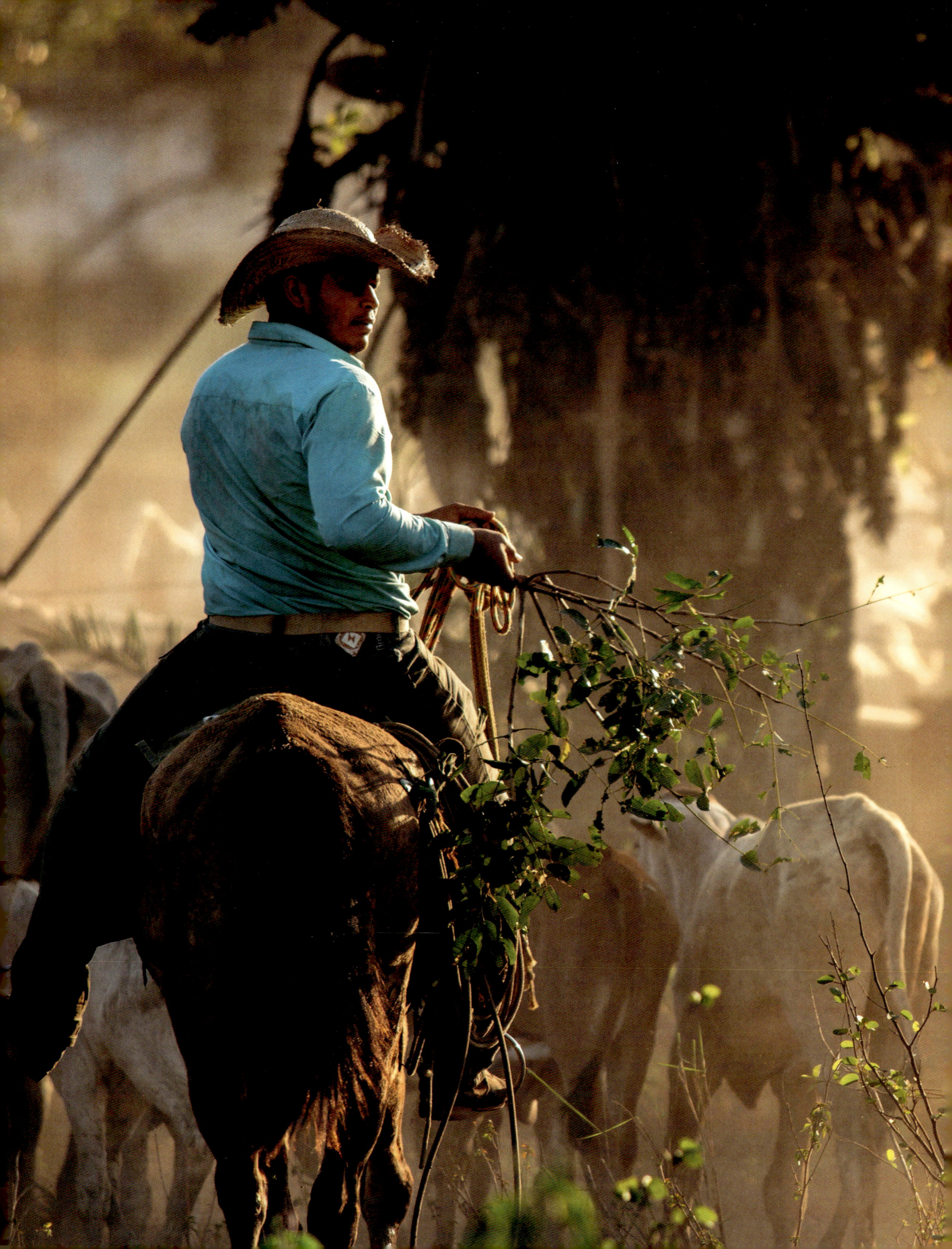

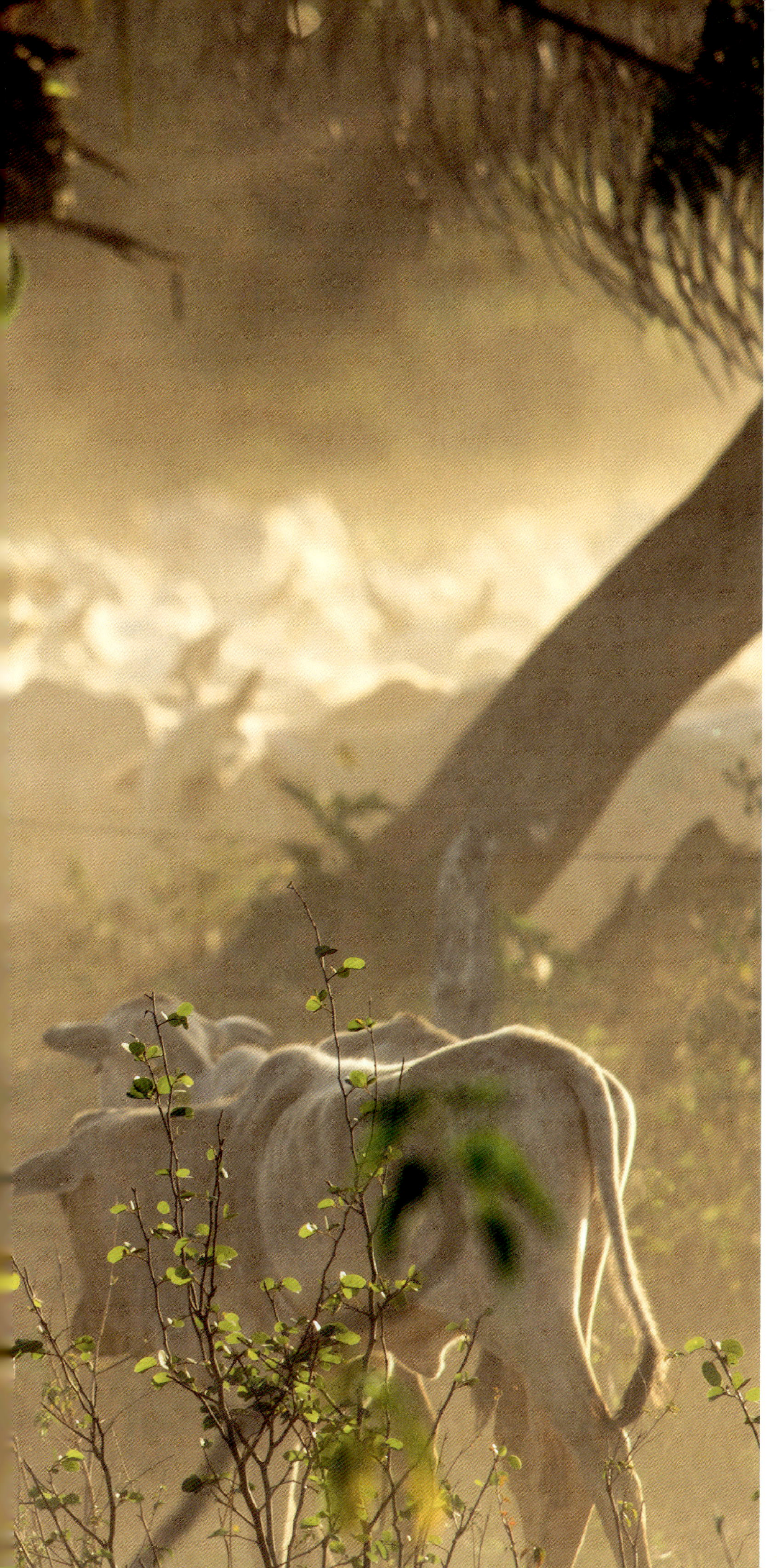

These pages: *A Brazilian cowboy guiding a herd of cattle along the Transpantaneira Road in the Pantanal region of Mato Grosso, Brazil.*

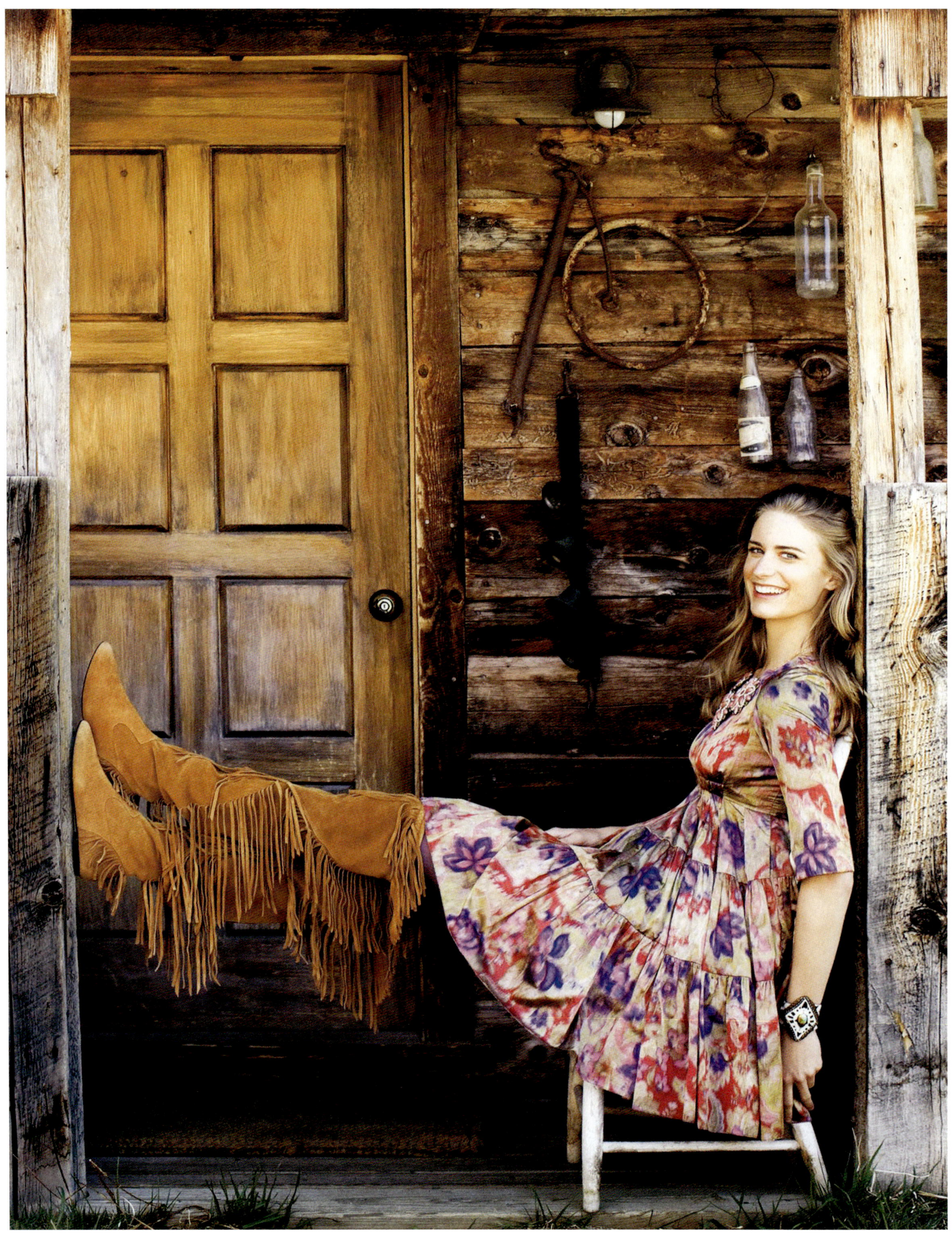

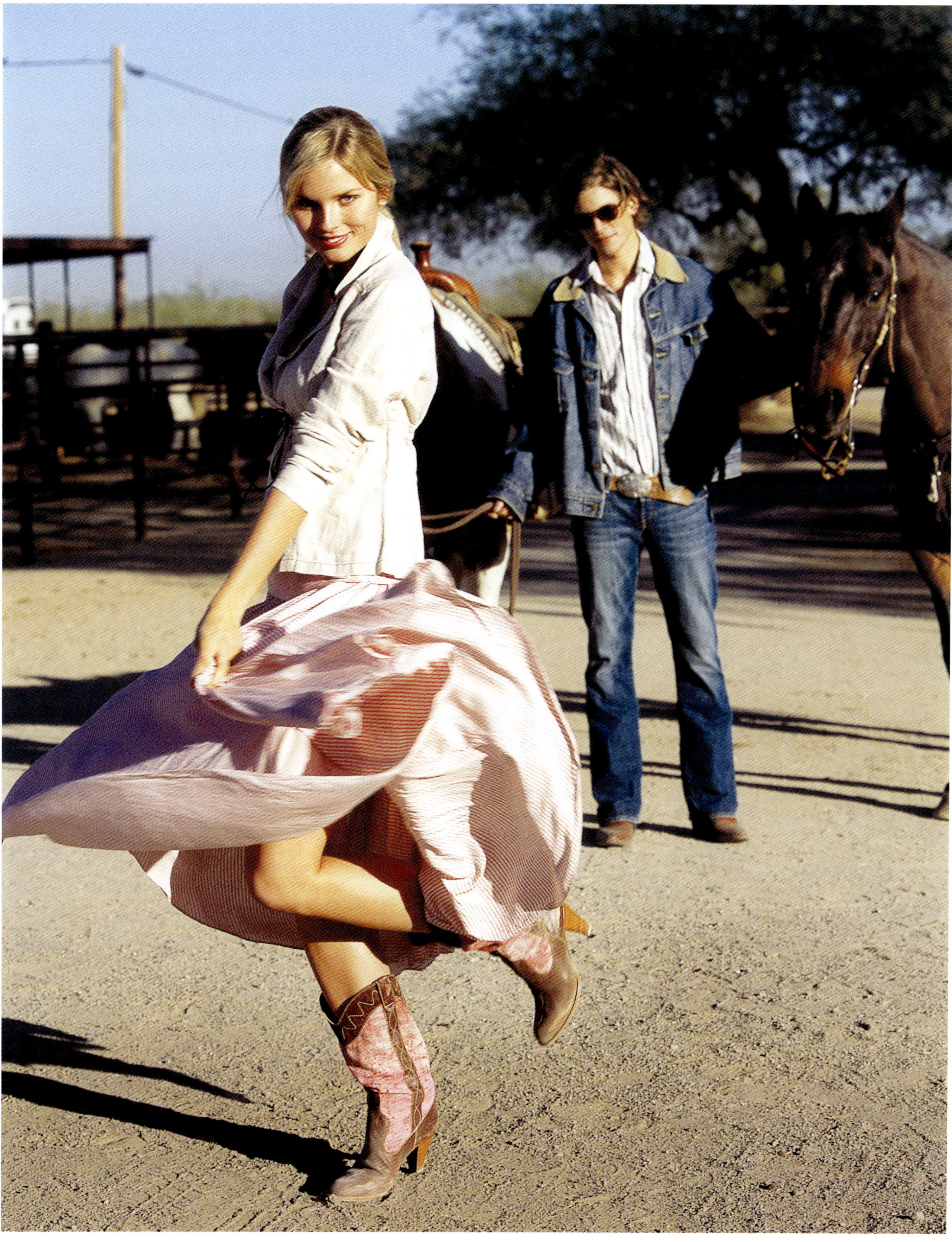

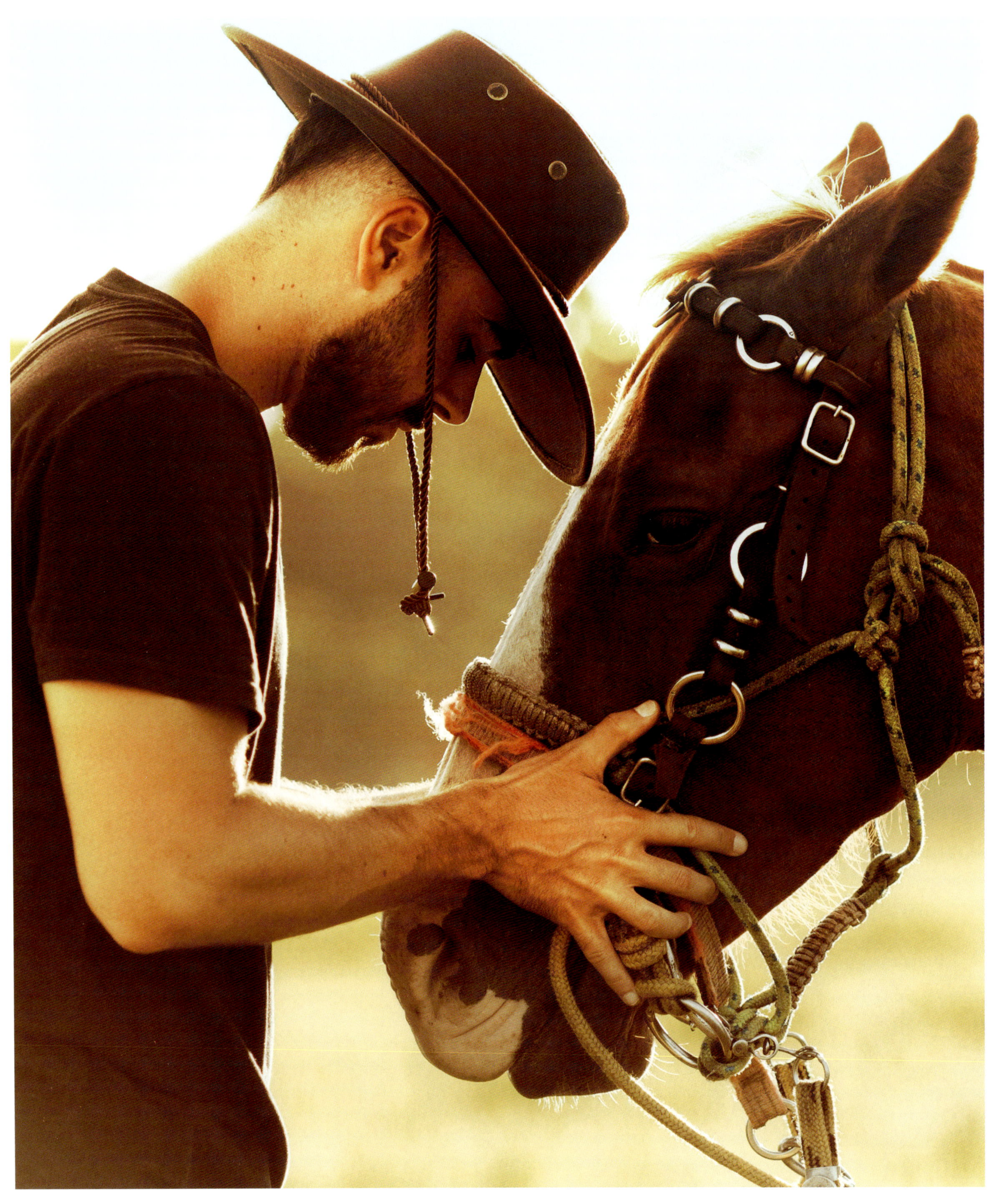

Opposite: *Matt Damon in ALL THE PRETTY HORSES (Thornton, 2000).*

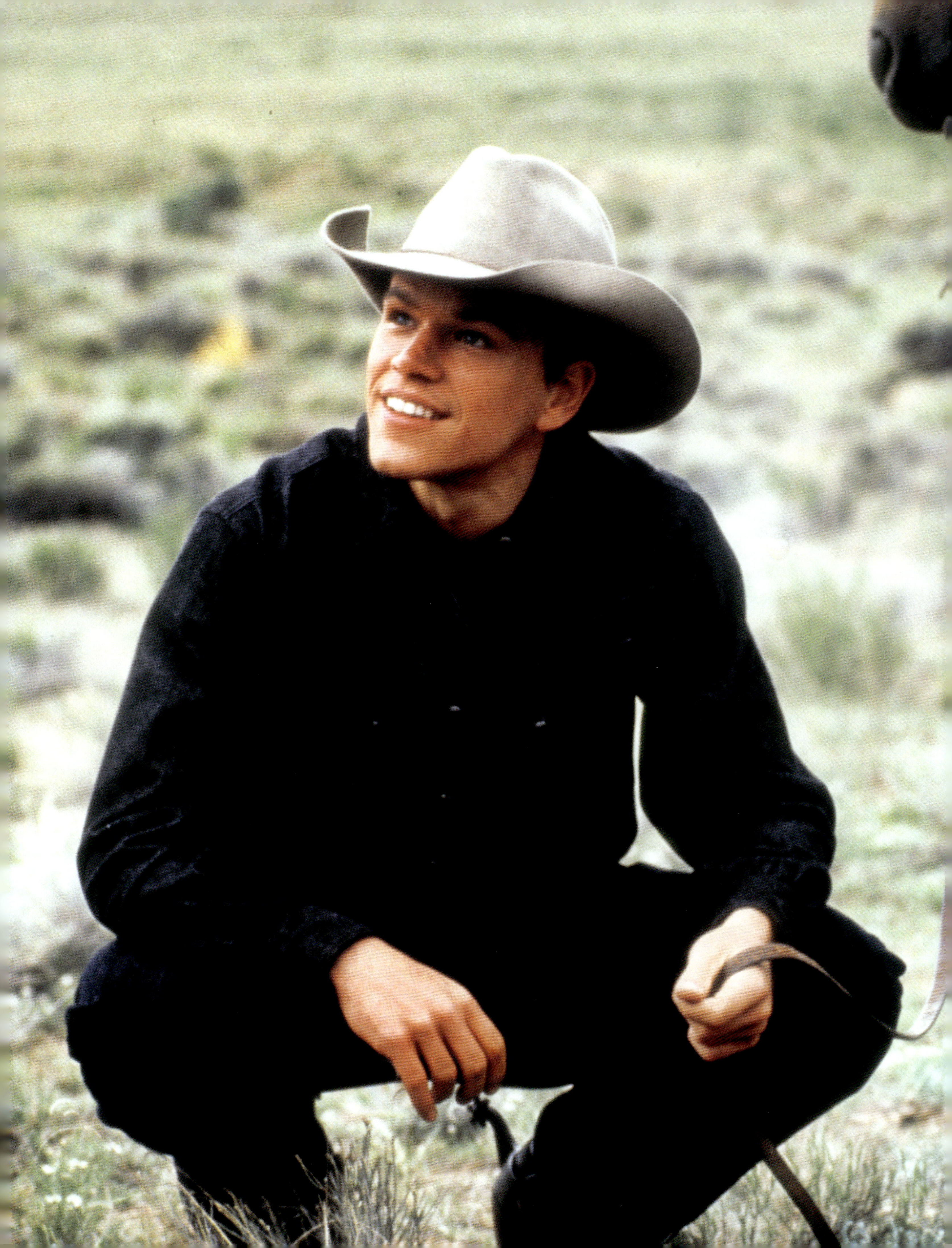

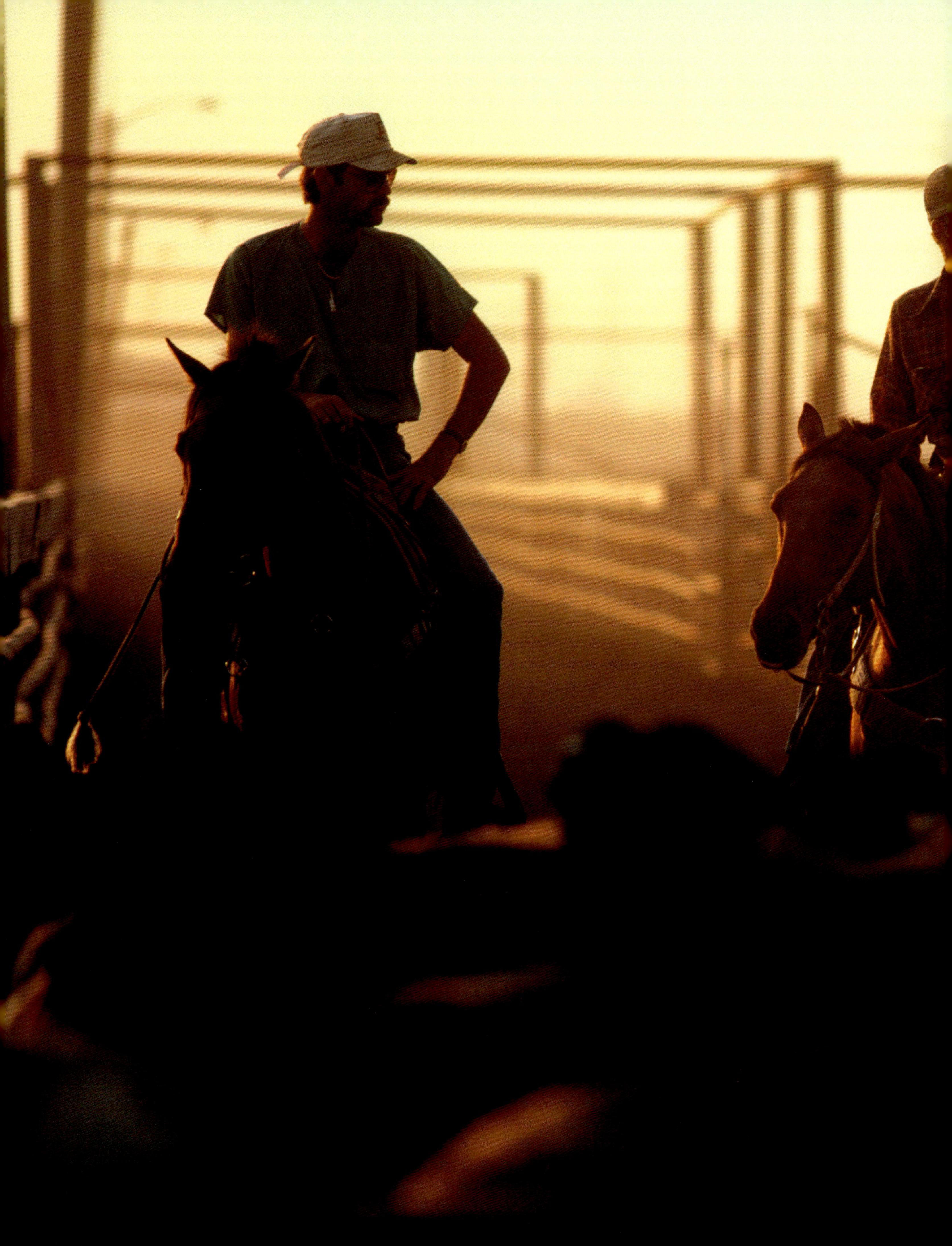

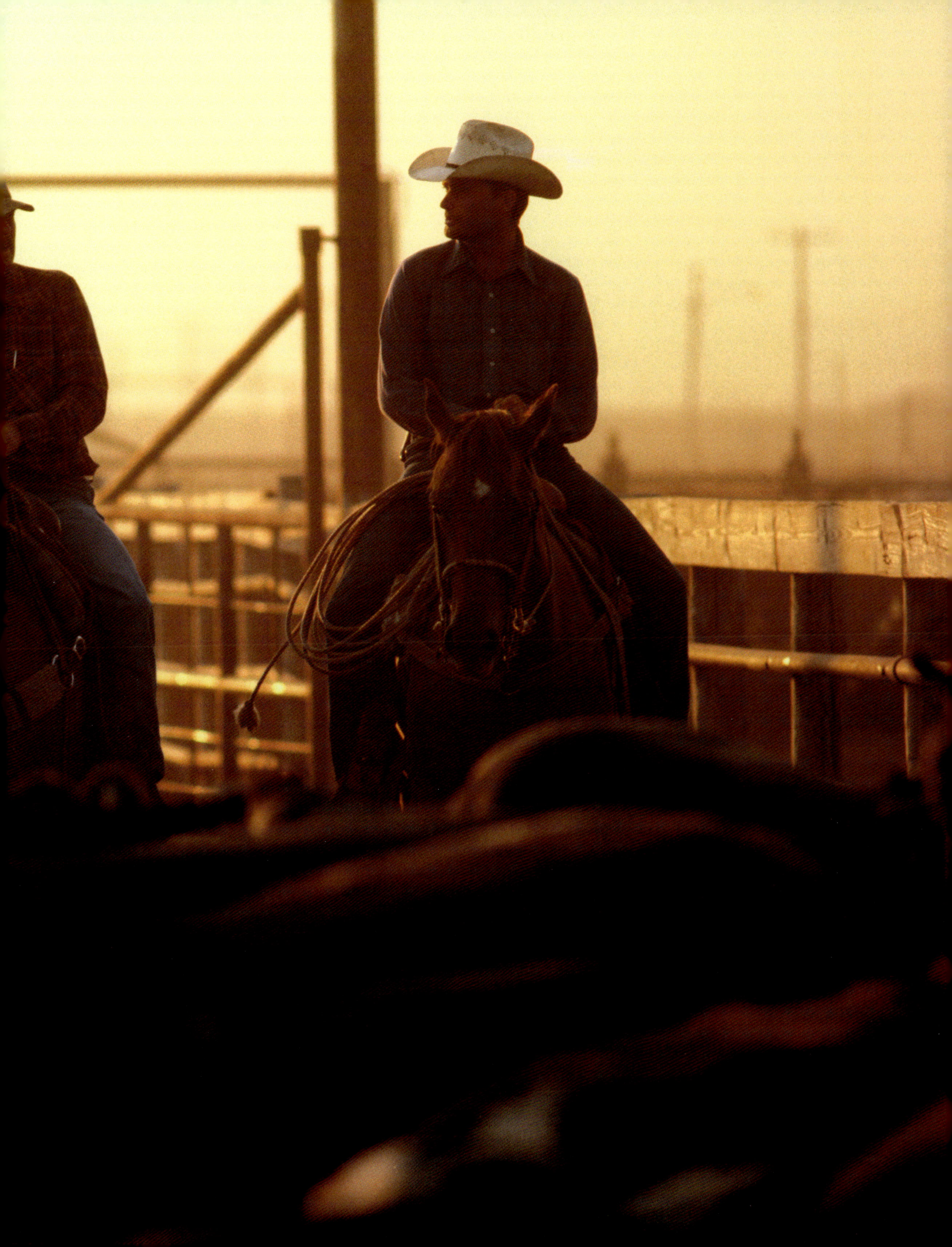

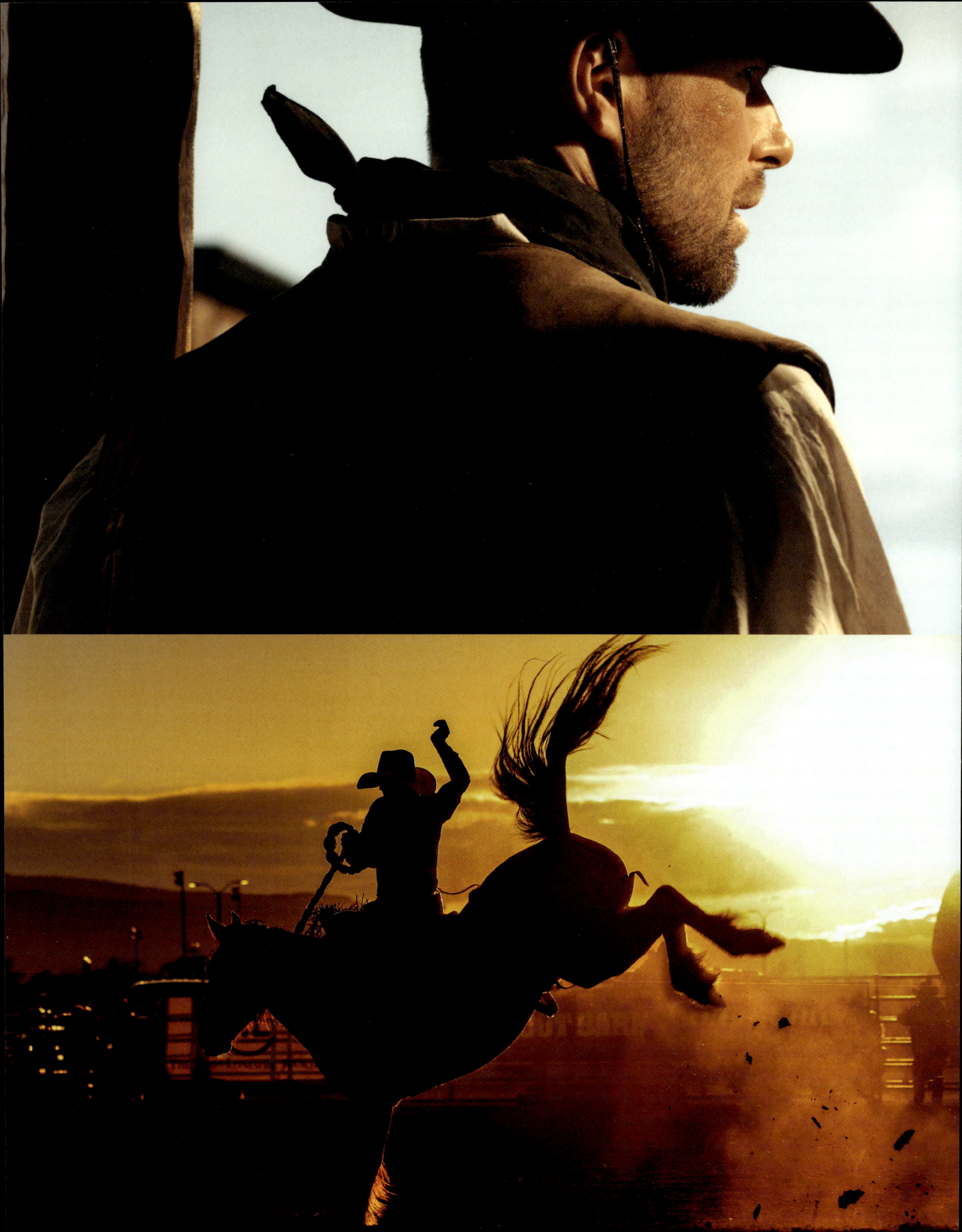

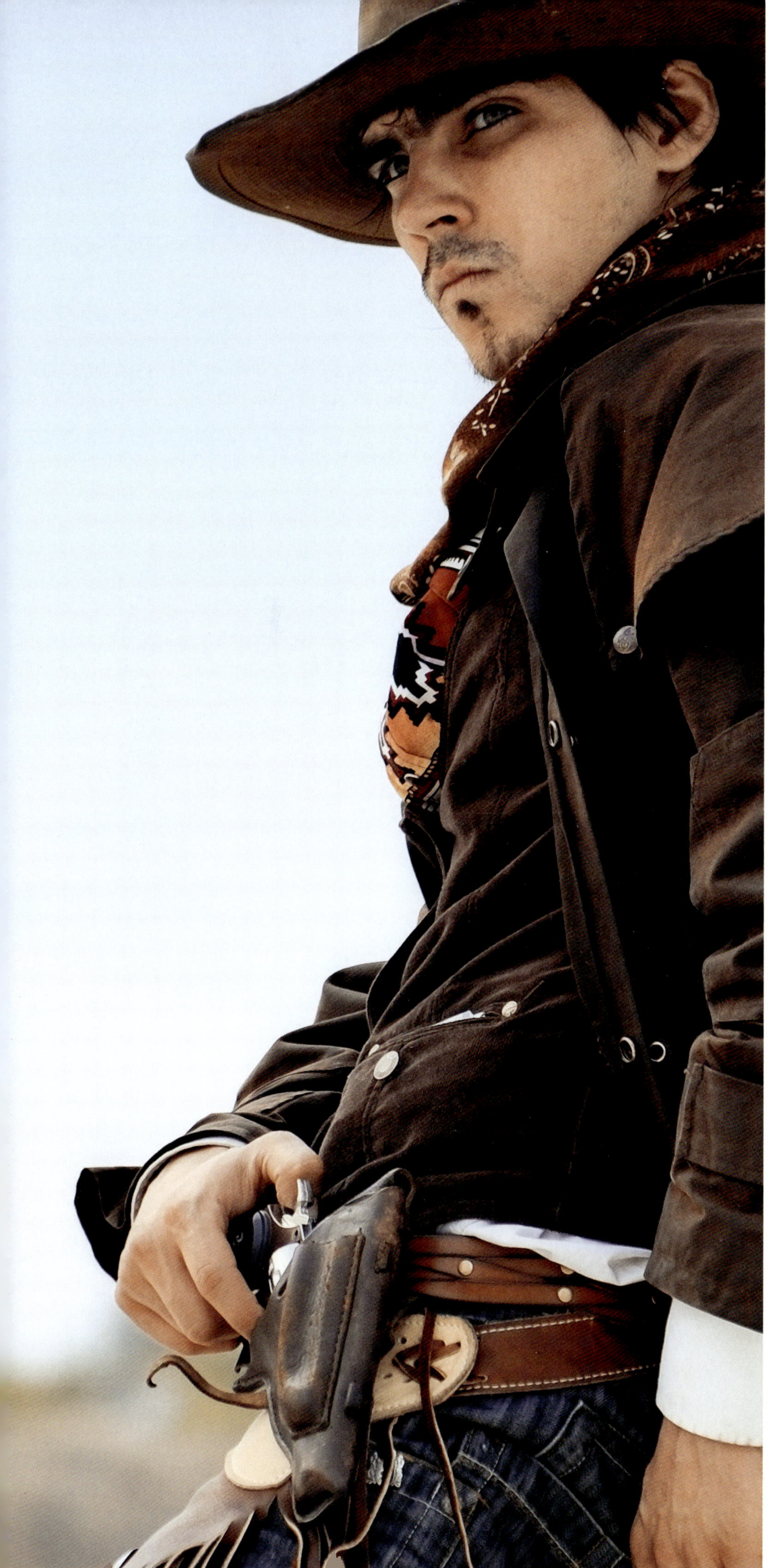

Page 157: *Models Christy Turlington and Naomi Campbell, wearing gold outfits by Mark Jacobs for Perry Ellis, relaxing on the porch at Parlange Plantation outside New Orleans.*

Page 158: *Street Style, New York Fashion Week September 2019, Day 3. Corin Christian is seen wearing a white cowboy hat, blue striped shirt, blue jeans and a white studded belt outside the Longchamp show on September 7, 2019.*

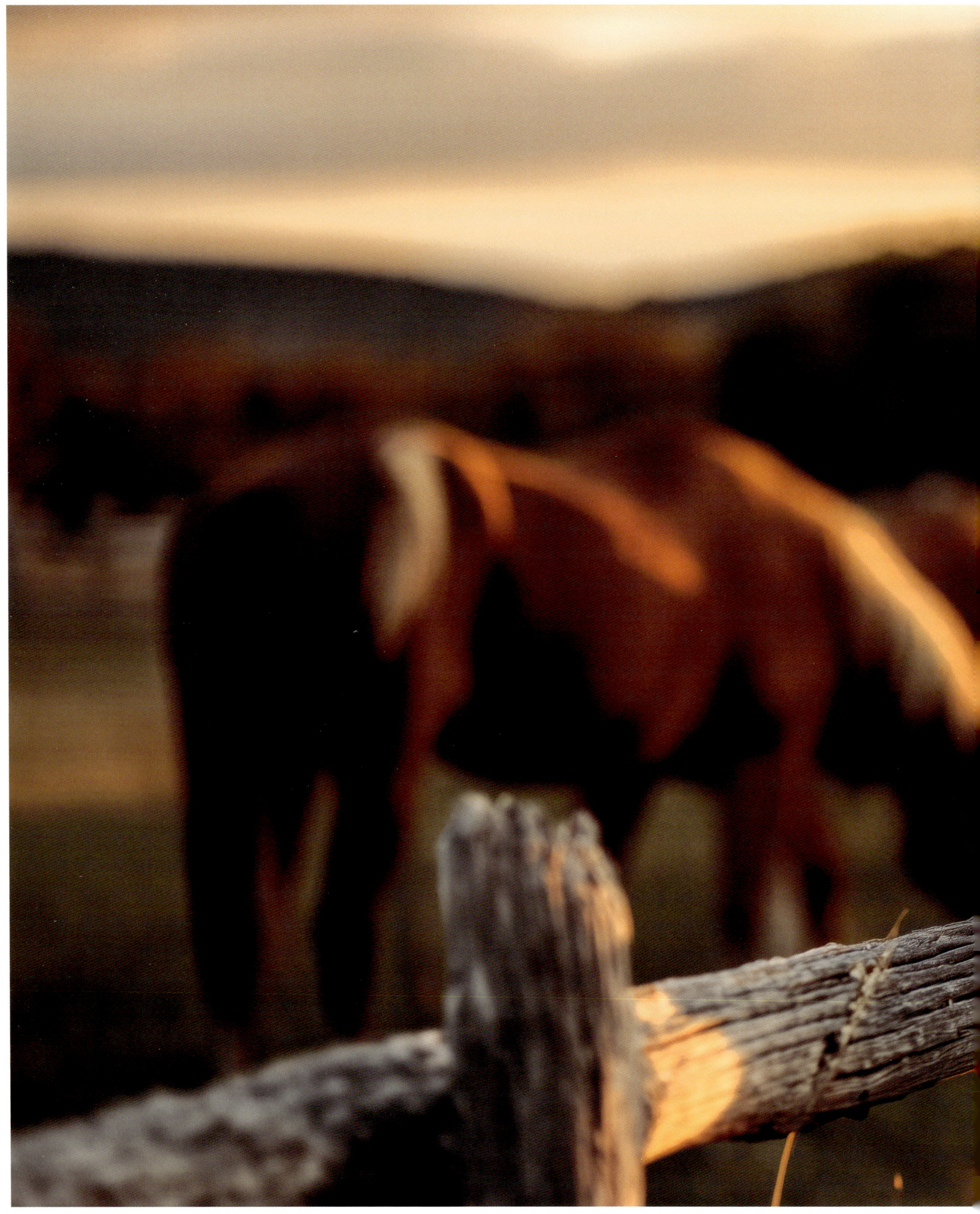

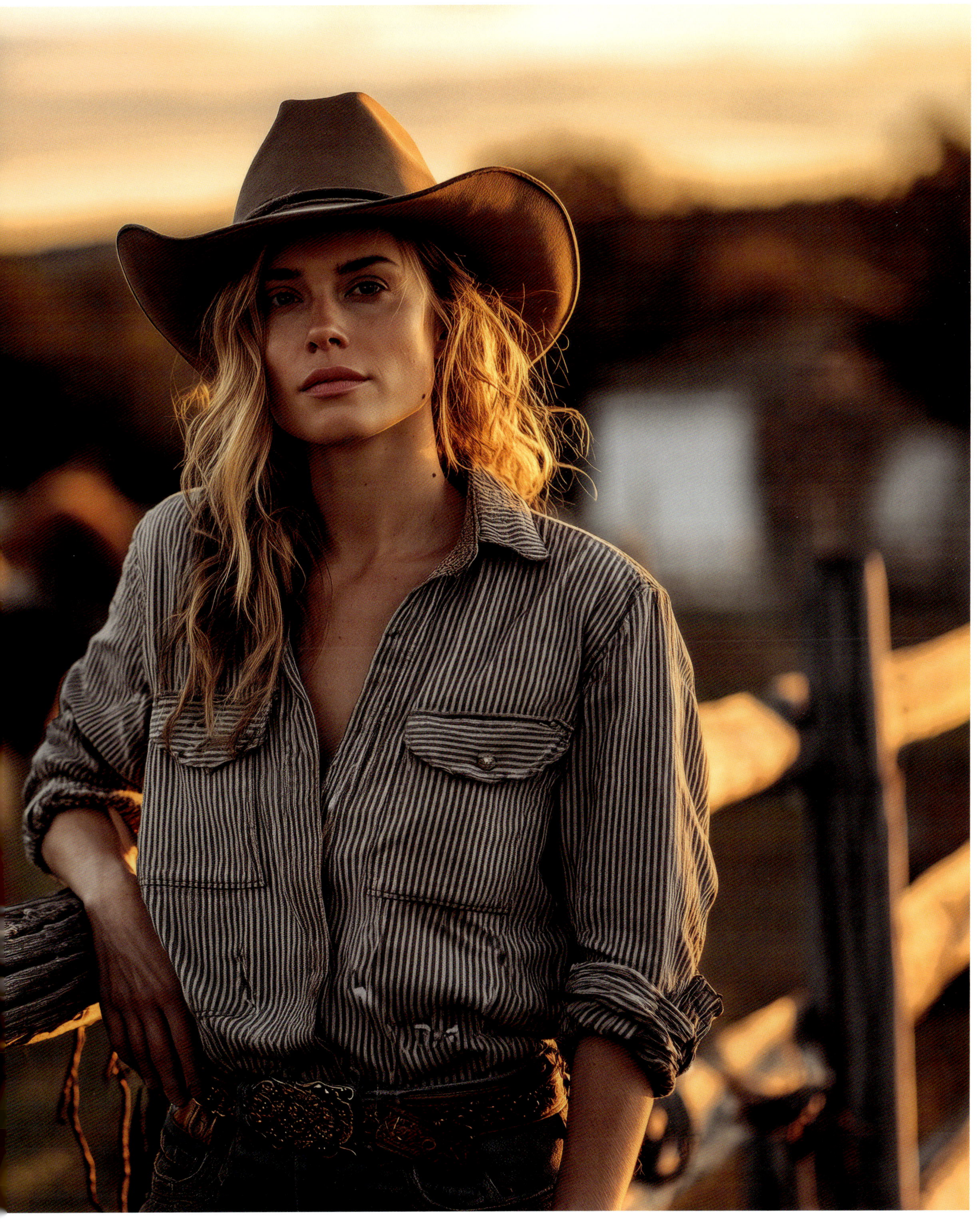

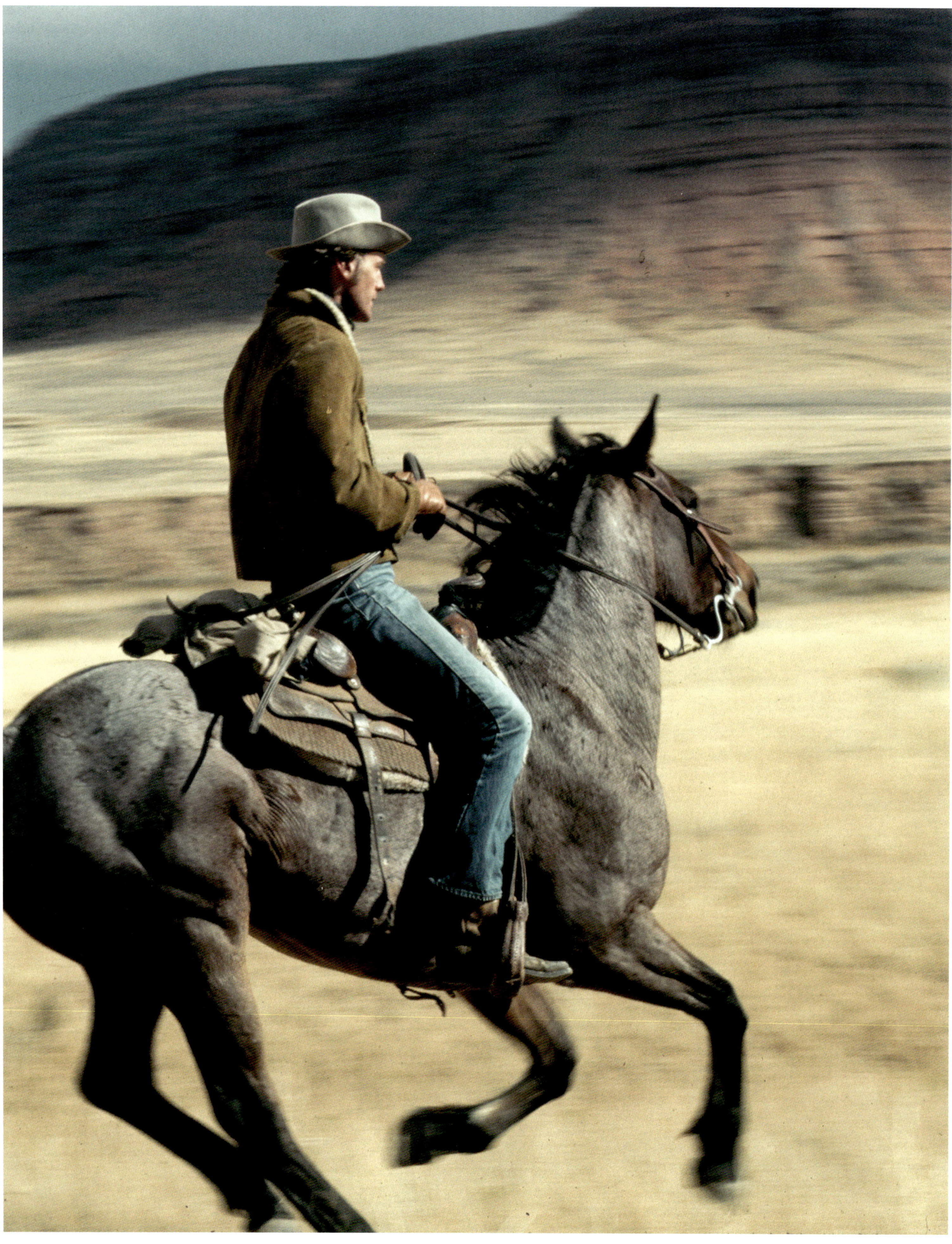

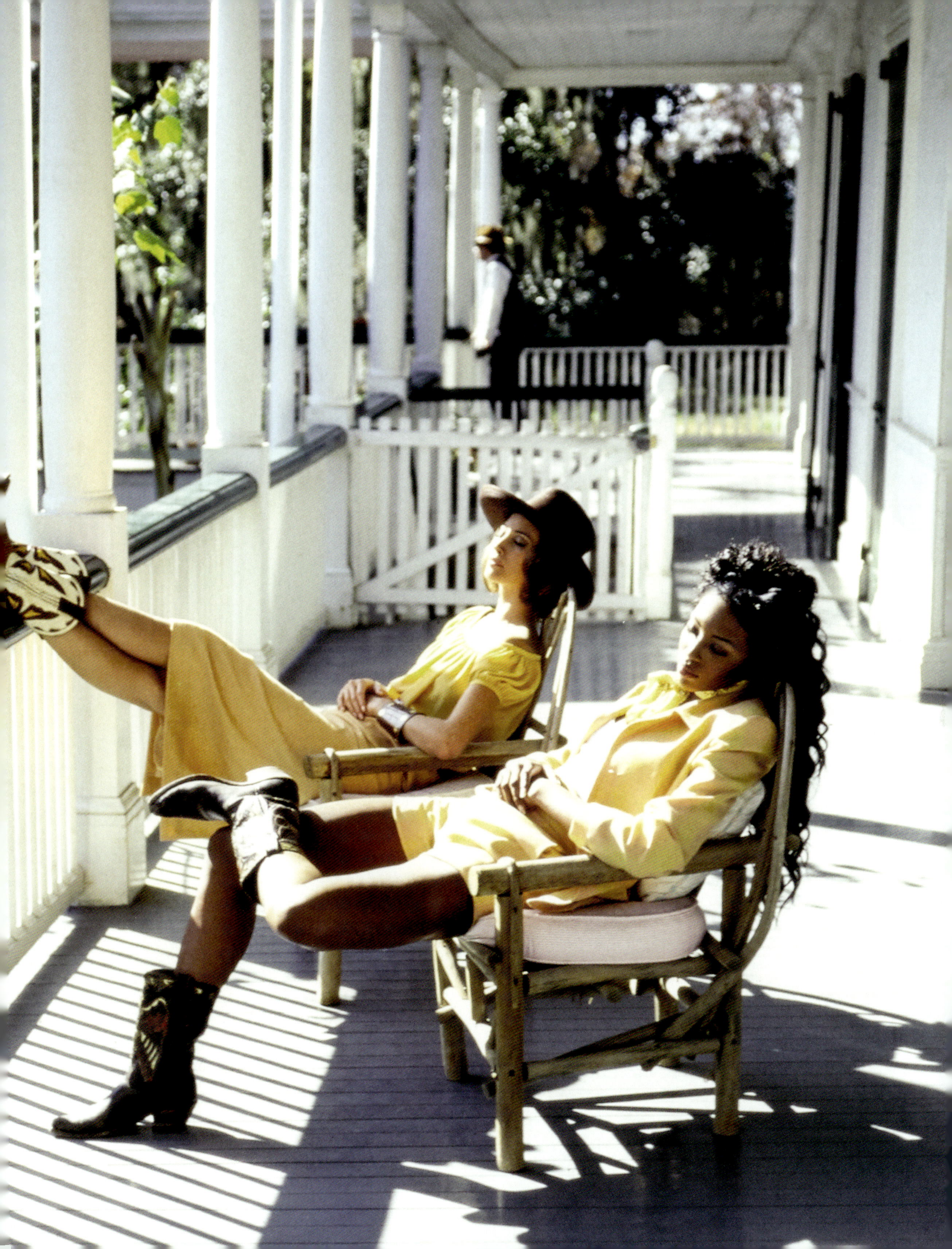

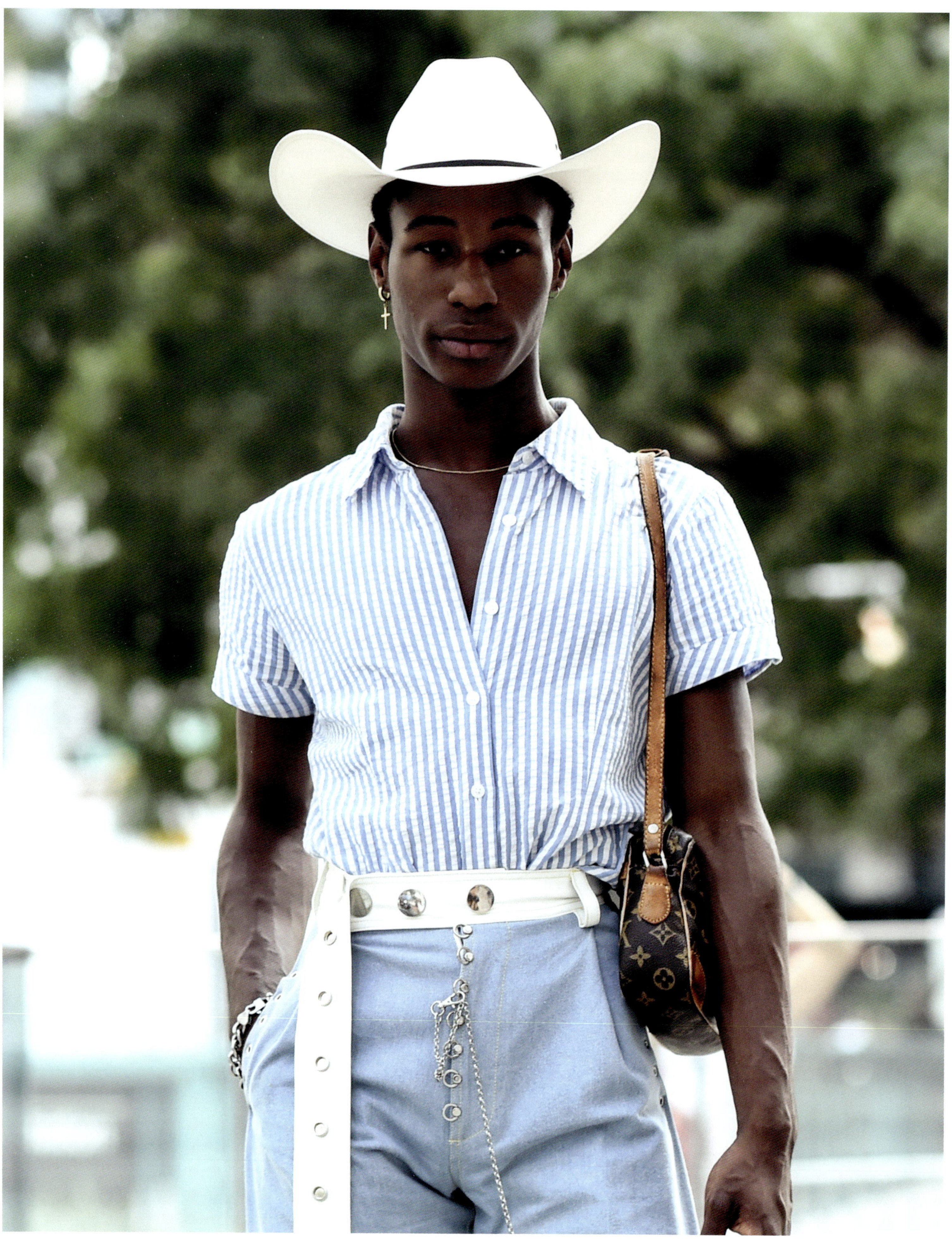

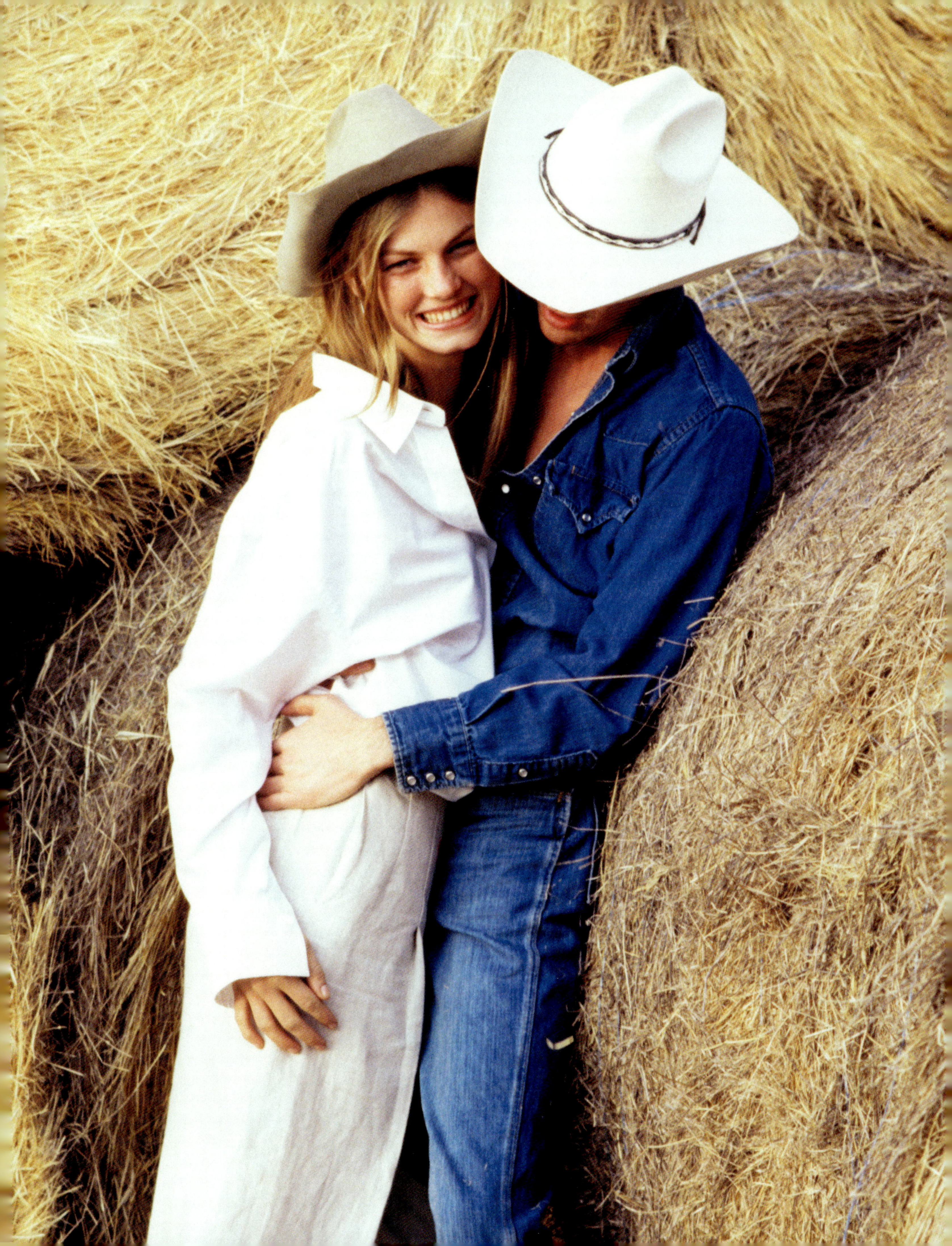

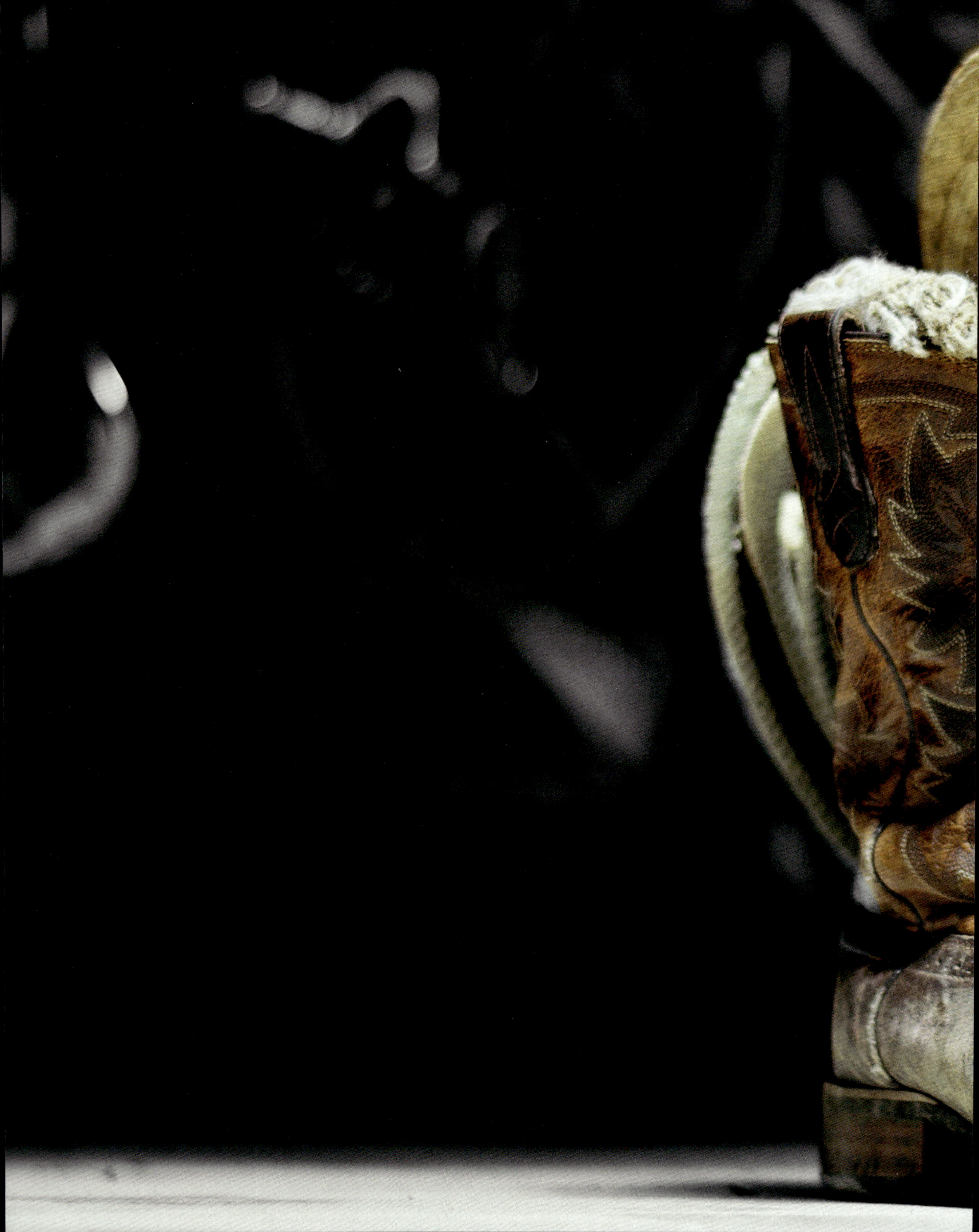

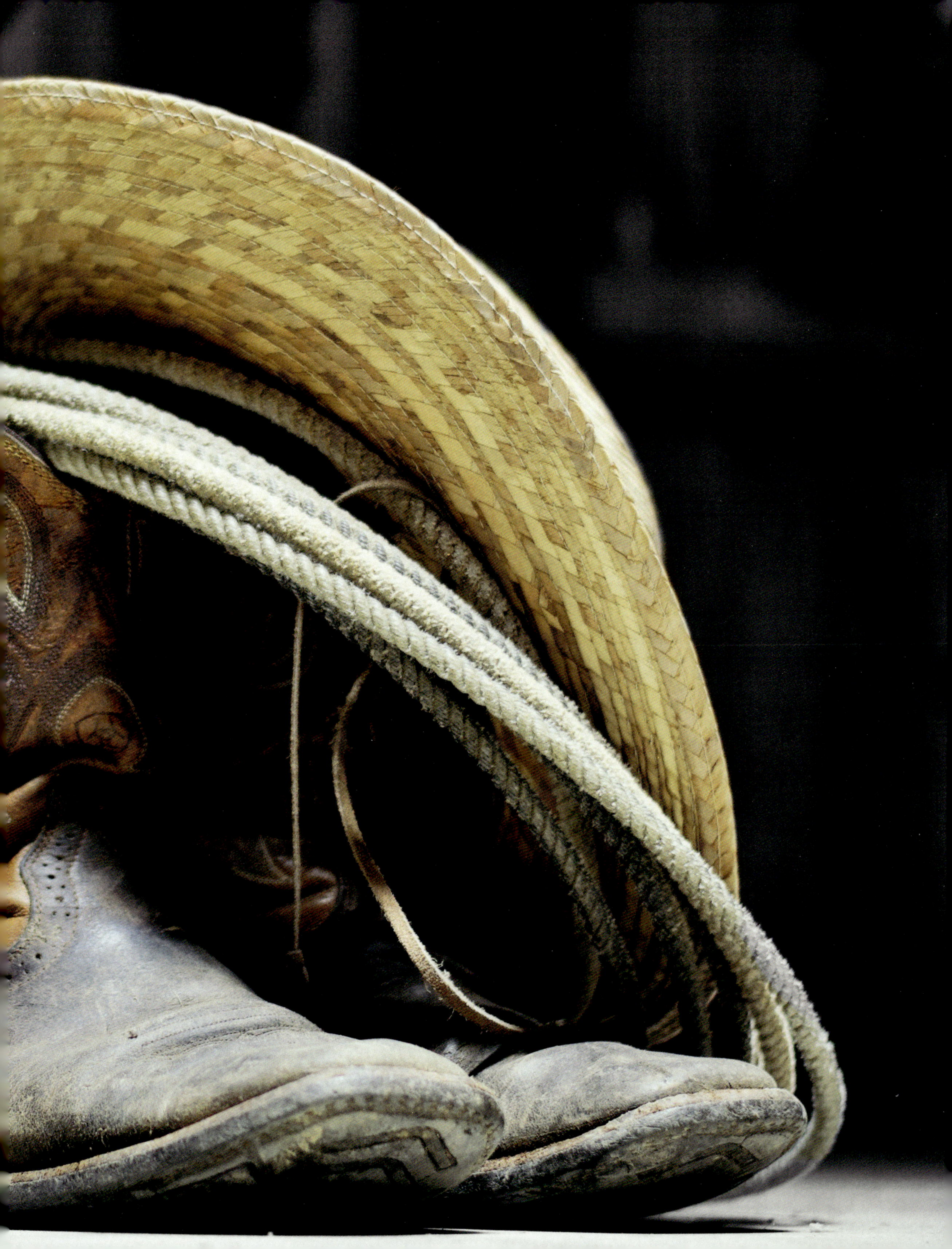

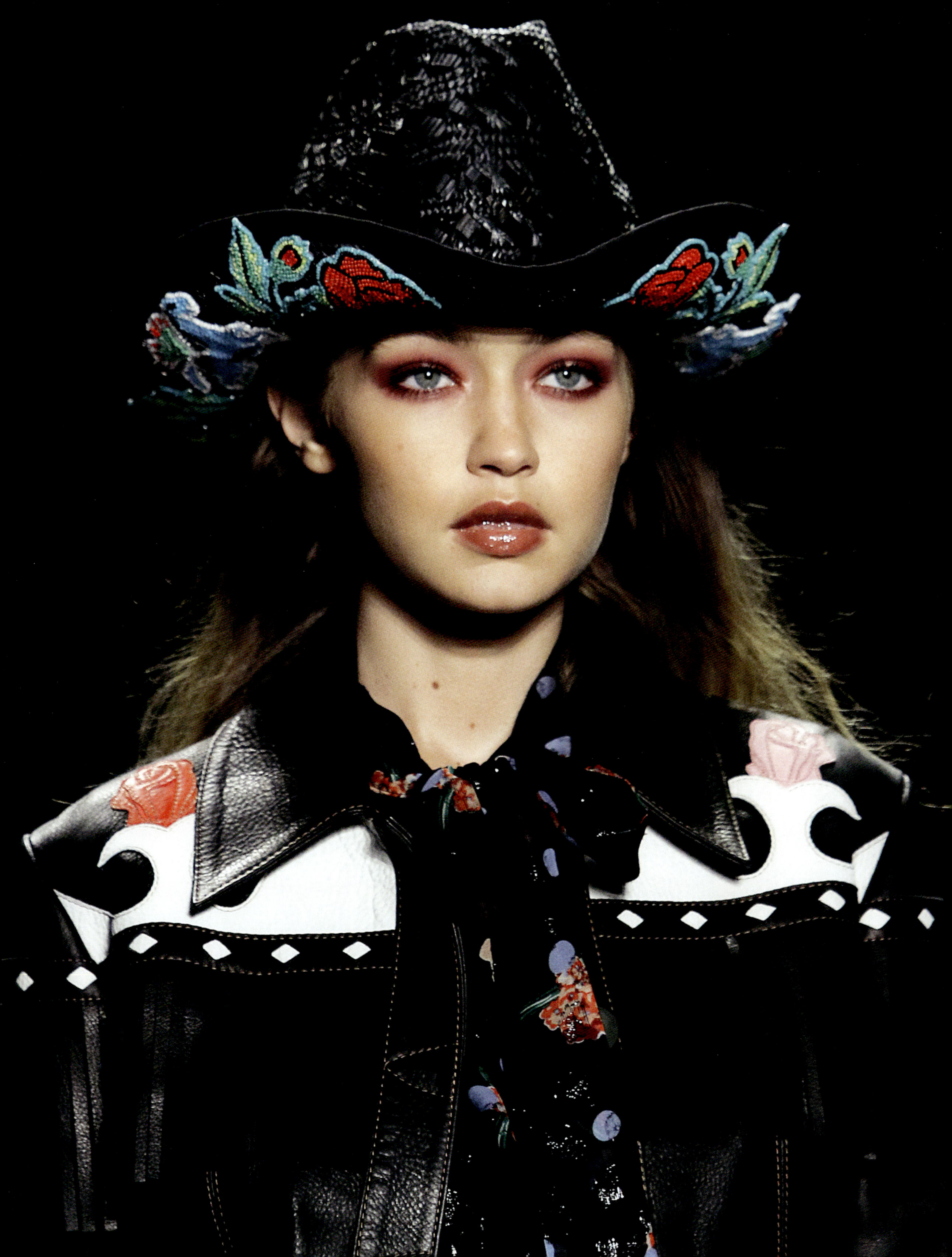

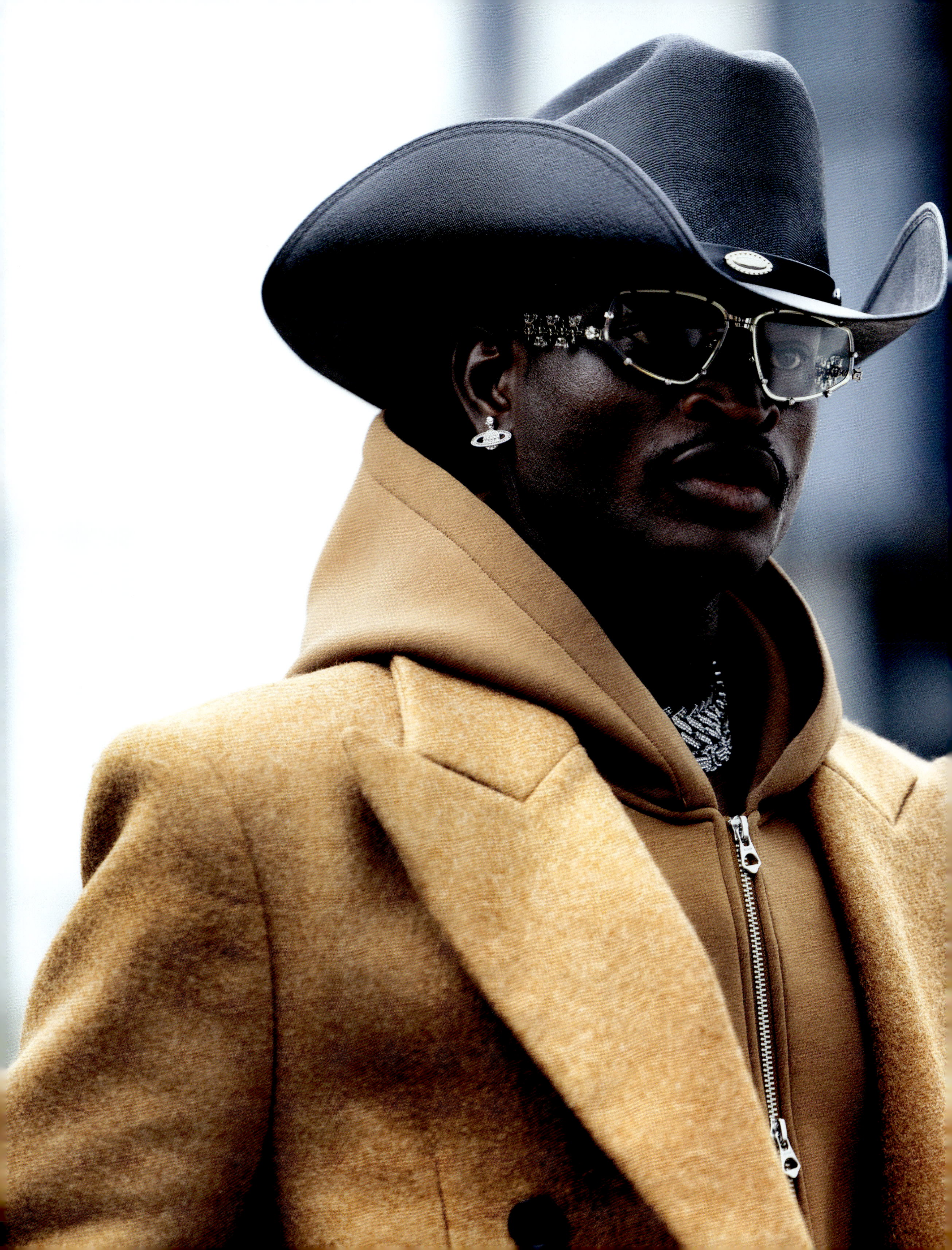

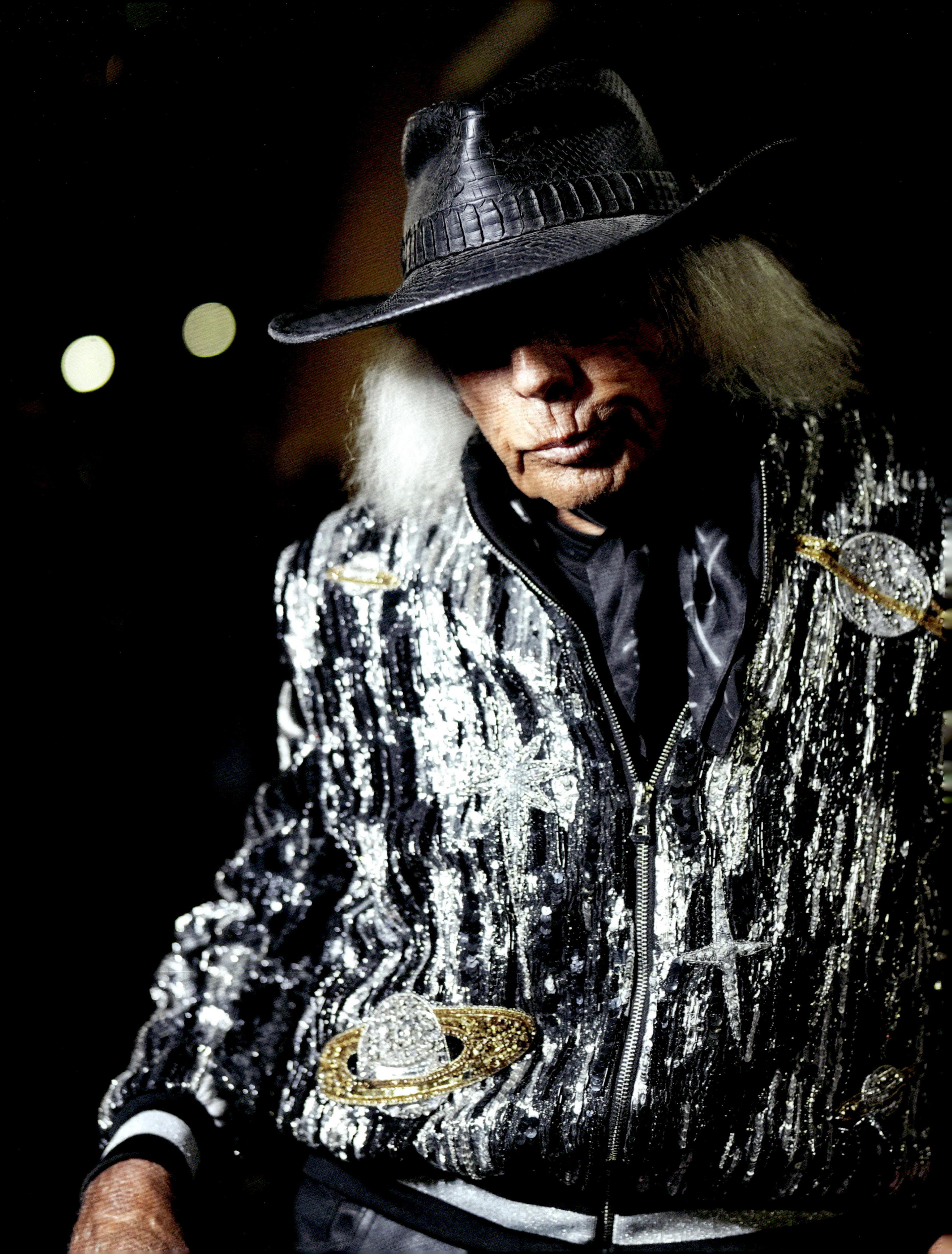

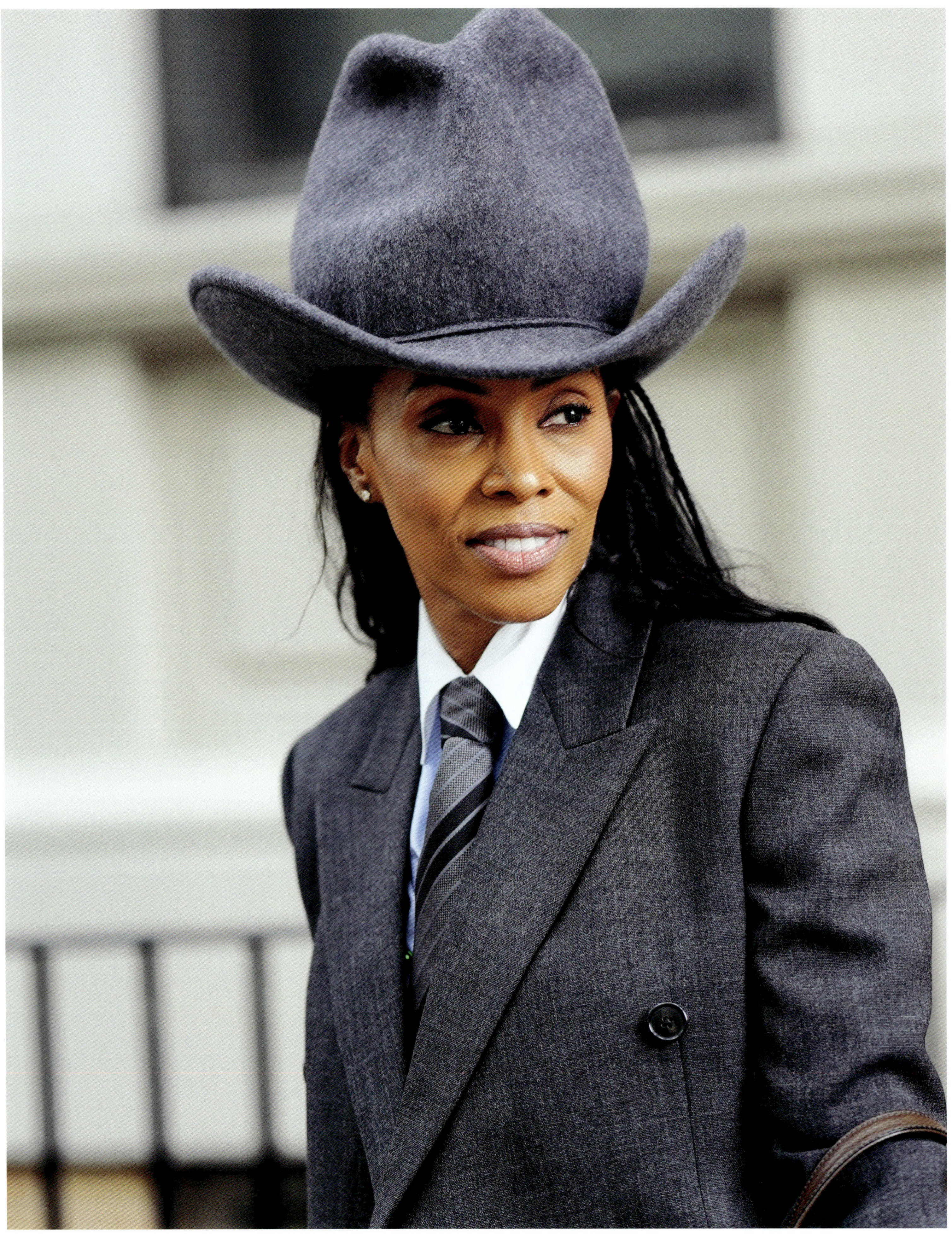

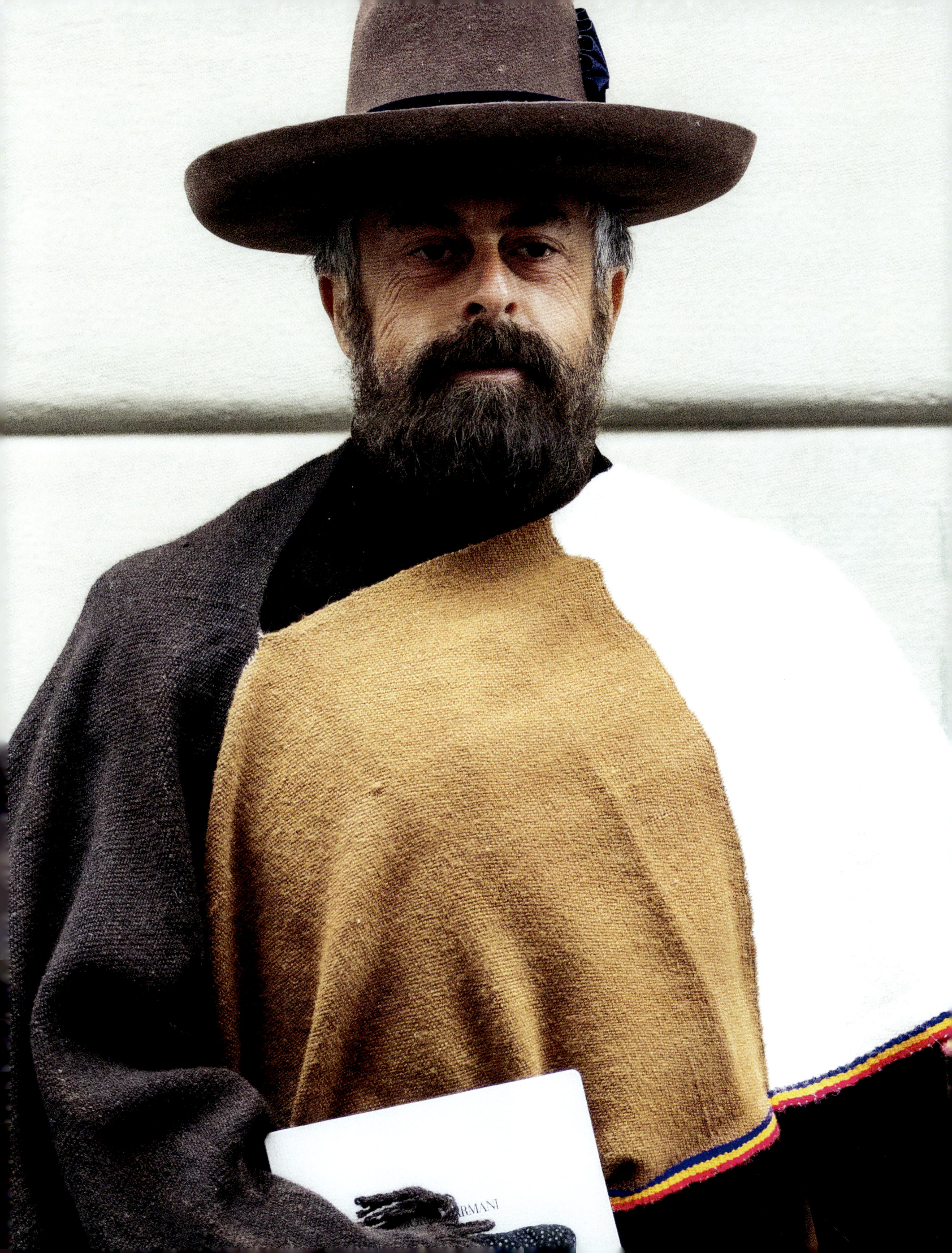

ARMANI

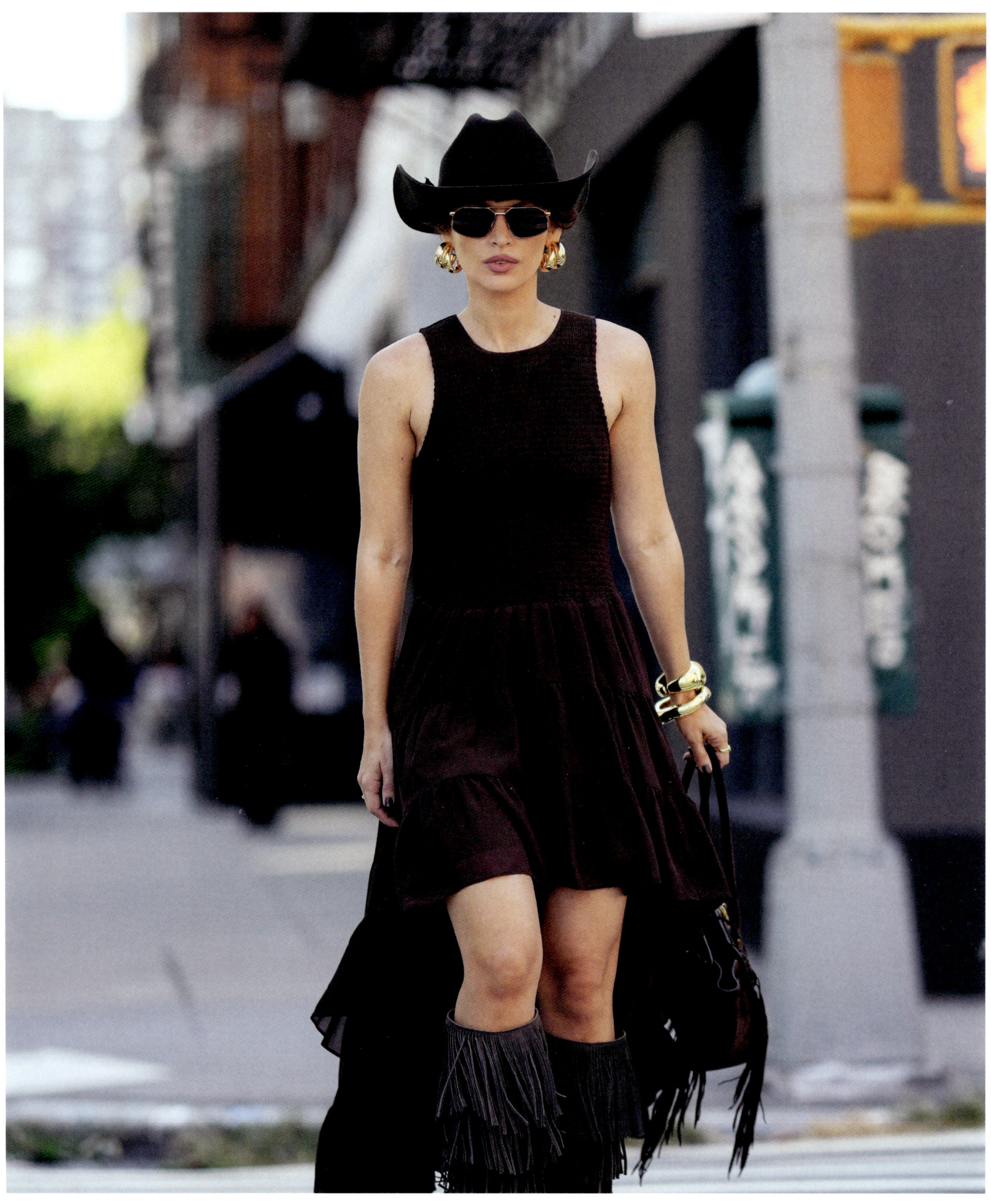

This page: *Irina Kro wears a sleeveless dark chocolate dress and fringed charcoal gray suede knee-high boots accessorized with a black felt cowboy hat, aviator sunglasses, gold-tone jewelry, and a dark brown suede Michael Kors handbag at the Michael Kors show during New York Fashion Week on September 11, 2025.*

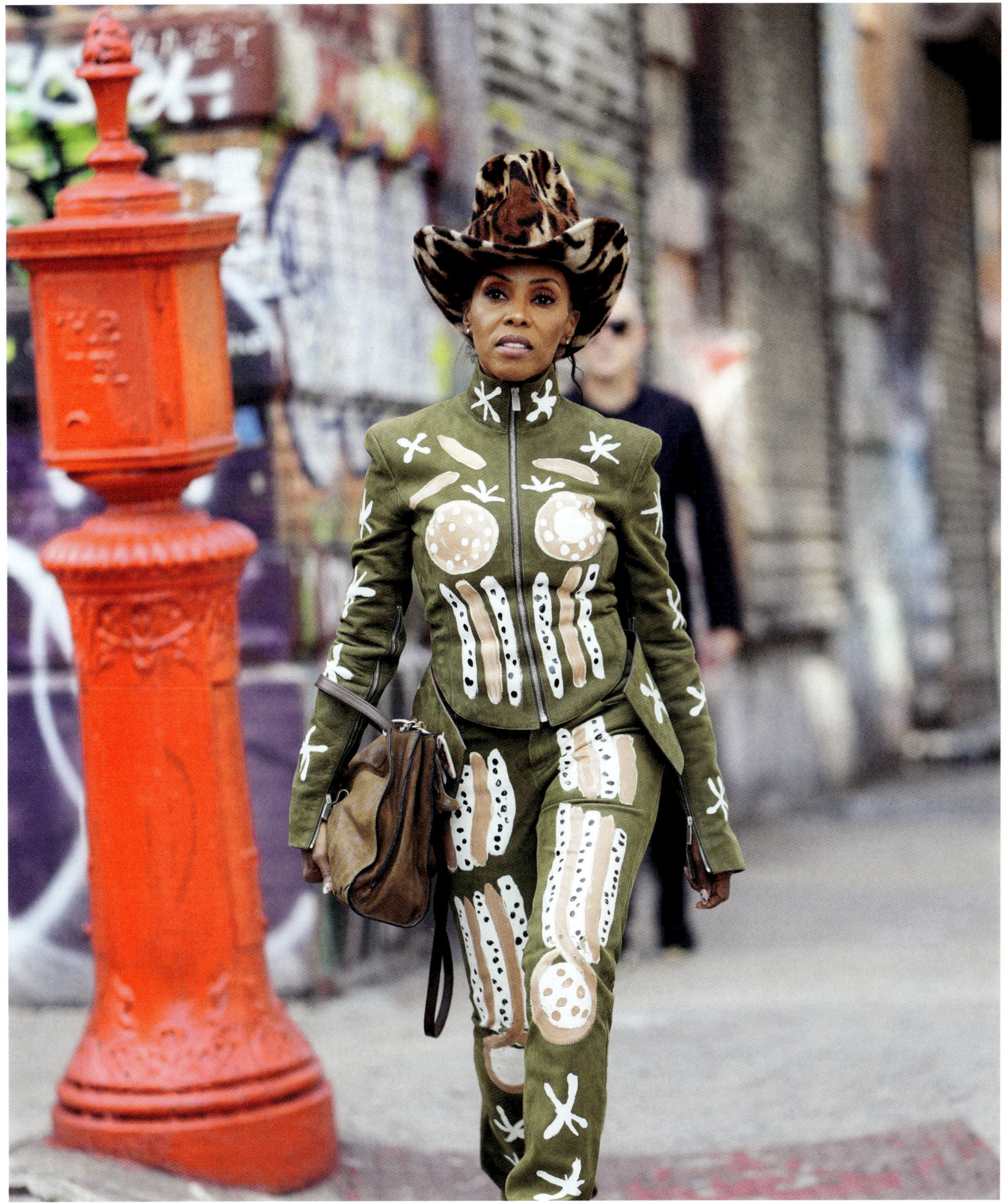

This page: *June Ambrose wears a brown and black leopard-print cowboy hat and olive-green zip-up jacket with matching trousers (featuring abstract motifs) during New York Fashion Week on September 12, 2025.*

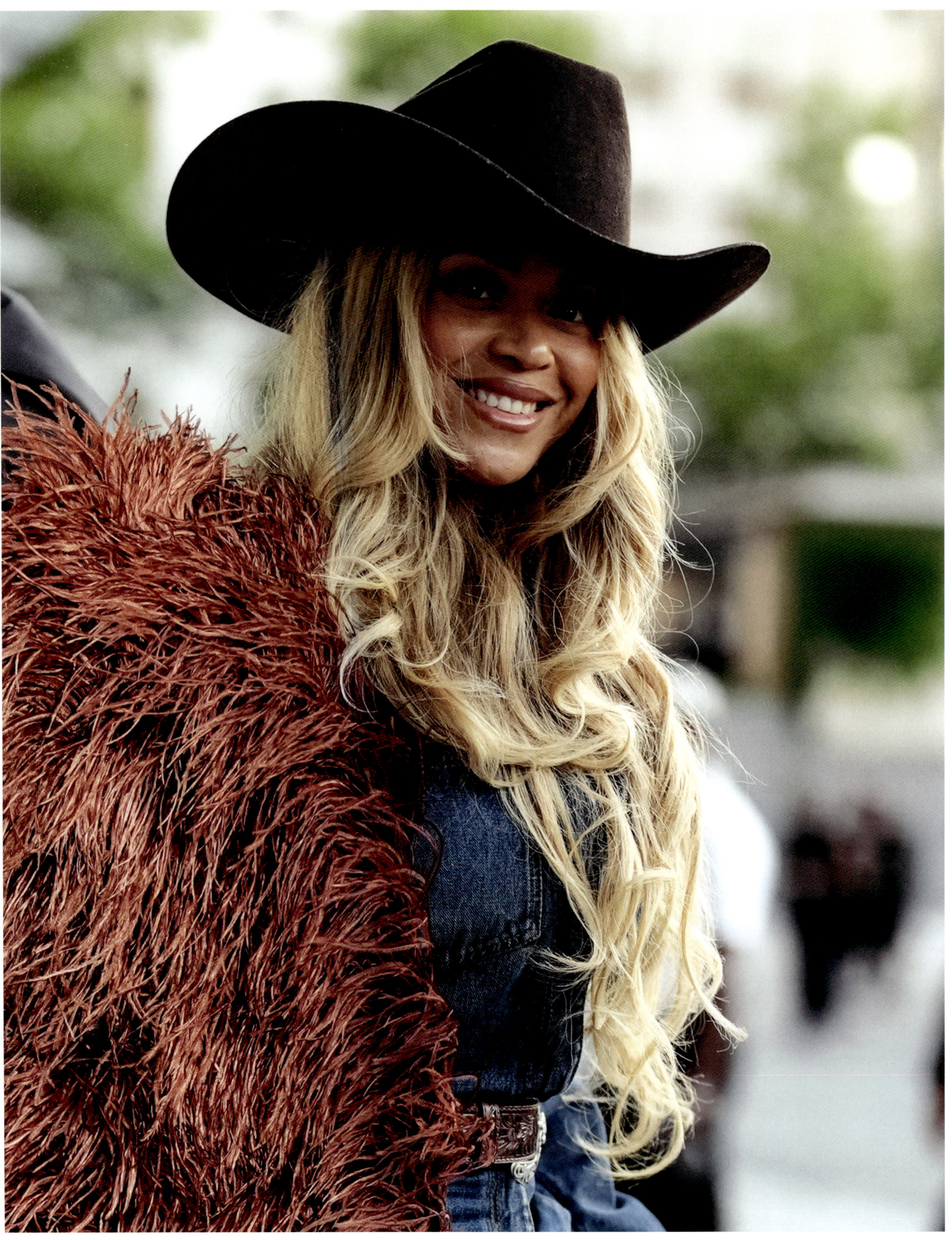

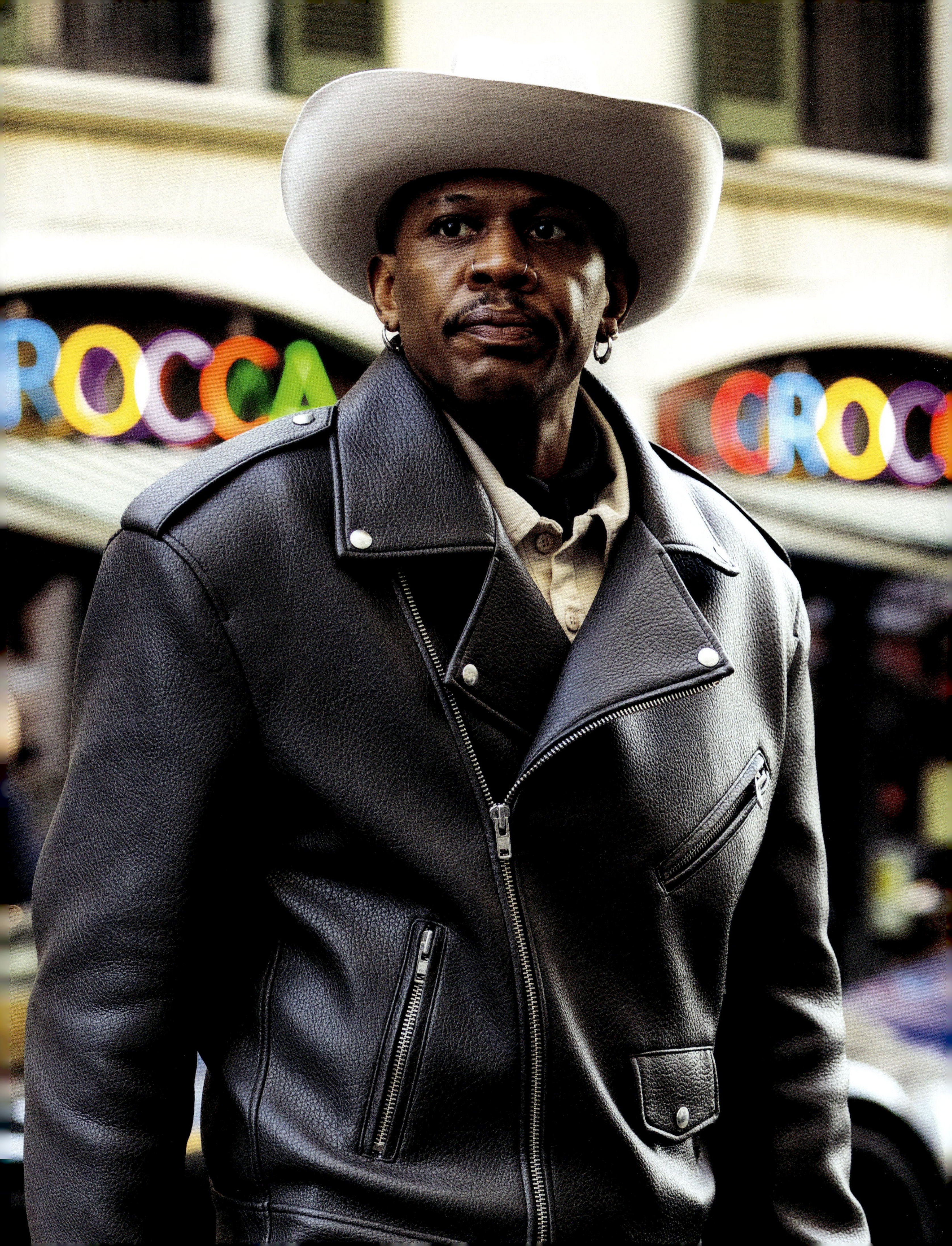
ROCCA
CROC

Cover: H.Armstrong Roberts/Classic Stock
Backcover: Darrell Gulin/Getty Images

p. 2 Darrell Gulin/Getty Images, p. 5 Arthur Elgort/Conde Nast/Getty Images, p.6 Nicoli/Adobe Stock, p.10, 11 Arthur Elgort/Conde Nast/ Getty Images, p.12 The Denver Post/Getty Images, p.13 Hulton Archive/ Getty Images, p. 14, 15 Michael Ochs Archives/Getty Images, p.16 Amy Susmann/WireImage/Getty Images, p.17 NDZ/Star Max/Gettyimages, p.18 Edward Berthelot/Getty Images, p.19 Ethan Miller/Getty Images, p. 20, 21 Martin Mills/Getty Images, p. 22, 23 Susan Wood/Getty Images, p. 24, 25 Arthur Elgort/Conde Nast/Getty Images, p. 26 Devaney-Superstock/Devaney Collection/ClassicStock, p. 30, 31 Dolkan/Adobe Stock, p.32 Alamy Stock Photos/mauritius images, p. 33 Keystone/ Getty Images, p. 34 H. Armstrong Roberts/ClassicStock/Getty Images, p. 35 Alamy Stock Photos/mauritius images, p. 36 Devaney Collection/ ClassicStock, p.38 H. Armstrong Roberts/ClassicStock/Getty Images, p. 39 H. Armstrong Roberts/ClassisStock/GettyImages, p. 40, 41 Emin Yildiz/ shutterstock, p. 42, 43 Devaney Collection/ClassicStock, p.44 Hulton Archive/Getty Images Hulton Archive/Getty Images, p. 45 H. Armstrong Roberts/ClassisStock/GettyImages, p. 46, 47 Taylor Brandon/unsplash, p. 48 Devaney Collection/ClassicStock, p. 49 Devaney Collection/ ClassicStock, p. 50 above: Pictureguy32/Adobe Stock, p. 50 bottom: Danmir12/Adobe Stock, p. 51 Lukas/Adobe Stock, p. 52, 53 Matthias Clamer/Getty Images, p. 54 Octavio Campos Salles/Alamy/mauritius images, p. 55 Dick Hoogerdijk/unsplash, p. 56 Everettovrk/Adobe Stock, p. 61 DEA/G.A. Rossi/Getty Images, p. 62 Bettmann/Getty Images, p. 63 Library of Congress/Getty Images, p. 64, 65 Library of Congress/Corbis/ VCG/Getty Images, p. 66 Jim Heimann Collection/Getty Images, p. 67 Bettmann/Getty Images, p. 68 Corbis/Getty Images, p. 69 Bettmann/Getty Images, p. 70 Fotosearch/Getty Images, p. 71 Everettovrk/Adobe Stock, p. 72 Gado/Getty Images, p. 73 Studio F./Adobe Stock, p. 74 Pictorial Press/Alamy/mauritius images, p. 78, 79 Pictorial Press/Alamy/mauritius images, p. 80, 81 Screen Prod/mauritius images, p. 82, 83 Pictorial Press/ Alamy/mauritius images, p. 84 Screen Prod/mauritius images, p. 85 Select Images/Alamy/mauritius images, p. 86 Screen Prod/mauritius images, p. 87 TopFoto/mauritius images, p. 88, 89 Collection Christophel/Spanky/ mauritius images, p. 90, 91 Pictorial Press/Alamy/mauritius images, p. 92 Everett Collection/IMAGO, p. 93 World Book Inc/mauritius images, p. 94, 95 Michael Ochs Archives/Getty Images, p. 96 Everett Collection/ IMAGO, p. 97 Everett Collection/IMAGO, p. 98 World History Archive/ picture alliance, p. 99 Everett Collection/IMAGO, p. 100 Pictorial Press/ Alamy/mauritius images, p. 101 Screen Prod/mauritius images, p. 102 Screen Prod/mauritius images, p. 103 Pictorial Press/Alamy/mauritius images, p. 104 Moviestore Collection/Alamy/mauritius images, p. 105 Screen Prod/mauritius images, p. 106 Screen Prod/mauritius images, p. 108, 109 IFA Film/United Archives/ Alamy/mauritius images, p. 110, 111 Kpa Publictiy Stills, United Archives/Alamy/mauritius images, p. 112, 113 Moviestore Collection/Alamy/mauritius images, p. 114 Alyssa Jane/ unsplash+, p. 118, 119 Arthur Elgort/Conde Nast/Getty Images, p. 120 Sunset Boulevard/Corbis/Getty Images, p. 121 Arthur Elgort/Conde Nast/ Getty Images, p. 122 Archive Photos/Getty Images, p. 123 Bettmann/Getty Images, p. 124 H. Armstrong Roberts/ClassicStock, p. 125 Keystone/Getty Images, p. 126, 127 Archive Photos/Getty Images, p. 128 Blake Little/ Getty Images, p. 129 Bert Stern/Getty Images, p. 130 Michael Smith/ Getty Images, p. 131 Michael Smith/Getty Images, p. 132, 133 Jackson Photography/Adobe Stock, p. 134, 135 Tom Kelley Archive/Getty Images, p. 136 Venti Views/unsplash, p. 137 Neale Haynes, Buzz Pictures/Alamy/ mauritius images, p. 138, 139 Dean Conger/Getty Images, p. 140, 141 Avalon/Getty Images, p. 142 Archive Photos/Getty Image,s p. 143 Tom Kelley Archive/Getty Images, p. 144 Renato Granieri/Alamy/mauritius images, p. 145, 146 Arthur Elgort/Conde Nast/Getty Images, p. 147 Arthur Elgort/Conde Nast/Getty Images, p. 148 Jsb-co/unsplash+, p. 149 Columbia Pictures, p. 150, 151 Design Pics Editorial/Getty Images, p. 152 above: Supamotion/Adobe Stock, p. 152 bottom: Nikki/Adobe Stock, p. 153 Sad/Adobe Stock, p. 154, 155 Ala/Adobe Stock, p. 156 Jonathan Blair/Getty Images, p. 157 Arthur Elgort/Conde Nast/Getty Images, p. 158 Daniel Zuchnik/Getty Images, p. 159 Arthur Elgort/Conde Nast/ Getty Images p. 160, 161 Joseph Hersch Media/unsplash p. 162 Robert Mitra/WWD/Penske Media/Getty Images, p. 163 Valentina Frugiuele/ Getty Images, p. 164, 165 Edward Berthelot/Getty Images, p. 166 Edward Berthelot/Getty Images, p. 167 Valentina Frugiuele/Getty Images, p. 168 Edward Berthelot/Getty Images, p. 169 Edward Berthelot/Getty Images, p. 170 Edward Berthelot/Getty Images, p. 171 Valentina Frugiuele/Getty Images, p. 173 Claudia Lavenia/Getty Images, p. 174, 175 Arthur Elgort/ Conde Nast/Getty Images

Page 170: *Beyoncé wears a blue denim shirt and cowboy hat, with a burgundy faux fur fluff coat on one shoulder, at the Louis Vuitton Menswear show during Paris Fashion Week on June 24, 2025.*

Page 171: *A guest wears a black leather jacket, beige shirt and cowboy hat to the Pierre-Louis Mascia show during Milan Fashion Week on January 17, 2025.*

Opposite: *Two guests attend the MSGM show during Milan Fashion Week on January 13, 2024.*

Following pages: *Model Nadja Auermann sits on back of a tinker's caravan in Ireland wearing a turtleneck and cut velvet coat , both by Ozbeck, and a washed velvet coat by Donna Karan, VOGUE, 1993.*

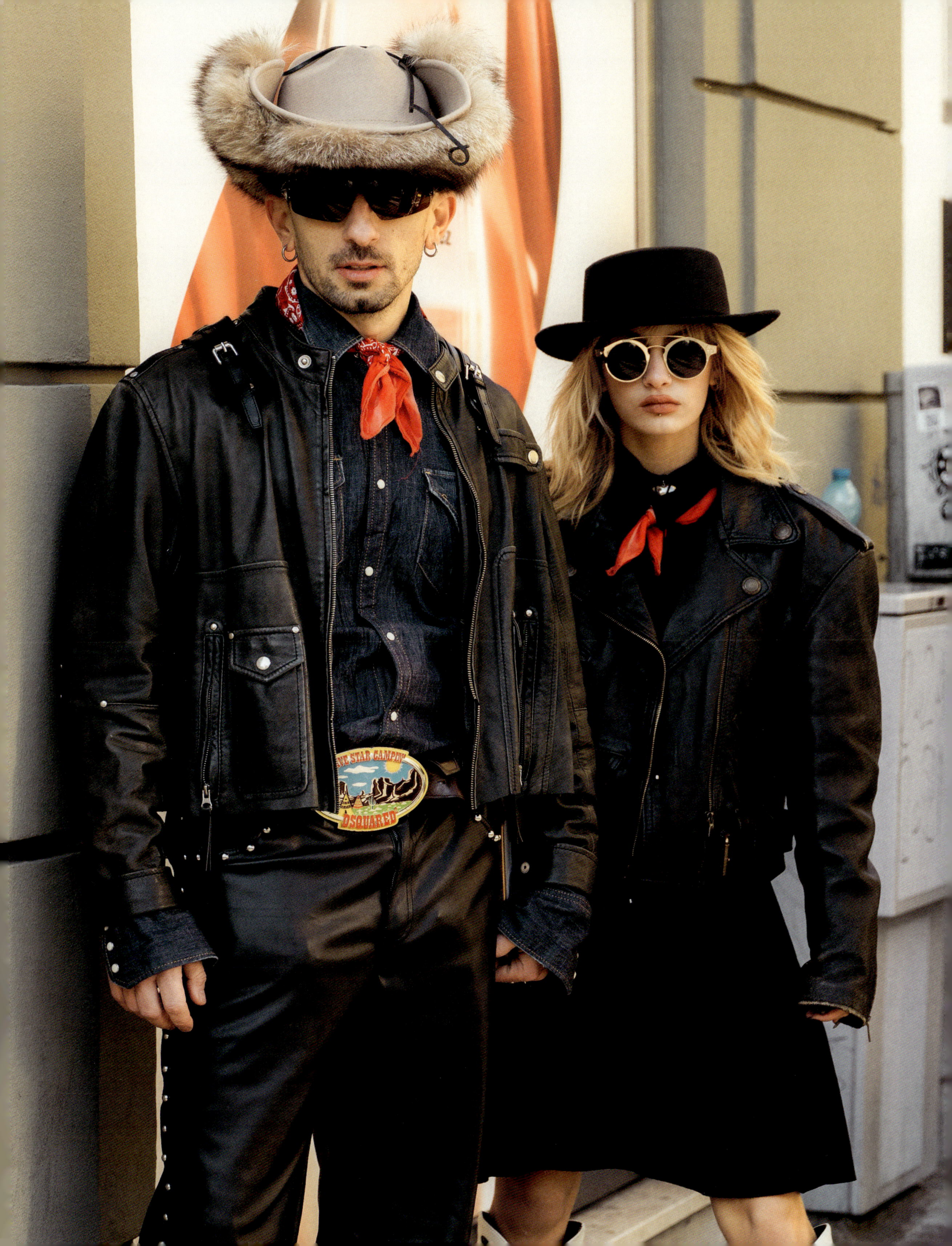

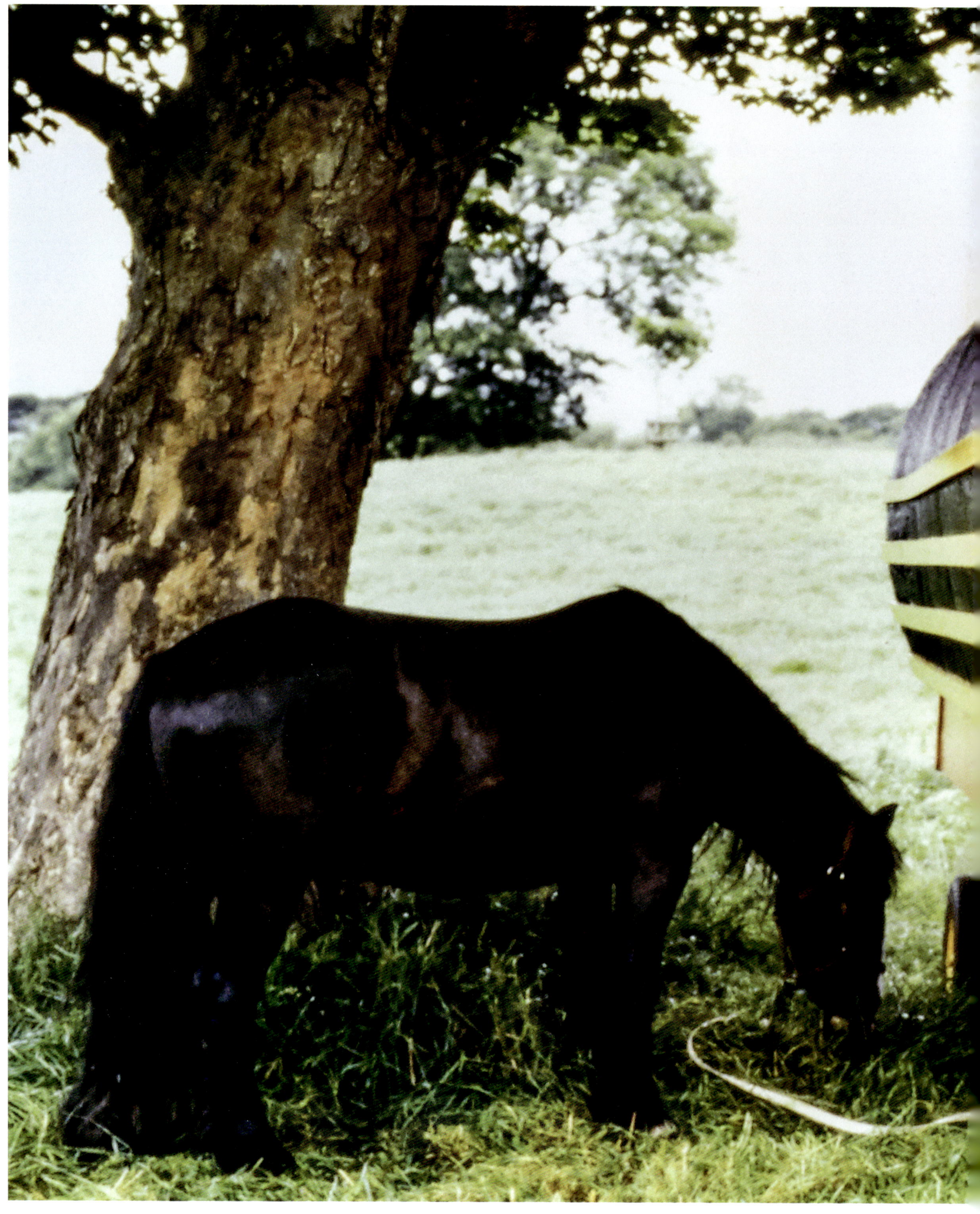

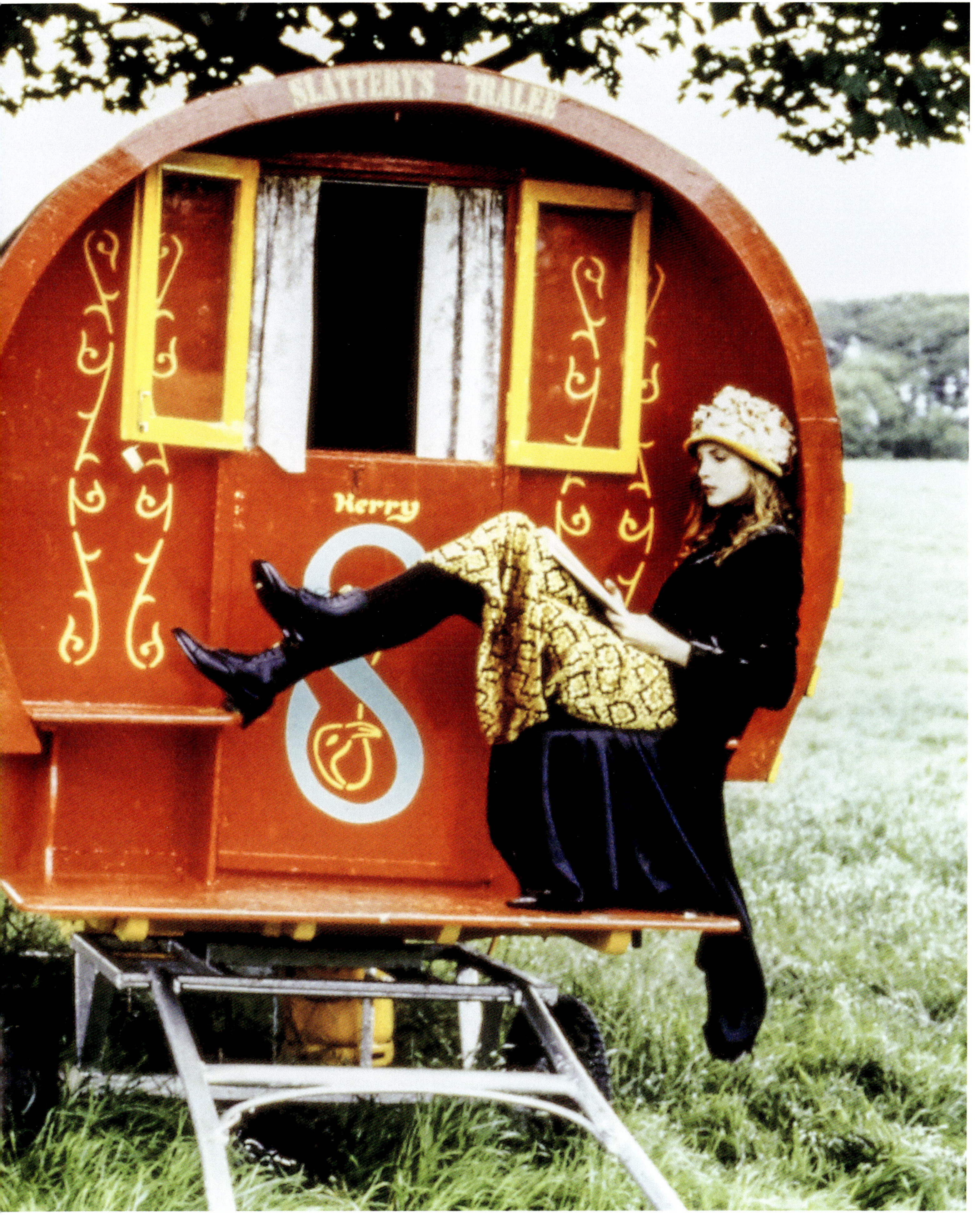
SLATTERY'S   TRALEE
Kerry

IMPRINT

THE STYLISH LIFE COWBOYS
ABE DAVIES
This book was conceived, edited, and designed by teNeues.

Text and preface by Abe Davies
Copyediting by Amanda Ennis
Editorial Management by Stephanie Rebel, gestalten
Design by Marcus Taeschner
Layout by Marcus Taeschner
Picture Editing by Heide Christiansen
Color Separation by Jens Grundei
Production by Sandra Jansen-Dorn, gestalten

Printed by Schleunungdruck GmbH,
Marktheidenfeld, Germany
Produced in Europe

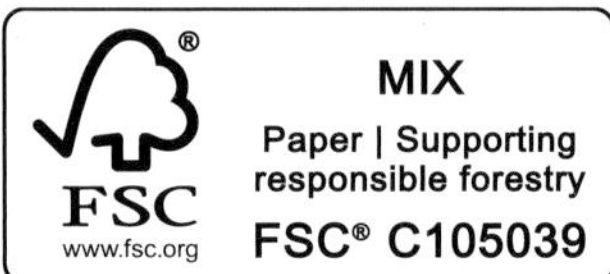

Published by gestalten, Berlin 2026
ISBN 978-3-96171-736-1

1st printing, 2026

© teNeues, an Imprint of
Die Gestalten Verlag GmbH & Co. KG, Berlin 2026

For more information, and to order books, please visit
www.teneues.com and www.gestalten.com

Die Gestalten Verlag GmbH & Co. KG
Mariannenstrasse 9–10
10999 Berlin, Germany
hello@gestalten.com

Krefeld Office
Uerdinger Str. 265 / Villa Pattberg
47800 Krefeld, Germany
verlag@teneues.com

teNeues Press Department
press@gestalten.com

Bibliographic information published by the Deutsche
Nationalbibliothek. The Deutsche Nationalbibliothek lists
this publication in the Deutsche Nationalbibliografie;
detailed bibliographic data is available online at
www.dnb.de

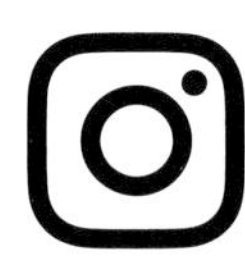

https://instagram.com/teneuespublishing

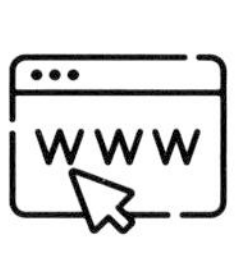

www.teneues.com